C000268834

DANCING

IN THE RAIN

Maggie Silk *2016*

MAGGIE SILK

Matador
9 Priory Business Park,
Wistow Road, Kibworth Beauchamp,
Leicestershire. LE8 0RX
Tel: (+44) 116 279 2299
Fax: (+44) 116 279 2277
Email: books@troubador.co.uk
Web: www.troubador.co.uk/matador

ISBN 978 1785892 585

British Library Cataloguing in Publication Data.
A catalogue record for this book is available from the British Library.

Printed and bound in the UK by TJ International, Padstow, Cornwall
Typeset in 11pt Aldine by Troubador Publishing Ltd, Leicester, UK

Matador is an imprint of Troubador Publishing Ltd

To Kerry, Mam & Ann

ACKNOWLEDGEMENTS

For the constant encouragement and advice, many thanks to everyone in my creative writing group. A special thank you to Liz Ringrose who taught me all I know.

My sincere gratitude goes to Lauren and Chelsea from Matador who helped me to believe in myself.

LIFE ISN'T ABOUT WAITING FOR THE STORM TO PASS,
IT'S ABOUT LEARNING TO DANCE IN THE RAIN

Anonymous

CLEETHORPES, 1943

I was drowning. One minute I was sitting on the edge of the lake watching the boats with the boys. Then I felt two hands on my back. Somebody pushed me. It was so quick there was no time to cry out. The dirty water enveloped me, going up my nose, into my eyes, then in my mouth as I tried to scream. Water seemed to go into my lungs as I panicked and kicked. I reached out with my arms in a struggle to stay afloat. For a moment I seemed to rise before I went down for the second time. Terror seized me. I swallowed more water and was really struggling to breathe. Suddenly I felt someone grabbing my hair and was hauled out. The bright sunshine hurt my eyes, which were streaming with a mixture of water and hot tears. I gasped and sobbed unable to speak. I felt the strong arms of a man as he hoisted me up onto his shoulders. I could feel his body warmth and the texture of rough cloth on my bare legs. Although I was only four years old I knew at once from his khaki uniform that he was a soldier. I felt safe again. Perhaps he knew my daddy, who was a soldier as well. I clung to his outstretched hands as I shivered in my wet clothes. The water from my hair was still dripping down my face. His hands were warm, big and comforting. He walked with huge strides away from the lake, crossed by the sandpit and asked whether anyone recognised me. At last he came to the grassy area where he found my mammy sitting with her friends. They were all knitting. It was wartime and because all the dads were away fighting Hitler and his Germans, we went there every Sunday with a picnic. Mammy's friends had children, too, and we all played together either on the grass or in the sandpit. This particular time I'd wandered over to watch the boats following Bobby and John. They were brothers, a little bit older than me.

After thanking the soldier Mammy gave me a big cuddle before she dried me. She dressed me in a pair of borrowed shorts and a spare jumper and told me not to wander off again.

Had that young man not been there I wouldn't have lived to tell my story.

A WARTIME CHRISTMAS

It's a late December afternoon, it's drizzling outside and nearly dark, but in our living room it's warm and cosy. There's a smell of wood smoke and the burning logs in the grate are spitting and hissing. Mammam, my mammy's mam, is sitting in the soft comfy armchair right next to the blazing fire. She's holding a saucer in her left hand and a cup of tea in the other. We are watching her from our den. She pours a few drops from the cup into the saucer before she puts the cup down into the hearth. Then she holds the saucer in two hands and blows over it before taking little sips and making loud slurping noises. We get told off if we do that.

Ann and I are under the living room table pretending it's our house. The green cloth on the table overhangs and I like flicking the little tassels with my finger and thumb. We have our own tea set that Father Christmas brought. It's doll-sized, made of tin, painted pink and has cups and saucers, a teapot, a jug and a sugar bowl. Mammam has filled the pot with real tea and given us milk and sugar. The tea is warm and sweet and tastes a bit tinny, but I like it that way. Ann copies Mammam and pours some tea into the saucer. It overflows and goes down her dress, so instead we both decide to sip it from the cup and make the loudest slurps we can. It makes us laugh and the tea runs down my chin.

We know Mammam won't be cross because she never is. Ann's told me that Mammy's gone to hospital to fetch a new baby home but I don't believe her. She often tells me things that aren't true. Anyway I'd like a real baby to play with.

Christmas time was exciting in our house. I used to listen for the click of the letterbox and rush into the hall to pick up the cards. I couldn't understand how Mammy knew so many people. I wished every year that someone would send a card just for me. Auntie Dora, my mammy's friend was a teacher and she always sent a little calendar that she'd painted. It was a picture of winter or spring with a robin sitting on a farm gate, or tiny blue violets and yellow primroses growing in a wood. Auntie Dora taught me the names of the flowers and promised to take us all to Irby Woods to look for the first violets.

Mammy put the cards on the mantelpiece, sideboard and windowsill but there were still some left over. We helped her to make coloured paper chains then she had to stand on the table or a chair to reach the picture rail where she tied them up. She kept dropping the drawing pins and I had to find them. Once I knelt on one and it stuck in my knee. I didn't cry because it didn't really hurt till she pulled it out. Then I yelled and Ann called me a cry-baby so I stuck my tongue out. Once we had a real Christmas tree that Mammy stood in some soil in a pretty biscuit barrel. She said it was a part of a tea service that was a wedding present but it couldn't be used for biscuits anymore because the lid was broken. We painted shells that we'd collected off the sands to decorate the tree. There were long, sharp razor shells and round cockleshells with pretty wavy edges. Mammy made a hole in each one with a darning needle, then threaded a piece of cotton through and knotted it before hanging it on a branch. A few shells broke but we had plenty more.

On Christmas Eve we all wrote our own letter to Father Christmas. We watched Mammy fold it and throw it up the chimney. It fell back into the fire, then the burned black pieces floated up and disappeared one by one. I knew it was on its way. Next morning I crawled to the foot of the bed where I'd left my long woolly knee sock. It was a funny knobbly shape. I felt inside and pulled out an apple, a tangerine and some nuts. We found other presents left in the living room. I loved my colouring book and crayons but best of all was a teddy who wore a red knitted jumper. If I pressed his tummy he squeaked. Ann and John got card games and board games like Ludo, or Snakes and Ladders. We each got one book. Mammy said they cost a lot of money so we had to look after them. My very first book was called *The Nursery Peter Pan* about a boy that could fly. I used to sit on Auntie Dora's knee while she read it to me over and over again and sometimes I read it to her. I couldn't really read the words, I'd just remembered them, but I think she believed I could. I learned how to fasten the buttons on Auntie Dora's navy blue cardigan, counting each one up to ten.

We didn't have many sweets and chocolates because Mammy couldn't afford them and they were rationed. Instead she swapped our sweet coupons for sugar coupons with the lady next door. Mammy needed the extra sugar especially at Christmas for a cake and pudding and even homemade mincemeat if she could get any dried fruit. Mince pies were my favourite part of Christmas tea. Mammy had a friend who was married to a farmer and once he gave us a chicken for Christmas Day. We kids didn't really like it as we'd never tasted it before so we had a slice of tongue. I liked that with gravy and roast potatoes, but I hated the Brussels sprouts and always hid them under my knife and fork when I'd finished.

THE AIR-RAID SHELTER, 1943

The long, loud whine of the siren woke me. It was a sound I hated, one that made my tummy turn over. Ann was pulling at my nightie and I scrambled out of bed to put on my coat, socks and shoes that Mammam was holding ready. We followed her and the others out of the house. The shelter was right opposite the back door but we had to go down steps to get into it because it was under the ground. They were steep so John was allowed to go first because he had the matches and the candle. Mammy went next, then Mammam passed David to her, before she let Ann and I go. That meant she was always last but she could give me a hand and didn't seem to mind. John once forgot to take the matches back into the house and the next time he tried to use them, they were no good.

It was cold down there and always smelt of damp earth, like the garden after it had rained. There was no electric light or heat. The yellow flame of the small candle stuck in a saucer flickered and danced in a draught. It cast long shadows on the corrugated metal sides of the air-raid shelter. David, my younger brother, was lying on a camp bed. Mammy had taken a blanket off his own bed and wrapped it round him over his 'jamas before she carried him down there. He hadn't even woken up. She'd thrown an army overcoat on the top for extra warmth but I could still see one foot sticking out, showing his little knitted sock. I curled up on Mammam's lap. She had an old armchair that someone had been chucking out. Mammy told them it would be ideal for the shelter and she'd managed to find a nice piece of old red curtain material to drape over it. John called it the throne because it was the best seat down there. Mammy was good at making things look better and she'd even put a piece of carpet on the floor to hide the stones and the soil. Ann and John knelt on it, still wearing their shoes and socks with their school coats over their 'jamas. They played cards and argued now and then, but Mammy never told them off. I liked to hear people talking 'cos it made me forget about the planes as I snuggled up to Mammam with my thumb in my mouth, listening to her chatting to my mammy. She was sitting on an old wooden fruit crate covered with a torn grey army blanket. We'd laughed when she said it was to stop the splinters going in her bum.

I didn't like the sound of the German planes when they flew low overhead; it made me feel funny inside. As soon as I heard a low drone in the distance I put my hands over my ears. John and Ann stopped playing their game. They sat still and looked up as though they could see through the roof. Then my mammy started us all singing.

'*She'll be coming round the mountains when she comes,*

she'll be coming round the mountains when she comes.' I couldn't wait to sing the chorus after every verse.

'*Singing I yi yippee yippee yi. Singing I yi yippee yippee yi.*' I sang as loud as I could to drown out the noise of the planes. When we stopped, they'd gone.

'Can I sing one I learned at school? You have to put your hands together and close your eyes like this.'

This time I didn't shout.

'*Thank you for the world so sweet,*
Thank you for the food we eat,
Thank you for the birds that sing,
Thank you God for everything. Amen.'

When I opened my eyes and looked at Mammy. I could see a tear running down her cheek.

'Didn't you like it?' I was puzzled.

She wiped away the tear with the back of her hand and smiled at me. 'Course I did, I loved it and I'm so proud of you.' Mammam gave me a big cuddle.

When it was safe to go into the house we heard the all-clear. It was different from the siren, sort of friendly; it meant that we could go back to our warm beds. Sometimes when I scrambled out and looked up at the stars, John showed me the beam of the searchlights as they swept across the dark sky. He said even though we lived right next to the North Sea and the Germans came from the other side of the water, that was good because they were more interested in flying over us. They wanted to get to the big cities like Coventry and Sheffield. He knew a lot about the war and planes and could even tell whether it was one of ours or the enemy just by the sound of the engine. Once, when Ann was climbing out, she put one hand on the wet grass and the other one touched a hedgehog. Everyone jumped when she screamed. I was glad it was her and not me.

A HAIRCUT

I was sitting on the bottom step and Shirley was sitting behind me on the one above, holding the scissors in her hand. The back door of the house was wide open and I could hear her mother singing as she worked somewhere inside. I liked playing with Shirley; she had no brothers or sisters. Her dad was a sailor who hardly ever came home because of the war. I saw my dad once or twice even though he never stayed for long. Shirley's dad was miles away in another country. I think it was called "The Pacific".

She called me "her little sister" because although she was only a year older than me and had started school, she was much taller. I loved her brown hair, which parted in the middle and hung down in two long plaits tied with fat shiny ribbons.

'Sit still,' she said, as she began to cut, lifting each corkscrew of hair one by one. I sat, enjoying the attention, trying to catch the curls as they drifted down, helped by a warm summer breeze. It didn't seem to take long before Shirley stood up. She brushed some hair off her lap, put the scissors on the step and said, 'There, finished. Let's play again.'

The grass at the foot of the steps was covered with a fine layer of my hair.

We ran down the garden and played hide-and-seek. There were plenty of bushes to go behind and an old wooden shed, where you could actually go inside and hide under some smelly sacks on the floor. Suddenly, we heard Shirley's mam shouting. Her voice sounded funny; sort of half cross and half upset. I ran back, expecting the usual treat of a glass of milk and a chocolate biscuit. My mammy couldn't afford chocolate biscuits.

Shirley's mam looked at me in horror and put her hand in front her mouth. I could see her lips moving through her fingers and just heard the words, 'Oh my God, oh my God.' She picked up the tray with the drinks, which had been sitting on the step.

'Get inside,' she snapped as she pushed Shirley into the house. I could tell she was cross.

'You'd better go home,' she said to me more kindly, before she went inside, too. I heard the key being turned in the lock. Not fully understanding, I went home. It was only up the street anyway. All I could think about was the chocolate biscuit she'd forgotten to give me.

Mammy was chopping carrots as I walked into the scullery.

'Shirley cut my hair, do you like it?'

'What with? A knife and fork?' That was an expression she often used. I could see she was trying not to laugh.

She took me to Auntie Mona's, one of her best friends, who was a hairdresser. She trimmed it again so at least it was all the same length.

'Cutting her hair is like pruning a rose,' Mona said to Mammy. 'The harder you do it, the better it grows back.'

She was right; within weeks my head was a mass of curls again. Mammy wasn't at all cross with me or Shirley. She had too many more important things to worry about with four children and a husband away fighting the Germans.

I didn't see Shirley for ages. Mammy told me later that her mother was so upset that she'd locked up the house and gone to stay with her own mother for a couple of weeks.

I knew I was lost and began to cry. I wanted Mammy. Then I heard a voice I recognised.

'Hey liddle lady, what are you doing here all on your own? Where's your mom?'

I stopped crying and sniffed. 'She's at home.'

'Well let's go find her; she'll be worried. She'll be missing you.'

The tall American serviceman smiled, took a white handkerchief from his pocket and gently patted my tears away. Not like Mammy, who usually spat on the hanky before she rubbed my face clean.

He took my hand and we crossed the main road, then walked round the next corner up Queens Parade. He walked slowly so that I could keep up with his long legs. He was chatting all the time but sometimes I didn't understand what he meant because he didn't speak like my dad. When we got back to the bungalow he knocked loudly on the front door. Mammy opened it.

'I think this liddle lady belongs to you,' said her friend. He grinned.

'Good God,' she said, looking at me. 'What *have* you been doing?'

'Don't be mad at her,' he said. 'She got lost and I'd know those curls anywhere. I've gotta shoot. I'll see you later.' He touched his cap and left.

'Is he going to shoot the Germans?' I asked.

'No, he meant he's in a hurry,' said Mammy. 'Come in the bathroom and let's wipe your snotty nose and clean your face.' This time, she used a warm flannel.

TOILETS AND GAS MASKS

In winter we stood and shivered on the cold lino as we waited for Mammy to run the water. I hugged my naked body, shoulders hunched and arms crossed over my chest with my little hands thrust deep into my armpits. We were only bathed once a week, two by two in the same water; David and I were first being the youngest, then Ann and John. The water hardly went over our legs in the steep-sided iron bath but Mammy said it was because of the war and we weren't allowed to waste it. She said we were lucky to even have a bathroom inside, as a lot of houses didn't and some children had to go in a tin bath in front of the fire. I secretly thought that would be nicer and much warmer. Once, we all had scabies. We were scratching like mad and my body was red and sore. Mammy had to scrub us in the bath with a nailbrush to kill the itchy mite and that was even worse. I wriggled and cried because it hurt and she got cross, but when David screamed she didn't tell him off. Ann called us both cry-babies.

Next to the bath was a white handbasin where Mammy washed our hair. I hated that, too, because I was afraid of the water going into my eyes and mouth and had to hold a flannel over my face.

The lavatory was opposite the door with a water cistern high up near the ceiling. It had a long chain with a wooden handle that I couldn't quite reach so Mammy had to tie a piece of string on it for David and me. When I pulled it, it shot back with such a jerk and a loud clang that I ran out of the bathroom and slammed the door.

At least our lavatory was inside. Not like the one at Great Aunt Ann's. She was Mammam's sister. She lived in a little village in the country and her lav was down the garden near the hen run. I had to perch on the huge wooden seat holding tight, scared of slipping through and landing in the stinky earth closet down below. We made lavatory paper at home from old newspapers that we kids cut into squares. Then Mammy threaded it onto string and hung it up on a nail that someone had bashed into the wall. John laughed and told me that the print came off the paper and made your bum black, but I couldn't see it anyway.

At school we had real lavatory paper, shiny and medicated, called Izal, but like the bathwater that was rationed as well.

My infant school was at the top of our street. It was also where my big brother John went, but he wasn't in my class because he was twelve and I was only five. I liked it on Monday mornings when I had to go to his class to get my dinner money. Mammy wouldn't let me take it because she thought I might lose it. My teacher was called Miss Nottle. She had dark brown hair and was very kind. We did all sorts of things as well as learning to read and doing really hard sums. I liked cutting out and sticking because we had better paste and scissors at school. If we wanted to stick pictures at home Mammy made the paste with flour and water; it was all right but it smelled funny. In my class we had a tin with white powder in. It looked a bit like flour but you could pour it like sugar. After Miss Nottle had given us all a spoonful that she'd already mixed with water she said, 'Take a pinch of your favourite colour of powder paint and stir it in the wet paste.' I chose orange. Then I took a paintbrush and slathered the gooey mess all over the cover of my dull grey exercise book. We'd all made a comb from a piece of card by cutting jagged edges like sharp teeth, so next, Miss Nottle told us to drag it over the wet paint to make a wavy pattern. That was fun especially when the comb got soggy and my hands started to turn orange. We left the paint to dry, then went into the infant cloakroom to wash. We weren't allowed to go alone; it was always one boy and one girl. I think that was to make sure the boys didn't mess about and start water fights.

One afternoon we had to line up and follow the teacher out of the classroom. We were all wearing a gas mask, the one that we took to school every day. There was a big white truck parked outside with the back doors wide open and another class was already climbing in. I didn't want to go inside because it looked dark and I couldn't see any windows, but we had to follow Miss Nottle. She led us up the wooden steps, helped us in and told us to make a circle so we could play ring-a-ring o' roses. There was another lady with us who had a nice smiley face and she started singing just as someone closed the double doors. It was so black it hurt my eyes. Someone in the class screamed and a girl started to cry. I was terrified. Standing between two friends, I could feel their hands squeezing mine and I knew that they were scared like me. I stumbled round in the dark fiercely holding on to the next person pulling me round. Suddenly, the doors were opened. The daylight was blinding and I almost tripped over in the rush to get out. Next morning, I told my mammy I was never *ever* going to school again.

MISUNDERSTANDINGS

I sat on a wooden chair in the hospital corridor swinging my legs waiting for the present. I could hear people talking. Doors opened and closed. There was a funny smell. A man came along whistling, pushing a trolley filled with silver shiny things that rattled on the tray as he walked. He slowed down as he steered it past me, turned his head and winked. Then he stopped whistling and said, 'What's your name? Curly Locks?'

'No, Margaret. I'm waiting for the present.'

'Stay there then, else they won't know where you are.' He smiled at me as he left. I was beginning to feel a bit lonely and wondered when my mammy was coming back to fetch me. We'd come together on the double-decker bus, leaving Mammam at home looking after the others. Mammy took me upstairs so I could look out of the window because it was quite a long ride to Grimsby. It had been hard climbing the steep steps so I'd used my hands to help me scramble up in case the bus started. Mammy laughed when I told her and said that the driver could see us in the big, round mirror at the top of the stairs. We sat in the front seats so that I could see where we were going. There were only two girls sitting right at the back. They were smoking cigarettes. It wasn't allowed downstairs.

'One and a half please,' Mammy said to the conductor, who took the money and put it in his black shoulder bag. He turned the handle twice on his ticket machine and out popped two tickets. He passed them to me.

'Don't lose them, Shirley,' he said and walked away.

I looked at Mammy. 'Why did he call me Shirley? That's not my name.'

She laughed, then told me that there was a little girl in films called Shirley Temple who was famous.

'Well, it's not me. I'm sick of people calling me different names as well as mixing me up with Ann.'

When we got off the bus it wasn't far to the hospital, but Mammy held me with one hand and in the other carried a small brown suitcase. A lady wearing a white dress that had a belt with a big shiny buckle met us just inside the building. I didn't listen to what they said; I was too busy looking around me at the high windows and corridors. It reminded me of school a bit. They stopped talking and Mammy bent down to kiss me.

'Be a good girl for the sister,' she said. 'I'll come back tomorrow to see you.' She hugged me and smiled and I thought I saw tears in her eyes before she turned and disappeared out of the door. I knew that I'd come to the hospital to have my sore throat made better because Mammy had told me. She'd said that I would have blancmange and jelly and even ice cream when they'd sorted it.

It was the same nurse who'd taken my hand and left me sitting on the chair in the corridor. Another nurse came not long after she'd gone and asked me if Sister had left me there.

'No, no, my sister's at home. It was my mammy who brought me.' I didn't understand why she laughed as she patted my knee.

'You're a good girl. Well, wait there for the present and someone will soon come.' So I sat very still, wondering what the present would be.

THE LAUGHING POLICEMAN, 1945

'It's my turn.'

'No it's not.'

'Yes it is, you did it last time.'

'What about me? I want a go.'

'You're not old enough.'

'Yes I am.'

'Leave him alone.'

'Shut up you, I'm in charge.'

'You're always in charge, it's not fair.'

'Leave it!' screamed Ann at David. He was daring to reach out and touch the machine. She leaned forward and slapped his hand. He began to cry loudly. My mammy rushed in from the scullery with her hands covered in flour.

'Why's he crying?' she asked, looking at me.

'Because she hit him.' I pointed to Ann, who glared at me.

'No I didn't,' she answered.

'Liar,' I said, looking at my mammy. 'Ask him.'

'You don't hit anyone,' Mammy said. She was cross. 'I'm the boss of hitting in this house.'

Ann was determined to have the last word.

'Well, John hits me,' she said, sticking out her bottom lip and pulling a face.

Mam ignored her. David had stopped crying now that he was the centre of attention.

'Anyway, what are you arguing about?'

That morning had begun with rain; normally we'd have been in the garden. Instead the three of us were kneeling on the living room floor quarrelling over the little record player someone had given to Mammy. It had a turntable, which was operated by a handle on the side. You turned that until it wouldn't go any further, a bit like the key that worked the dancing clockwork tin monkey.

Then the machine was ready for the small plate-sized record. You had to move the long arm with the needle at the end and place it gently on the record before it began to play. The sound came out good and loud from a trumpet-shaped loudspeaker on the back.

'Look,' said Mammy, 'now you've all calmed down, take it in turns. Let David wind it up, Maggie put the record on and Ann you start it because it has to be done carefully.'

Ann grinned at me and stuck her tongue out. I knew what she was thinking.

'But who chooses the record?' I asked.

'The person that puts it on,' said Mammy, forgetting that we only had two records anyway. She must have been sick to death of hearing them over and over again. 'If the sun comes out after dinner, we can all go on the sands if you like.' She headed back into the scullery.

Ann looked at me.

'What makes you think I want to go on the sands with you two?' She didn't even wait for an answer. 'Well, which record is it?' she asked grudgingly.

'"The Laughing Policeman".' I was already holding the precious piece of vinyl in my hand.

David was winding up the machine and looking pleased.

'Cry-baby,' muttered Ann, but he didn't hear her.

We listened to "The Laughing Policeman" twice, and joined in when he sang "*Hah hah hah*" which went on and on. David was rolling about on the floor holding his tummy; he couldn't stop laughing.

We stopped arguing and when *Workers' Playtime* came on the wireless and Mammy called from the scullery, 'Set the table girls,' we knew that dinner would soon be ready.

'We're all going to a party in Nicholson Street because there aren't enough children round here,' Mammy said one day. I was excited. I'd never been to a party. When I saw the tables lined up down the middle of the road I couldn't believe my eyes. There were plates and plates piled high with sandwiches, biscuits, little fairy cakes with icing on the top and huge jugs of orange juice. It was the first time I had seen so much food. When all the children were sitting down the mammies, grandmas and aunties passed the plates around. They said it was to stop the bigger, greedy lads from grabbing handfuls before the little ones. There were so many different kinds of sandwiches I didn't know which to choose first.

There was egg, meat paste, fish paste, cheese and spam. John was sitting opposite me so I took whatever he took and there was enough to have what you liked. We all had a little Union Jack that we waved when we stood up at the end and sang "God Save Our Gracious King". Then all the grown-ups clapped and shouted "Hip, hip hooray", so we joined in. Best of all, afterwards, there were donkey rides for the under tens only.

I was only six, too young to realise that it was a celebration to mark the end of the war and couldn't understand why it didn't happen again the following year.

IN THE JUNIOR SCHOOL

I had to change school when I was seven and, because it was too far to walk, I caught the number six bus every day. Ann was still at St Peter's and she had to take David with her.

'Why does she have to go to a different school?' she asked Mam.

'Because she went to the nearest infants during the war and now it's the rule she goes to Bursar St Junior.'

'H'mph,' Ann grunted and glared at me as if it was my fault. I was secretly glad. I was sick of being the younger sister who got bossed around.

I loved being in the juniors. We had two big playgrounds: one for the boys and the other for girls. The lads played football and chasing, or marbles and conkers when they were in season. We all had scabby knees from falling over. We played with skipping ropes; usually a piece cut off your Mam's washing line. If it was too long, you had to wrap it round and round your hand. No one seemed to decide when it was time to change from skipping to ball games, it just seemed to happen. I liked balls the best and played endless games of two ball or three ball against the school wall. Then whips and tops came into season and we decorated the tops with circles of coloured chalk. When it spun round, the colours merged so that it looked like a rainbow.

I enjoyed the English lessons that we had every day. Sometimes we just read aloud round the class, or we had dictation. I liked that because I was good at spelling. I was always reading at home and went to the public library with Mam once a week. I had my dinner at school, too, and all the dinner ladies called me Shirley. I didn't mind that though because I think they liked me and always asked if I wanted a second helping. I usually did. We had assembly in the hall every morning and also went in there for singing because that was where the piano was.

'"While the raging seas did roar,
And the stormy winds did blow
And we jolly sailor boys were sitting up aloft
With the landlubbers lying down below, below, below,
And the landlubbers lying down below",' we sang.

That was just the chorus that came after every verse. We knew that landlubbers were the people who were seasick. That was why they were lying down on their bunks.

Our big class of fifty, all eight and nine years old were sitting cross-legged on the floor in the hall. We'd only sung one verse.

'Sing up!' shouted Miss Ingham above the noise from the piano as she thumped the keys. 'Come on, I can't hear you.' Outside it seemed like the end of the world. Rain was streaming down in torrents, flooding the school playground. Lightning lit up the room and the thunder was roaring and grumbling like a hungry lion. Then, without warning, it seemed to pounce and there was an almighty crack overhead. Everyone jumped and some girls put their hands over their ears.

Miss Ingham stopped for a minute. She was smiling.

'Now stand up. That was just a practice. Let's try to raise the roof and shake the window panes.'

She put her foot down on the loud pedal and struck the keys, going straight into the chorus again. We were delighted and took up the challenge. Our voices seemed to resound off the walls and ceiling. I was sure even the photograph of King George VI and the one of Lord Montgomery shook a bit in their frames. We were fired up and forgot the noise outside. After six verses and six choruses, the piano playing finally stopped. Breathless and laughing, we sat down as the storm rumbled away into the distance. We all liked Miss Ingham. She chose good songs and everyone enjoyed the sea shanties, particularly the boys when they could let rip.

There was a strong tradition of singing in the junior school. I loved being in the choir and taking part in the musical festivals. They were annual events open to school choirs from all over North Lincolnshire. One was held in the big dance hall on the pier, where we competed against classes of the same age from different schools.

Whenever we won, my greatest wish was to be chosen to fetch the silver cup from the adjudicator on the stage. It was not to be.

However, I had had my own moment of glory in 1946 when I was just seven in the first year juniors. I had an amazing memory for words especially of songs and poetry. My teacher had entered me into the verse speaking class in the Grimsby musical festival. There were twenty-seven children competing. I recited *Waiting at the window* by A. A. Milne and, to my joy, I came third. I could see Mam's face when I went up to shake hands and receive my certificate. She was smiling and talking to the lady sitting next to her and I could tell she was as thrilled as me.

NANNY AND UNCLE CHARLIE, AGED 8

"If at first you don't succeed, try, try again." What did it mean?

It was written on a china plate, hanging on the wall opposite the dining table where I sat alone, on a hardback wooden chair, eating my breakfast. I still couldn't reach the floor with my feet even though I was eight years old. I hated such hard seats. Our chairs at home had soft shiny ones that Mammy could wipe down if we spilt anything. Underneath the writing was a coloured picture of a golfer dressed in a funny cap and a pair of green-check baggy trousers, swinging a golf club. I didn't understand the meaning of the saying. If he missed the ball, of course he'd try to hit it again; anyone would, wouldn't they?

Much more interesting was the painting beside the plate. It was nearly as big as our living-room window and had a beautiful shiny wooden frame; I think someone told me it was "mogamy". The writing said, "And when did you last see your Father?"

In this picture there's a young boy who's wearing

a blue satin suit with a white lace collar, leggings and silver-buckled shoes. His big sister, standing behind, is crying even though she's wearing a pretty white satin dress which comes right down to the floor. An old-fashioned soldier holding a spear and wearing a helmet is resting his arm around her shoulder. The boy is standing on a sort of small stool behind a table, facing a man on the other side, who's leaning towards him resting his elbows on the table. There are some more men sitting beside him, one wearing a tall black hat that looks like a chimney pot. It was all very puzzling, though I liked it. If we ever put our elbows on the table Mammy shouted "ELBOWS" and we all jumped back.

Those pictures were in my nanny's house. She was my dad's mother. She was tall with a red face and a big nose and wore dark brown glasses. She was married to Uncle Charlie; he was her second husband. I liked him but was a bit afraid of her 'cos she was always asking me questions like "Does Ann still wet the bed?" or "Do you still suck your thumb?"

When I went to stay, there was nothing much to do and she left me alone for ages. I knew three different kinds of Patience and sat on the floor playing cards, inventing new games and waiting for dinner.

On the third morning after breakfast, I'd had enough. I decided to run away so I packed my little brown suitcase and crept downstairs. I tiptoed past the big grandfather clock ticking in the hall and out of the back door, round to the front of the house. Then I squatted down out of sight on the furthest side of the big bay window. It was too far to walk home and I didn't have any money for a bus. Anyway I didn't even know where the bus stop was. As I was wondering what to do next, I heard someone shouting.

'Maggie, Maggie, where are you?'

I crouched down even lower and shut my eyes. The next minute I felt a hand grasp my collar and heard her horrible voice above me.

'You naughty girl, what do you think you're doing?'

'I want to go home,' I said and burst into tears.

Uncle Charlie took me home in his car and I was never asked to go again.

MAMMAM'S HOUSE

We were upstairs on a double-decker bus travelling over the Corporation Street Bridge in Grimsby because I was going home with Mammam for a few days. She lived in a long terrace of houses opposite the railway line at number 6 Clayden Street. My granddad used to work on the railway but he died before I was born. I bet I would have liked him as much as I loved her.

'What would happen if the bridge opens when we're on it?' I asked.

'It'll never do that. It only operates for the ships to go through into the dock,' said Mammam. 'Don't you worry; it closes long before they need it and when all the traffic is safely off a big barrier swings across.'

I felt happier knowing this and grateful that she didn't laugh at me. I think she knew I was still afraid of water even though I never mentioned it.

The front door of her house opened into a passage that led to the living room. I thought that it was much cosier than ours because she had a shiny black cast-iron range with a massive grate for the fire. There was an oven at the side like the one in the story of Hansel and Gretel that the witch got shoved into. In front of the grate, down on the floor, was a pretty, twisted gold-coloured fender that went all the way round the tiled hearth. It stopped any pieces of coal that fell from rolling on to a rug. The water in the huge kettle was always kept on the boil ready for use and the nice smells from the oven made me feel hungry. Mammam kept the tea caddy on the mantelpiece, next to the box of matches for the gas mantel. She had no electricity and as it got darker I watched her pull the little chain and wait for the gas to hiss before she put a lighted match to the mantle. It always made a loud pop and made me jump every time.

I liked to sit on the floor in front of the fire on the coloured peg rug that she had made. She'd cut up bits of cloth from old skirts, coats, curtains, anything she found that was suitable. I watched her making one and tried to have a go but it was too hard, so instead she taught me to knit. She made dishcloths and tea cosies and pan and kettle holders. She showed me some burn marks on her fingers and told me that the handles got *very* hot and I must never ever touch them. I decided to knit a scarf for my teddy, making the first half blue and the second half red. Then I ran out of wool. It didn't matter though, because every time it was washed it seemed to get longer. After tea I used to sit on the rug and play Patience while Mammam sat knitting and chatting. She told me that when she left school she went to work in a jam factory called Ticklers. It was a funny name that made me laugh. She said that during the First World War, hundreds of big tins of plum and apple jam were made for all the brave men fighting away from home.

I think my favourite game was playing with the buttons. She always kept the small, round tin with the picture of Prince Albert on the lid ready for me on the mantelpiece. It was crammed full of so many different shapes, sizes and colours of buttons that I was never stuck for ideas.

A door from the living room led into the small scullery where Mammam washed up in a white enamel sink. She had to carry a pan of hot water through because there was only a cold tap. There was no bathroom either, just a lavatory in a shed, next door to the coalhouse in the backyard. If I wanted to wee in the night or early morning in the winter when it was dark and Mammam was still asleep at the side of me, I slipped quietly out of the warm sheets and used the po that was kept under the bed. My other nanny, the one with the red face, called it a "chamber pot" but I thought that was posh and daft.

When I was ten I was allowed to go to Mammam's house on my own because I'd been going to the junior school on the bus with friends since I was seven. Once, Mammy gave me an egg that Mammam could boil for my tea so I put it in my pocket. I kept my hand over it all the way until I arrived at the front door. When I knocked there was no answer, so I twiddled the knob. The door opened a bit, then stuck again. I put my shoulder to it and pushed. Then I remembered the egg. It was too late. It had smashed to bits leaving a yellow gooey mess on my fingers and all inside the pocket. I was so upset that Mammam made me my favourite tea; condensed milk sandwiches.

WINTER
(ON THE SANDS), 1947

We were on the prom, standing on the bottom bar of the icy cold railings, holding tight and leaning over in order to look down. Sparkling below us lay a dazzling desert of pure white; it looked like icing on a massive cake. It sparkled and glistened in the sun, seeming to stretch for miles in both directions. Deep and crisp and even. Untouched and so inviting. Despite the bitter east wind blowing from the direction of Spurn Point Lighthouse, I turned to Paddy and said, 'Shall we jump?'

It was a daft question to ask because Paddy, who was nearly ten, dared do anything. I don't think my mam approved of our friendship but we both liked horses and doing the same things. I was sorry when a few months later the family suddenly left the area. She nodded and grinned.

We scrambled through the railings, then balanced on the slippery edge holding hands.

'One, two, three!' We had to shout above the wind. We jumped. The drop to the sands was at least twelve foot, and my excitement turned into shock and horror as I landed in the drift. The snow went up to my waist and I gasped as the piercing cold hit my bare legs. As I fought to struggle through the drift, the snow began to melt against my warm body and icy water began to seep into my shoes. We headed for the foreshore where the tide was gently lapping at the frozen seaweed and all the rubbish that it had brought in that morning. It became easier to walk and we crunched along towards the slipway near the pier, where we slithered and slid back up onto the deserted promenade. Paddy ran straight home but at that point I realised that I would get into trouble. I'd been to Sunday school in St Peter's Avenue and had only bumped into Paddy when I was leaving. It had been my idea to go to the sands to see how deep the snow was.

Mammy had a friend called Emmie; she was actually Mona, the hairdresser's mother, and I had to pass her house on the way home. She was quite old with several grandchildren and I liked her, so I decided to go there. Ten minutes later I was standing at her door, knocking hard. With my soaking underclothes, skirt and socks clinging to cold skin I couldn't stop my teeth chattering. The minute she opened the door, I burst into tears. Kind Auntie Emmie stripped off the wet socks, skirt and knickers and hung them over the fireguard in front of a blazing fire. I stood and shivered with my hands under my armpits as she gently dried me.

The tops of my legs were bright red and the gap between my skirt and the top of my three-quarter-length socks was raw and chapped. Every winter I had chilblains on my toes and angry red marks between my knees where they rubbed together. Auntie Emmie fetched a blanket off her bed and wrapped it around me before she made me a warm drink of Oxo. I sat cradling it between my hands, subdued and quiet as I gradually thawed out, feeling the warmth seep back into my body and watching the steam rise from the wet clothes.

'You won't tell Mammy, will you?' I asked. 'I'll get into trouble.'

'Course I won't, it's our little secret, she doesn't need to know. I think you've learned a lesson.' When I finally got home, it was nearly dinner time. Mammy was cross.

'Where do you think you've been, young lady? You should have been back an hour ago'

'I'm sorry. I only went to look at the snow on the sands with Paddy.'

'I didn't know she went to Sunday school.' Mammy sounded surprised.

'No, she doesn't. I met her, it was my idea.'

'Well, don't do anything like that in future; I was beginning to get worried.' Ann, who'd been listening, smirked as I pushed past her.

'Miss Goody-Goody got told off,' she whispered.

'Shut up you,' I said. I was starving hungry and wanted my dinner.

It happened in 1947, when the first snow started in January and lasted until the middle of March. The newspapers said that with record low temperatures of 21 degrees Fahrenheit (-30 Celsius) and the persistent snow cover, it was the worst winter of the twentieth century.

Transport almost ground to a halt and lorries carrying coal couldn't get to the power stations. Consequently, electricity in shops, factories and homes was turned off during certain hours. Some families put a brick in the oven or even on a fire to get hot before wrapping it in a piece of cloth to warm the bed. We had heavy khaki army coats thrown on top of the thin sheets and blankets and sometimes wore our socks and a cardigan. Mammam and Mammy unpicked old jumpers and I helped, sitting on the floor to wind up the corkscrew wool nice and tight into a big ball so that it could be used again. They knitted mittens, gloves and a balaclava hat each for John and David. I would have loved one but Mammy said only boys wore them, so Ann and I had to have a silly hat that buttoned under the chin. She lost hers the first time she wore it and told Mammy someone at school had pinched it. Mammy was mad and said she'd have to do without.

'I don't care,' Ann said. 'I never liked it anyway.' I think she'd chucked it away on purpose but I daren't say anything.

Dad started using coke on the fire, which he said was cheaper and easier to get hold of than coal. It glowed red hot without the flames we were used to seeing but it was much better for making toast. We had a long-handled wire toasting fork and took it in turns kneeling in front of the fire to do our own slice. Sometimes it burned if you took your eye off it or even fell into the fire. You could smell it before you saw it. We had to scrape off the black bits because Mammy said she couldn't afford to throw bread away while it was still rationed. It tasted a bit smoky but the margarine and homemade jam helped to hide it. Dad never ate butter or marge, only dripping. He said it was because he'd grown up in a family of butchers. Whenever we had roast lamb and beef for Sunday dinner, Mammy always had a little dish ready to fill with the brown fat. As a treat, sometimes we had it on toast with a sprinkling of salt.

School carried on despite the cold weather and we made snowmen in the playground and threw snowballs at one another. Every day, the milk froze in the little bottles standing in the crate outside our classroom. The cardboard tops were pushed up and seemed to sit on white stumps of snow. They looked like rows of frozen toy soldiers each wearing a beret. The crate was brought in to stand by the huge radiator until the milk began to thaw, but there were still frozen lumps floating in it so we pretended it was ice cream.

AN EVENING AT HOME

We were in the living room, with both doors closed and a warm fire burning in the grate. Dad had stoked it up before he went to the pub. David was in bed, sung to sleep by Ann, who had come back to Mam's chair by the fire. She had her arms crossed tightly over her chest in an attempt to get warm again after ten minutes in the unheated bedroom. We had to take it in turns to sing to him in bed each night. Mammy was ironing while she was listening to a play on the wireless. One of my jobs was to set the board up for her. As she was left-handed I'd learned to do it that way so she could rest the hot iron on the asbestos sheet. Before she got an ironing board, she used to put a thick blanket on a table like Mammam. When I was older and needed to iron a dress for dancing, I couldn't for the life of me put the board up the opposite way round. I did it Mam's way and had to walk round to the other side.

It was 1948 and John was sitting at the table putting his new Olympic stamps in his album. When the games had been in London that summer the papers said that the world went to London on 29 July for the opening ceremony. No one we knew went. Mam said she had more important things to think about, like food rationing and shortages. I loved looking at John's stamps and was fascinated by the strange names of places I'd never even heard of. I wondered how he knew that the words "Magyar Ker" meant Hungary or "Helvetia" meant Switzerland. He had lots of boring old stamps with Hitler's face on, which we all knew were German. When I was only five years old I'd heard of Germany because Hitler owned it. He seemed to have lots of American stamps that were more colourful and interesting. They had pictures of buffaloes, covered wagons, big sailing ships and even bigger aeroplanes. My favourite stamp of all had a picture of a man with brown skin called Ghandi who'd lived in India. In his white robe, with his shaven head and big, round glasses, he seemed to have a kind face – a bit like I imagined a grandfather could have. Mammy told me that someone had shot him in January and that it was a wicked shame because he'd only wanted peace for his country.

I was sitting in Dad's chair right by the fire looking at Mammy's big green poetry book. Inside the cover, she'd written "Christine Gorbutt, 22 Parker St. Cleethorpes 1943".

I knew that her American friend had given it to her and that I wasn't allowed to read it if Dad was around. It had over 700 pages of poems, ballads and sonnets and a few speeches of famous people.

I knew by heart the ones I liked and those too long to learn I read over and over again. My second favourite, after "The Man on the Flying Trapeze", was about two soldiers who killed each other with a sword. One was called Abdul Abulbul Amir and the other Ivan Skavinsky Skavor. By the time I'd read aloud all seventeen verses with funny names in every one, I was expert at the tongue-twisters and made John and Mammy laugh.

Halfway through the evening, the lights went out and Mammy had to get her purse and find a shilling to go in the meter. As she shook the coins into her hand, she could see by the light from the fire. It was lucky she had one, or John would have had to go next door and ask the neighbour if she could change a shilling for two sixpences. John went into the hall and put the coin in the meter and the lights came on again.

Mammy finished the ironing and sat down in her chair while Ann went to make her a cup of tea and I put the board away. Then she lit a cigarette and started doing the crossword in the newspaper. I went back to my book and kept very quiet, hoping that she wouldn't notice that it was past my bedtime.

SHARING A BEDROOM

Our bedroom had a big curved bay window facing the street but no one was able to see in through the net curtains. We slept together, Ann and I, in a small bed with an iron-sprung base and a lumpy flock mattress, where I was on the inside pinned against the wall. I was not allowed to breathe on my sister, so if she turned over I had to face the other way. She made the rules in bed. When she wanted to sing, I had to sing the melody and she sang the descant. She made me do gymnastics, like balancing and handstands. It was easy for her to support me, younger and lighter, as she lay on her back, legs bent and arms outstretched while I stood and wobbled on her knees in my bare feet. But when I tried to hold her my knees parted, unable to take the weight and she collapsed on top of me. We often ended up giggling on the floor; the bed wrecked, with the sheets and blankets a tangled mess, just like when Mam stripped them off for washing. After one such session, I got straight back into bed because I was cold.

'Get out,' said Ann

'No,' I said, curling up smaller and trying not to shiver.

That made her mad. She grabbed the side of the bed,

meaning to pull it away from the wall, but she tugged so hard that the iron frame came off the base. I bashed into the wall and there was a loud bang as the frame hit the floorboards. I landed half off the mattress, wedged in by the springs and the bedstead. I couldn't move. The noise woke up Mam, who came rushing in. We both got into trouble.

In the winter the bedroom was so cold that we often woke in the morning unable to see out of the window. Frost covered the panes inside, creating the most amazing patterns. A ten-foot brass rail was fixed to the wall for thicker curtains to be drawn across the bay as the weather got colder. It took courage to leave a warm bed and stand on the cold lino with nightie off and teeth chattering before we had a race to see who could get dressed first. I usually lost; Ann knew this, because I had to put on my liberty bodice with the rubber buttons after my vest, as an extra layer. Mam said it was because I was prone to bronchitis in the winter. It wasn't fair because Ann never wore one. In the summer we did monkey swings across the curtain rail; left hand, right hand, legs swinging wildly from side to side. By standing on the iron bedhead it was easy to get a hold and launch off, but on reaching the other side, breathless with arms aching, there was of course a ten-foot drop to the floor. It made me feel good though because at least this was something I could do without being scoffed at.

September evenings were not times I looked forward to. All the kids I knew went scrumping on the allotments, but that was usually in the daytime. Sometimes you were seen and chased by a man with a spade but no one was ever caught and we did manage to stuff our mouths with the juicy, fat goosegogs as we ran away. Ann's favourite secret place though, was right next door where Fanny Crosspatch lived with her overweight white bull terrier. She was usually on her own because her husband worked nights as a long-distance lorry driver. Ann reckoned that it wasn't fair because they had the best apple tree in the street and no kids, whereas we had no apple tree and there were four of us. On Monday evenings Mam and Dad normally went to the pub around half past eight, so Ann waited until it got a bit darker.

'Come on, Maggie, they won't be back till ten.' Reluctantly I followed her in my nightie, clambering out of the bedroom window and jumping, landing on the front grass in bare feet. We sneaked down the side of the house, keeping low so the small fence would hide us. Sometimes we had to stop and wait if the scullery light was on next door. We could see straight in because she only had a net curtain.

'I bet she's getting herself some sweets and biscuits for the fat dog,' Ann whispered. I had to put a hand over my mouth so she couldn't hear me laugh.

As soon as the light went off, we ducked past the window and tiptoed to the high fence that separated her garden from ours.

'If the light comes on hiss-s-s-s like a cat,' said Ann.

I wanted to make an owl noise.

'Don't be daft,' she said. 'We don't get owls round here. Anyway if Fanny heard "whoo-hoo, whoo-hoo" she'd open the back door to look, then fat dog would get out, stupid.' It was true; we often heard blinking cats at night, squalling, hissing and spitting. I knew that that dog was one of the few things Ann was frightened of.

'Yeah, but what if she lets fat dog out to chase the cats,' I argued.

'Just do what I say, but not too loud. I'll hear you but she won't.' With those words Ann disappeared over the six-foot fence and I stood in the dark, keeping guard. After she'd picked four or five of the ripest apples, she leaned over the top and dropped them into my outstretched nightie before she jumped down. We scooted up the passage and back through the open window. All I wanted to do was get back to the security of my bed. Sometimes I was still awake when I heard footsteps going past the window then Dad's key in the door, but more often I fell asleep listening to the regular sound of Ann scrunching and munching her way through a third or fourth apple.

BROTHERS AND SISTERS

The first time I went to the pictures with a boy I was only nine. The film was called *The Beast with Five Fingers*. I didn't see much after the first person was strangled as I spent most of the time slouched down so I couldn't see the screen. Being small for my age I didn't have to slide far before the seat in front of me blocked the view. I don't remember much about the film, only being terrified of the cut-off hand that dripped blood all over the white piano keys. The cinema was the Plaza in Grimsby and the boy was my big brother, John.

When the war started on 3 September 1939, it was John's and Mammy's birthday. She was thirty-one and he was six. Dad soon went into the army and Mam was left alone at home bringing up three children before David was born in 1941, making it four. Although John was the eldest and still quite young, he had to grow up quickly and take on responsibilities beyond his age. He didn't have the freedom to go out and play football with his friends or go down on the sands to mess about.

Mam needed him to lift heavy buckets of coal and take out the ashes. He helped her to empty the dirty water from the copper after Monday washday, and in the summer he cut the grass. Once, the woman next door asked Mammy if he could cut her grass and Mammy was cross and said no. She said it was because the woman was afraid there might be a "butterfly bomb" hidden in the grass. Apparently there'd been a German raid the night before with these new secret weapons. John also had to keep an eye on us little ones or run errands, carrying home heavy bags of sugar, flour and potatoes. It was a good thing that he was tall for his age but he always seemed to be hungry. It must have been a nightmare for Mam when food was rationed, feeding a big lad who eventually grew to six-foot-four. I remember her putting a padlock on the pantry door to stop us kids raiding it when she was out.

One day, when John and Ann were coming home from St Peter's Junior School, they met a lad called Billy who was in John's class. He was well known for being a bully and tried to start a fight with John. John didn't want to be involved (it wasn't in his nature) and tried to ignore him despite the name-calling. Ann took the matter into her own hands. Sticking up for her brother, she took out the gas mask that she carried every day, swung it and swiped Billy on the head. He ran away screaming, with blood pouring down his face. Next day, there was a knock on the back door. Mam opened it and there stood Billy's mam.

'Your Ann tried to kill our Billy!' she shouted. 'I'm going to the police.'

Billy was nearly eleven and Ann was still eight.

John paid for me to go to the pictures because he was allowed to have a job when he turned fourteen. He worked for Ernie the butcher, delivering meat and sausages, which he carried in a basket on the front of the butcher's bike. Some customers even gave him a tip and said what a nice, polite lad he was. I loved my big brother.

On the other hand, Ann was bossy and made my life a misery. She seemed to take every opportunity she could to mock or belittle me.

I was actually scared of her and didn't dare tell Mam half of what she did, sometimes physically hurting, because I knew what would happen when we were alone again. I must have been fourteen or fifteen before I had the guts to stand up to her and even then it was because she needed my co-operation in some form.

The routine never changed after a Sunday dinner.

'I'll wash, you dry,' Ann ordered as she pushed up the sleeves of her cardigan and shoved the plug into the sink. I never bothered to argue, knowing full well that Mam would hear and shout from the living room, 'Stop arguing, you two, else I'll bang your heads together.' She never carried out the threat but the vision of it was enough to stop me.

Hot water, heated by a back boiler behind the living-room fire, gushed into the sink raising a cloud of steam. Ann threw in a couple of handfuls of soda crystals from a blue cardboard box before dropping all of the cutlery into the water and making a splash. Mam always stressed it was important to do the knives and forks first. Ann attacked the pots and pans with her usual force and in no time everything was precariously piled high on the wooden draining board. I dawdled because I liked to let it drain a bit, then the tea cloth didn't get so wet. Meanwhile, she swept the scullery floor, slamming and banging the wooden head of the long-handled brush against the skirting boards. Then she gave the red tiles a quick wipe with a wet floor cloth, before leaving me in peace to daydream.

By the time I was eleven we were allowed to go to the ABC Minors at the Ritz Cinema near Grimsby Town's football ground on a Saturday morning, but we had to take it in turns. Mam paid our bus fare and the sixpence to get in and although it was crammed and noisy I loved the atmosphere and liked to sit upstairs where I could look down over the safety rail and see the rough kids larking about. When the lights were dimmed and the picture started, everybody went quiet. First there was a cartoon like *Tom and Jerry* or something funny like *Laurel and Hardy*, then the serial. It was often about cowboys and Indians and some kids in the audience became so involved that they shouted for the goodies and jeered the baddies. Everyone groaned when it finished on a really exciting part. I always told Ann what happened so that she could follow it the next week, but sometimes she deliberately wouldn't tell me, knowing full well it would make me mad.

I got my own back when it was my turn to clean the bedroom that we shared. It was a job on hands and knees with a dustpan and a small, soft brush. The floor was mostly covered in a light brown lino apart from a small rug by the fireplace. During the summer there was usually a small amount of sand on our bedroom floor from my shoes, but rather than carry it through the whole house and chuck it on the garden I hid it under the hearthrug where Ann always found it the following week.

We never did have a real fire in our room, but sometimes when we were poorly we went into Mam and Dad's bed. Before he went to work, Dad would carry a shovelful of red-hot coals from the living room and use it to start a fire going in the small grate in their room. After I had my tonsils out, I remember snuggling under the covers watching the firelight make shadows on the walls.

To supplement pocket money, we collected lemonade bottles that people had chucked away because the shopkeeper gave us tuppence a bottle. If we were really lucky and found six, that was a shilling or sixpence each if we shared. We walked everywhere because although Dad worked at a garage, he never owned a car. Sometimes he borrowed one from his friend Oscar and took us to Skegness, but Ann was usually carsick and for once I could have a jibe at her. We both learned to ride a bike on Mam's "sit up and beg". It was so big I had to stand on the pedals to reach the handlebars, which were almost level with my face. Ann held it steady while I got on and then pushed it off before I lost my balance. We took it down a cinder-track road to practise on, which, apart from tractors, had no traffic. I learned to stop by applying the brakes and steering it into a wall where I fell off. My first bike was a second-hand one when I was twelve. I used it to fetch Dad's beer on a Tuesday night when he didn't go to the pub. In a bass, a woven-fibre bag used for carrying fish, two empty quart bottles clanked together as it dangled from the handlebars. I felt embarrassed when a woman heard the noise and turned to tut at me. The man in the off-licence filled the bottles with four pints of best bitter from a barrel on the floor. The extra weight made the bike unsteady and harder to steer as I rode even more precariously back home. I grew up hating the smell of beer, but it was worth it for the sixpence Dad gave me.

WASH DAYS -
(about nine years old)

On rainy Mondays I could smell warm, wet washing the minute I walked in after school. It was draped on an airing rack suspended from the scullery ceiling. Each of the five long wooden slats could hold a big white sheet and two pillowcases. The gas-fired copper, a huge tank that held gallons and gallons of water stood in a corner by the back door. Although it was empty, it was still warm to the touch. Dad lit it first thing in the morning before anyone else was up. When he'd gone to work and we kids had left for school, Mammy could start without any interruptions.

Using the tap on the side she filled a tin bucket with very hot water from the copper. She poured it into the metal dolly tub, a large barrel-shaped container so big it must have taken at least twenty bucketfuls before there was enough water to cover the clothes. Then she shook wash powder in from an orange cardboard box, which said "Tide" in big letters on the side. We all thought it was a funny name because the tide was where we went paddling or swimming. Someone always cracked the same joke: "Is the tide in Mam?" She never laughed, just groaned and pulled a face.

Mammam told me that in the olden days she'd had to wash her clothes and sheets in cold water outside in the wash house. There was no powder, only a big bar of green soap. After she'd soaped the dirty clothes, she'd rub them hard with a scrubbing brush against a wooden washboard. In the winter her hands were chapped red raw, so she lathered them in Germolene. Once when I fell over she put that on my sore knee; it was pink and smelled nice and came in a little round tin. I thought Mammy was luckier. She used a long wooden pole with a T-shaped handle at the top and a three-legged stool at the bottom. It was called a dolly. I don't know why; it didn't look like any doll I'd ever seen. She swished the dolly and the clothes went backwards and forwards, backwards and forwards as it bashed out the dirt. When we were tall enough to reach she let us have a go, but what had looked like fun was hard work especially with my little arms. Next Mammy very carefully picked up the scalding, dripping washing from the tub with a pair of long-handled wooden tongs. She dropped it into the sink to rinse under cold running water where all the bubbles and soapsuds took ages to disappear down the plughole.

After she had squeezed and twisted the rinsed clothes, she needed to put them through the wringer. It must have been difficult holding the washing with one hand to guide it through the two rubber rollers, while turning the handle with the other. I could help with little things like tea cloths, socks and hankies, but I couldn't shift it for the heavy, wet sheets. John was able to help, though, and used two hands to turn it. The water dropped into a bucket under the wringer, which had to be tipped down the sink.

If it was fine, everything dried outside on a washing line supported by a long wooden prop. On good windy days it slapped and flapped, and sometimes in a gusty wind, little things, like girls' knickers, sailed over the fence into next door's garden. On rainy, dull Mondays the washing took twice as long to dry inside. In the living room straight off the scullery, Mammy draped it over a wooden clothes-horse in front of a blazing fire. The windows soon steamed up and we drew pictures or wrote our names, which we had to clear off later. I loved the smell of the washing drying, it was warm and familiar, but what I liked even more was the smell of bubble and squeak cooking in lard in the frying pan. After a dinner of roast beef, Yorkshire pudding and vegetables, followed by jam roly-poly with custard on a Sunday, we always had cold meat with piccalilli, red cabbage and pickled onions, and a big helping of bubble and squeak every Monday.

CRIME AND PUNISHMENT

As I waited I was biting my lower lip, determined not to make a sound. Seconds later I was nursing a stinging left hand, where across the palm an angry red wheal was already forming. I blinked back the tears as I stumbled over to my desk. As I picked up my sewing, averting my eyes from the children around me, I tried to do a few stitches with a shaky hand in the offending piece of screwed up material. Words tumbled round in my head.

"I hate you, bitch. Everyone hates you in your stupid high heels and tarty red lipstick."

She was only five-foot tall, and even though some of the lads now ten or eleven years old were bigger, they admitted that they were still scared of her. They nicknamed her "wacko Jacko". She didn't have any rules about using the cane but made them up as she went along. I only did it for a laugh, balancing the thimble on my nose I mean. They did laugh and that was when she caught me. Once, she caned the whole class just for drawing a line with a pencil and ruler under a completed piece of work. She said she hadn't told us to, so how come every single person did it? At least I sat in a row furthest away from her. There were fifty of us in the scholarship class, sitting in six rows of seven and one row of eight. Boys were on the left and girls on the right. The boys she liked to keep an eye on sat directly in line with her high desk, where she perched like a preacher barely able to see over the top. I felt sorry for poor Anthony, with his black National Health glasses, sitting right under her nose. He wasn't disruptive, just a quiet, nervous lad, maybe a bit slow in answering for fear of getting it wrong. We were all envious of the children in Mr Brown's class next door; he was young and didn't even have a cane.

Playtime was a welcome escape and a chance for the boys to let off steam. Their playground was noisy as they charged around playing their war games. They dashed about with arms outstretched, swooping, swerving and colliding as they machine-gunned each other out of the sky. The noise changed to a long, high whine as they spun around pretending to be hit before falling to the ground. Sometimes a few lads kicked an empty tin can round the playground if there was no ball available, and some groups knelt out of the way playing a game with marbles.

In our separate playground, we skipped to the familiar rhymes that we knew by heart. Every girl owned a skipping rope, usually an end piece from a washing line. If like me you were quite small and the rope was too long, it had to be wrapped several times round your hand.

We skipped fast and even twice as fast for what we called "big jumps". Even though the playground was hard if you tripped and fell, we still loved the risk of jumping over a rope held by one girl at each end. With our gingham dresses tucked into the legs of navy blue knickers, we sailed over as it was slowly raised higher and higher until there was a winner. Games had a season and skipping ropes were changed for balls; one, two or three depending on your ability. It was then the turn of whips and tops. We competed to see who could keep them going the longest.

When the whistle was blown for the end of play we ran to line up single-file, boys on the left, girls on the right. There was no touching, no talking and no laughing, especially if a teacher called Miss Armstrong was on duty. She only came in if another teacher was away. We were all scared of her, even the boys, because she was tall with black hair and faint signs of a moustache, heavily built, more like a man than a woman. I never saw her smile. If the line wasn't straight she'd march up to the person concerned, grab hold of an arm and shove them into place. The poor boy or girl, taken by surprise, usually staggered and nearly fell over. It was no wonder that her nickname was Miss Strongarm.

TRADESMEN

I heard music on the wireless and smelled the dinner cooking as I walked into the scullery. It was late on a Friday morning and Dad must still have been at work. He was usually home just after twelve. There in the living room, hands clasped, their bodies close together, was my mam with Albert. They were dancing and laughing to the unmistakeable music of Victor Silvester. Albert was the insurance man who came weekly to collect Mam's regular payment of a shilling. It was innocent flirting between old friends but I wasn't old enough to understand. I hated him for touching my mam and always calling her Chrissie. Nobody else did. She was Chris to everybody.

Charlie Wilson the grocer also came on a Friday but I liked him. He didn't flirt or dance but I think he was fond of Mam. I could tell by the easy way they chatted and joked. He wore a big white apron and had a little stubby pencil tucked behind his ear. He wrote her order in his red book, sometimes licking the end of the pencil to make it write better. He and his wife didn't have a family and he always made a fuss of us kids, often bringing a few sweets while they were still rationed. Mam stayed loyal to him even when the first self-service shops began to operate. He finally had to retire, though, because of the competition.

The coalman only came during the winter. He looked really funny with his smudged dirty face and filthy black hands. He must have been strong because he could carry big hundredweight sacks of coal on his back from the coal lorry parked on the street, right down the side of our house. Dad usually ordered ten bags. The man had to tip them through a small door outside where the coal fell into the coalhouse inside, in the corner of the scullery.

'What a mucky job,' I said to Mam when he'd gone. 'I bet you're glad Dad isn't a coalman.'

Other tradesmen called at houses in the late forties and fifties, some knocking on doors and others shouting or ringing a bell from the street.

I can remember a time when I was four or five, running to the front gate holding a two-pint jug. Standing patiently at the roadside was a huge black and white Shire horse with a shaggy mane and big brown eyes. The cart behind him was tipping with the weight of the heavy churns full of milk. The milkman, dressed in a long white coat, held a long-handled, tin measuring cup which he dipped into an open churn. He filled my jug with two level cupfuls of the white frothy milk. As I walked slowly back down the side of the house, I dipped a finger in and was still sucking it as I handed it to Mam.

'Is it good?' she said.

'Mmm, can I have a drop more please?'

A knife grinder came three or four times a year and was always surrounded by a group of children. The grindstone was on a small cart with wheels so the man could easily move it from street to street. We watched it revolve as he worked it with his feet a bit like the old-fashioned treadle sewing machine that Mam's friend had. While he sharpened the knife, which he held in two hands, the stone turned, and as the blade hit the metal there was a loud screeching noise. We all put our hands over our ears while we watched the sparks flying off like fireworks.

Sometimes the rag-and-bone man came down the street with his horse and cart. If we gave him some old clothes, even dirty ones, he'd give you tuppence. As he walked on down the road all the kids echoed him shouting, "Enyoleraggabone!" It was such a lovely word.

GROWING UP

I was helping Mam to change the big sheets on her bed when she stopped and looked at me.

'I need to talk to you about periods before you go back to school.'

'I know,' I snapped, deliberately keeping my head down and not looking at her. 'Don't bother, I already know about it.' I snatched at the top sheet and, trying to hide my embarrassment, straightened the corner, pushing it hard under the mattress, hoping she wouldn't go on.

It was bad enough having to share a bed with Ann and sometimes waking up to find her blood on my nightie. That was when I'd learned about what happened to girls. How could anyone sleep so close to an older sister night after night and not become aware of such awful bodily functions? The other thing that I'd recently found out was that babies weren't born through the woman's tummy. I was only eleven and didn't want to grow up.

It wouldn't be long until September when I'd be starting at the grammar school. Mam had had to borrow the money to buy my uniform from Albert the dancing man who collected the insurance each week. He gave her something called a credit note, and in return she'd pay him a fixed sum each time he came. We'd been on the bus to the Co-op department store in Grimsby because they stocked the uniform but also took "tickets", as Mam called them. I'd been fitted out with a navy blue gymslip – only the older girls wore skirts – two white blouses, an orange and navy tie, a navy blazer and a matching beret. The blazer had a gold badge on, which said Cleethorpes Girls' Grammar School. If you paid with money in the big Co-op, they didn't put it in a till like other shops. The notes and coins were placed in a hand-sized metal cylinder that whizzed up a tube behind the assistant. It was then propelled along a tram wire overhead to the cash desk. Sitting behind a glass window in a tiny office upstairs I could see the cashier, who put the change and receipt in the tube and sent it back the same way. Sometimes there appeared to be several cylinders flying through the air at once; it was fun watching them.

Alice, one of Mam's best friends, bought my leather school satchel and the hockey stick. I liked Auntie Alice; she only had one son and he was in the navy. I know she missed him. Mam said that was why she spoiled us girls. I remember once going out with her in a bread delivery van that she drove during the war. I sat next to her in the front seat and loved the smell of the baked bread and rolls piled in the trays behind us.

'Promise me you won't move,' she said, each time she got out to make a delivery. I sat quite still, knowing that she'd give me an iced bun if I was a good girl. She didn't seem to have a husband; maybe he'd been killed in the war.

'Would you like to go to Aunt Ann's for a few days?' asked Mam, after we'd finished making the bed in silence. She must have realised that I was embarrassed and changed the subject.

'Yes please.' I jumped at the chance. Although Annie was Mammam's sister, we didn't call her Great Aunt Ann because it was too much of a mouthful. She didn't have any children because Uncle Jack, her husband, had been gassed in the First World War. They lived in Holton Le Clay about ten miles away and I had to go on two buses. First I caught a number six, the one that took me to junior school every day. I knew to get off at the Old Market in Grimsby. That was where all the town buses turned round. Then it was a short walk through the square to the other bus station, where I looked for one that said Louth because that went through Holton.

Maureen, the little girl who lived next door to Aunt Ann, was always across the road waiting for me with her dad. He owned the garage opposite the bus stop and always seemed to know what time I was arriving. Maureen was just a year younger than me and had no brothers and sisters, so we got on very well. Every day we went exploring in the fields behind her house. She showed me where there was a robins' nest, we looked for frogspawn in the ditches, and she taught me how to recognise the mewling call of a buzzard miles away in the sky.

We made daisy chains and wore them like necklaces and held buttercups under chins to see who liked butter the best. One day I watched her from a distance as she stood gently stroking a big, fat bumblebee with the tip of her finger. It had come to rest on the back of her outstretched hand.

'Here,' she said, 'you have a go.'

'Um, no thanks.' I'd have loved to but didn't have the courage. Ann would never have believed me even if I'd dared.

John went into the RAF for five years about the same time that I went to the grammar school. In the 1950s all boys had to do National Service when they reached eighteen. They had to choose between going into the army, the Royal Navy or the Royal Air Force. It lasted for two years but they could stay in longer if they wanted to.

For the first six weeks they did something called square-bashing, which I didn't really understand apart from the fact that it involved being ordered about outside and in by a bossy man in uniform, who I thought must have had the loudest voice on the camp.

John happened to be home for a couple of days before the September term started for me, so Mam took the pair of us, John in his uniform and me in my new school blazer, to have our photo taken with her.

Her friend, Harry the newsagent, was a photographer but he didn't have a studio. He made the three of us walk together up Sea View Street towards the camera with Mam in the middle. She loved the black and white photo that Harry printed and gave to her and I loved it too because I was so proud of my big brother. When he was posted to the Far East for two years I wrote to him every week and put my letter in the blue and red airmail envelope along with Mam's.

I told him I was learning French at school and that I had quite an old teacher called Miss Oliver, but I liked her because she was sort of old-fashioned and quaint. Her grey hair was coiled over her head in two plaits and little wispy kiss curls hung at the side of her face. I was good at French and along with English it became one of my best subjects. We learned little songs and jingles like "Frere Jacques" and "Le Coucou", though I soon discovered that singing them aloud at home irritated Ann, who snapped.

'Stop showing off just because you're learning French.'

I didn't ever tell her that I'd been the only one in the class who couldn't do a handstand when we were asked to do one in the gym against the wall bars. I'd felt so daft as I struggled to kick my legs really high. It was pathetic. To my relief no one had laughed and when the teacher asked for two volunteers to act as side supports, several girls put a hand up. With a bit of help and a lot of laughing and encouragement, I soon learned to do it on my own.

In the second year, our two classes of twelve-year-olds were streamed into A and Alpha. In A we started to learn German and the other class did cookery and sewing. At the end of each year we had exams and it was always the same clever girls who came in the first five. I was quite happy to be in the top twelve for most subjects, except for maths. I never did understand the concepts of theorems, sine or cosines, logarithms and antilog. It was all double Dutch to me.

I preferred geography, which included so much more than learning the capital cities of countries. It opened up the new associated language of climates and weather patterns, rainforests and hanging valleys.

Television was still in its infancy and we could only look at illustrations in books of the natural world. I saw a mountain for the first time in my life when we went on a field trip to the Lake District when I was sixteen. I was overawed by the grandeur and beauty of it all.

HOLIDAYS AND EVENTS

It was in July, at the start of the long summer holiday, that Mam and Dad came back from a few days away to find a card propped up against the clock on the mantelpiece. Printed in black capital letters, it said:

GRIMSBY AND DISTRICT
GENERAL HOSPITAL

VISITING HOURS: 3pm to 4pm and 7pm to 8pm

They'd left us with Mammam and David had had an accident. We had no phone and there had been no way to tell them.

'Can't we ask the police to put an SOS on the wireless?' I suggested. 'Every week there seems to be one – *Here is an SOS for Mr and Mrs Charlie Brown believed to be touring in Cornwall. Will they please contact the Oxford Hospital where their son is seriously ill.*' I tried to say it like the man on the wireless. Mammam laughed.

'It's not that serious. He's only in for observation.'

On the morning they were coming home, she was

up early baking and I was helping her. As she put some bread buns into the oven, she said that she was a bit concerned about what Mam would say.

'She'll be fine,' I told her with all the wisdom of my eleven years. 'Don't worry; she's used to one of us doing something. Can't you remember Ann falling off the see-saw on the rec last year and knocking out four top teeth? Mam never went mad then. Let's make some Ambrose for a treat while the bread's baking; they're her favourite.' Ambrose was a made-up name for a special currant bun. It was called that after a friend of Mam's who'd given her the recipe.

When Mammam did tell my mam and dad I held her hand and squeezed it, because I loved her and didn't like to see her upset. I was right. They were fine about it, I knew they would be. Mammam made a cup of tea and I buttered some current buns, making sure there was one for them to take to David.

Although I was partly to blame, I didn't realise just how serious it could have been. I'd persuaded David to come on the sands with me and help with the horses. Not the little Shetlands but the bigger ones near the bathing pool. Although they were much taller and heavier in size they were steady and reliable, popular with older children and even some adults. The biggest horse called Dawn was a brown and white mare, who despite her huge frame was kind and gentle. She'd nuzzle you for a treat or sometimes rub her big head against your shoulder as if you were a scratching post. David had been leading her when he tripped and fell. One of her hooves had accidentally caught him in the corner of the eye and he was taken to hospital in an ambulance. When they carried him off on a stretcher, I felt quite important that it was my little brother. The ambulance men were very nice and said not to worry; it was just to make sure he was all right. They kept him in for two or three days but there appeared to be no long-lasting effects. It was lucky that the ponies were not wearing shoes, otherwise the damage could have been worse.

We never went away as a family but neither did my friends. It hardly mattered as the sands were less than a mile in one direction from the house, and fields, allotments and countryside even nearer at the bottom of the street. John went to scout camp one year and Ann went with the school to Stoke Rochford. She stayed in a large country house, which had been used by the army during the war before it became a training college for teachers. She must have been about twelve and all she remembered when she came back was the awful girl who snored all night. If it had been me, she'd have thumped me and woken me up.

When I was thirteen and at the grammar school, my attendance was a hundred per cent. John always said we weren't allowed to be ill. One day in June, after exams, I pleaded with Mam to let me go and help Ray with some donkeys for the day.

'Yes,' she said. 'Only this once, so don't ask again.'

We went to Barton-upon-Humber, which was thirty miles away. Apart from the day trip to London with the school when I was ten, my experience of the world was limited to a radius of seven or eight miles. As I sat with Ray in the front of the horsebox, perched high on a cushion in the passenger seat, I was so excited that Barton could have been the North Pole in my mind.

There must have been a school gala or a village fete because we parked in a field crammed full of tents and stalls. Young mums struggled over the bumpy grass with toddlers in pushchairs and children milled around clasping precious pocket money in hot sweaty hands. I was in my element giving them rides on the donkeys and told them each one had a name like Jack and Jill or Lucky and Silver.

Next day, which was a Friday, I went back to school with a nose that was starting to peel and telltale freckles that had appeared overnight. When I handed over the note Mam had written saying I'd been sick, my teacher gave me a look of sheer disbelief.

'Humph,' she sniffed. 'Well, you look all right to me!'

SUMMER SUN

The only sound is from the rhythmic beat of hooves galloping over the wet sand. The tide is still going out and the white seagulls wheeling above contrast sharply against the cloudless sky. We're both laughing as we ride together bareback on Billy the chestnut pony. Wendy, my best friend, is sitting in front of me holding the reins and grasping a hefty chunk of mane as she leans forward. I'm behind her, our bodies touching, with my arms encircling her waist. The pair of us weighs a fraction of what the pony could carry. Sometimes the wind blows Wendy's long hair into my face and I turn my head from side to side and spit it out. Billy's flanks feel warm against my bare legs, but now and again water splashes up as he gallops through a shallow pool left by the receding tide.

I learned to stay on a pony from the age of ten, with no lessons, no hat and no funny clothes.

After the war, holidays began again in the fifties with day trips to the seaside. The factories of the Midlands at that time would close down completely for a week but they staggered the holidays. I learned from Mam the expressions "Barnsley week", "Sheffield week" or "Wakefield week", not realising what it meant until I was older. I knew they were towns in Yorkshire nowhere near the coast.

Trains arrived in Cleethorpes full of excited parents and small children. They all trooped down to the sands with arms laden, the little ones clutching their tin buckets and spades. Some stayed near the station, not far from the pier, where there were donkeys, ice cream sellers, rock shops and a Punch and Judy. The smell of doughnuts and candyfloss mixed with the acrid air from the steam engines right alongside.

It was crowded and noisy, so many families wandered further along the prom towards the bathing pool. Here there was more room for them to sit and spread out with their belongings, where they stayed until it was time to go back for the train. There was only a small tea van on the sands that sold hot and cold drinks and sandwiches.

Instead of donkeys there were ponies and when I was eleven I started working down there for the whole of the long school holiday.

There were three Shetland ponies: Whisky, who was black and white; Brandy, a chestnut who was a little devil; and Soda, a quiet little grey. The fourth was a Welsh mountain pony, quite fast and very strong, called Silver.

The other children who led the ponies were like me. We did it partly for the money but more for the ride to the field at the end of the day. It wasn't hard work and we had lots of fun.

Visitors paid sixpence a go and we took it in turns to lead. It was easier to walk barefoot in the sand and we rarely got trodden on. Anyway, the ponies weren't shod. The ride was about a hundred yards and if it was with a small child, a parent walked by the side. Older kids, some cocky, would ask to go faster so we walked them up and pretended we hadn't heard. On turning, we warned "hold tight" and ran while the pony trotted. This usually bumped and shook them all over the place and was fast enough.

Occasionally Silver would canter and I had to hang onto the bridle, my feet scarcely touching the sand, as I was carried along. The rider would get off red-faced and grinning, half scared and half thrilled, while I flopped onto the ground to get my breath back.

I loved the freedom and fresh air and the smell of the ponies' coats on the days it rained. Then, the sands rapidly emptied as visitors scrambled to collect their stuff. They hurried up the steps onto the prom and across the road into the teashops with the steamed-up windows. Ray, the man who owned the ponies, would look at the sky to judge whether it was a passing shower or set for the day. Sometimes he waited for a while and bought us each a mug of tea from the stall. We sheltered under the awning cradling the warm drink between two hands, keeping an eye on the ponies that had turned their backs to the rain. They all stood heads down, patiently waiting to go home.

The best bit for us was the eventual ride to the field. We promised to take it easy and set off walking until we were safely out of sight, past the bathing pool. Then we kicked the ponies into a canter and, shrieking with laughter, had a race through the sand hills. Sometimes

Brandy got overexcited and bucked; the rider fell off but no one ever got badly hurt. At the field some thirty minutes later, we unsaddled and took off the bridles. The ponies usually rolled, shook themselves then went away to graze. We left the tack in a shed, locked the door and hid the key before we made our way back across the golf links. If we had any money we stopped to get two penn'orth of chips with scraps from the chip shop near the stables.

At the end of each week we got paid about thirty shillings, all in sixpences. It felt like a lot of money.

PASTIMES AND PLAYTIMES

The navy pram we pushed was a coach-built Silver Cross, sturdy and strong, with massive shiny wheels and a big rubber-handled brake on the left-hand side. I was in charge because it was my cousin who was fast asleep, snugly wrapped under the covers. I could barely see over the hood which was raised, but Wendy was younger than me and even smaller. The tide was right in that morning, so since we couldn't get on the sands we'd decided to do our good deed for the day. We would ride Billy later. We were walking along the prom, but as there was a cold east wind there were only a few brave souls out and about. It was what Mam called a good drying day, meaning the washing of course.

'I'm cold,' I said. 'Let's run.'

Wendy, on the left, grabbed a bit of the pram handle with one hand so that we'd stay together and we took off. As we picked up speed, we zigzagged in and out of the folk coming in the opposite direction. Ignoring the disapproving look on their faces we laughed and shouted against the wind, when horror of horrors the pram stopped abruptly and tipped over backwards. Wendy had accidently flipped the handbrake.

The wheels were still spinning in the air, but luckily the pram was balanced on the hood that we'd put up to protect the baby from the cold. Two bossy women rushed over fussing and tutting, taking charge and righting it, while we stood aside waiting for the worst in stunned silence. They found my cousin still blissfully asleep, safely cocooned beneath the blankets. One woman told us off and said we were totally irresponsible and naughty girls. We waited while they walked away, still talking loudly. I heard the words "too young" and "feckless mothers", whatever that meant. Somewhat chastened we turned round and headed slowly back home. We didn't bother to tell the baby's mam, my Auntie Joan; she might not have let us take him out anymore.

Sometimes in the summer, Wendy and I went off to Wonderland, the big indoor amusement park. It was right past the station at the far end, where the prom and the railings finished and the sand became muddy and stony. Mam called it the penny end.

When it opened again after the war, we were all given a free sheet of perforated tokens at school. The name of the ride or game was printed on each ticket, like dodgems, big dipper, crazy house or ghost train. I didn't like anything fast or things that swayed; even a garden swing or hammock made me feel dizzy and sick.

On the other hand, Ann loved them the faster the better. I'd swapped the tickets I wouldn't use with her.

I was happier with my feet on the ground where my stomach or heart would stay in its proper place.

The only time I did dare to go on the dips, I was sick all down the front of my cotton dress. It was miles to walk home, with the stinking wet material, where I'd tried to clean it, clinging to my legs. I never wore that dress again.

Most rides were only sixpence so if I'd been working on the sands I had a pocketful. Wendy's grandma gave her some money every time she saw her. I think she was quite rich because she owned a big fish and chip restaurant in the market place. If we went there and the fresh cream cakes had just been delivered, they'd be sitting on trays waiting to be taken into the kitchen. We were allowed to choose any we liked. I usually had two, because at home we *never* had fresh cream cakes, only the ones that Mam made with buttercream. I usually picked a cream slice with icing on the top, but my favourite was a butterfly cake with pastry so flaky it crumbled before it even went in your mouth. I think it must have been the cream that kept it stuck together.

Wendy and I always started with a ride on the roundabout. I loved the painted horses, each with its own special name written in fancy scroll on the neck below the mane. I liked to hear the music playing from the Wurlitzer pipe organ, and watch the arm of the little wooden man with a baton; it went up and down, keeping time as he conducted. According to Ann it was too slow and tame, but I didn't care. Anyway, she daren't even *sit* on a real horse, let alone gallop like Wendy and me.

The ghost train wasn't so frightening if you sat with a friend. Hairy spiders touched your face in the dark and grinning monsters suddenly leapt out to get you. We screamed and grabbed hold of each other in the little car. We weren't really scared but it did make us jump. The crazy house was a room of mirrors, reached by going over a wobbly bridge down a half-lit passage. We laughed like mad at the different reflections in the bent mirrors. Sometimes you looked really dumpy with a huge sticking-out belly and short, fat legs. Other times you were tall and skinny with a pointy head, long dangly arms and witch-like fingers. If no one else was in we danced around pulling a face and stuck out our tongues, trying to see who could be the funniest.

When we'd had enough we walked home, stopping to go in the arcades on the front, to have a go on the slot machines.

I couldn't see the point of losing all my hard-earned pennies, trying to ping a silver ball and win the jackpot. I was more likely to win something, even if it was only a toy watch or a few sweets, by trying to control the crane that hovered over and picked up a prize.

On the wall by the station steps, there was still an old chocolate-dispensing machine. The four tin drawers were rusty from lack of use, but the writing at the top was still readable. FRY'S CHOCOLATE BARS, it said in capital letters. I often rattled a drawer and dreamt of the day when I could put a coin in the slot at the top and, like magic, a bar of chocolate would shoot out of the bottom.

A QUESTION OF MONEY

'Lend me some money, Maggie.'

'What? Again? What for?'

'Cigarettes.'

'I've only got a shilling and I want that for some comics and stuff on Saturday.'

'Look, I get paid tomorrow; you'll have it back by then. Honest.'

Despite the fact that Ann was fifteen and had a job, she always ran out of money before pay day. I had to get by on pocket money, plus the little that Dad gave me for fetching his beer and in the summer what I could earn on the sands.

Ann met Shirley when they both started work doing the same job in an office at Smethursts. It was a large fish business that prepared and supplied fresh fish straight from the docks for wholesalers all over the country. Grimsby at that time was probably one of the largest fishing ports in Britain.

The two girls became best friends and did everything together; dancing on Saturday nights, drinking and smoking in the pubs and going out in a foursome when they each had a boyfriend. Shirley owned a motor scooter, which she used for work, and the pair of them regularly went off on it, though Ann never told me where they'd been.

Now and again on Fridays when Shirley came to our house, they made toffee in the scullery after Mam and Dad had gone out. They bought a green tin of Lyle's Golden Syrup and a bag of sugar and poured the whole lot into a pan. The gooey mixture bubbled and boiled till it was the right consistency and the scullery smelled like a sweet factory. My job, if I wanted a share, was to stand by the back door pushing it backwards and forwards in order to create a draught. It would hopefully get rid of the smell. At least I wasn't made to wash the sticky pan afterwards; it was a good job we had plenty of hot water.

On Saturday mornings I loved going to a second-hand shop that belonged to a woman called Amy Mills. She was even smaller than me and always had a great black shawl draped around her skinny body. It was dingy inside the shop, lit by a single bulb attached to a long flex hanging from the ceiling, which swayed to and fro every time the door was opened. There was a musty smell coming from the piles of old clothes stacked on the floor and spilling out from overfull cardboard boxes.

Hand-knitted jumpers and cardigans, even with holes, were piled up on a counter. These could be unpicked and the wool used again for mittens socks or scarfs.

There were torn cotton skirts and frocks that would be bought by a hard-up mum, who with her clever sewing skills could cut them up and remake the pieces into a dress for a little girl. Thick khaki army greatcoats hung from the picture rail and an old wooden chest was crammed with ladies' hats and men's flat caps. Amy sat on a stool behind a counter half hidden by a rusty birdcage, but her keen eyes were always watching.

Each week at home we got two comics that Mam paid for, *The Dandy* and *The Beano*. They featured Desperate Dan whose favourite food was cow pie, Korky the Kat who must have been on borrowed time having long used up his nine lives, Lord Snooty who lived up to his name, and Keyhole Kate whose nosiness was forever getting her into trouble. As I got older I discovered an American comic called *Captain Marvel* when I'd gone into Amy's shop to swap ours. She didn't always have them but if they were there I took as many as my money would allow. On the cover it said ten cents but if we had some to swap we only paid a penny. Captain Marvel was a superhero. In real life, he was a young reporter who'd met a wizard called Shazam after he'd been struck by lightning. If there was trouble, he would say the wizard's name and immediately he'd turn into the hero. He wore a bright red costume trimmed with gold, which had a lightning strike on the chest. The comics were first published in America in 1940 long before the later idea of Superman.

By the time I was fifteen I was able to do a part-time job. I worked in the tea stall on the sands, and in the shop near the pier selling seaside rock. It was situated near the railway station where day trippers walked by on their way back to catch the train home. They bought seven or eight small pink sticks of rock with Cleethorpes written all the way through and great black and white striped minty gobstoppers. I was glad we didn't sell candyfloss because I couldn't stand the smell of the sweet sickly stuff.

FIRST DANCE

'You can take Maggie with you tonight,' Mam said to Ann as we were eating dinner one Saturday.

'Why?'

'Because I'm asking you to, and because at least you can show your younger sister where the cloakroom and the lavatories are.'

'Doesn't the grammar school teach them that then?' Ann retorted. She was spoiling for an argument but Mam didn't rise to the bait. Dad might have been invisible for all his contribution; he just carried on eating, thinking no doubt about the forthcoming football that afternoon. Mam said she could never understand the animosity between the two of us. She'd been an only child herself and had wanted a brother or sister.

'She doesn't have to take me,' I said. I no more wanted to go with her than she did with me.

I'd just had my sixteenth birthday and was looking forward to the evening. We'd broken up for the summer holidays, finished O level exams, and a few of us had celebrated by going on the boating lake for the afternoon.

It would be the first time I was allowed to be out late on a Saturday night. We'd had a taste of dancing at school that term. For six weeks, boys from the grammar school up the road came to our all-girls school during the dinner hour. In the hall we'd been put into pairs matched only by approximate height, learning first how to hold your partner. I was teamed with a smallish boy who gazed at me through his glasses. He made me feel rather uncomfortable. We faced each other and I nervously placed my right hand in his left and put my left hand on his shoulder. He, with more confidence, put his right hand on my back, where I could feel the warmth from his palm through my white school blouse.

'Slow, slow, quick, quick, slow; slow, slow, quick, quick, slow,' chanted our gym mistress over and over. She walked it without the music as we stood and watched. 'Now you try.'

With heads bowed looking at our feet and chanting the rhythm, we moved slowly sideways, forwards and backwards.

It was difficult not to tread on each other's toes and even harder not to laugh. I relaxed more because I was concentrating so hard and we managed, albeit clumsily, to giggle our way through it.

We learned the basics of the waltz and the quickstep, and sometimes at home I persuaded Mam to practise with me when Victor Silvester was on the wireless.

After we'd washed up, Ann was banging the stuff on the wooden draining board harder than usual still trying to make her point. I left the pots to dry until later and got out the ironing board. My friend Janice, who was hoping to teach domestic science, namely cookery and needlework, made all my dresses. The one I ironed was white cotton with dainty blue flowers all over it. It had a scooped neck, no collar or sleeves and a full swirly skirt. I would wear my new waist petticoat made in stiff paper nylon, which puffed out the skirt. As it was July I wouldn't need to wear stockings. My legs were brown enough and, anyway, I just hated wearing suspender belts. The new fashion of girdles was just taking off, a garment that was meant to flatten your stomach and hold in your bottom. It also had suspenders. They were even more uncomfortable and really there was little need for us young girls with waists of twenty-four or twenty-six inches and tummies that were as flat as pancakes.

Although we left the house together that evening, not a word was exchanged as we walked to the bottom of the street. The minute we turned the corner Ann, spoke.

'You're on your own now, Maggie,' she announced and marched off.

I didn't care. I was meeting Janice outside the Winter Gardens. We'd arranged to go in and stay together all the evening. As we went through the glass swing doors, I heard the beat of the music and felt a flutter of excitement. In the dance hall to our immediate right, some girls were standing chatting in groups of two or three. Others were sitting round tables in fours, drinking glasses of fizzy Babycham.

Across the room in a large group stood the young lads, wearing open-necked shirts, trying to look suave with cigarette in hand as they eyed every girl who walked through the door.

The older men, who were sitting at tables drinking

beer, wore suits and ties, and those in RAF uniform looked so smart with their highly polished shoes and well-cut hair. With heads bent in earnest conversation, they appeared less concerned with their surroundings, naturally casual and more mature alongside the talent-spotting group of adolescents.

In the centre of the dance floor suspended from the ceiling, a large glass-faceted ball rotated slowly, its twinkling lights reflecting onto the dancers below and bouncing off the walls. A drum roll and a clash of cymbals from the band on the stage signified the end of that particular dance. Most men escorted their partners back to their friends but the younger lads beat a hasty retreat, leaving the poor girl to walk back to her seat alone.

We were both asked to dance pretty much all evening, the few lessons with the grammar school boys proving their worth. We left at midnight after the last waltz. Janice lived in a road just off the front facing the sea and the promenade so I walked the rest of the way home on my own. I carried my shoes, happy, but with aching feet unaccustomed to wearing high heels all evening. Mam was waiting up for me so I didn't mention Ann. I hadn't seen her all night anyway. I think she went with Shirley, probably to the Cafe Dansant across the road. She wouldn't be seen dead with her younger sister. Dancing became a routine every Saturday night and throughout the summer on Wednesdays and Thursdays, too, when the Pier Pavillion and the Cafe Dansant were also open.

Boyfriends came and went and we quickly learned

that servicemen and commercial travellers were much better dancers. They seemed more polite and worldly-wise compared with boys of our own age.

My first long-term boyfriend called John had a car, which was my chief reason for going out with him. He was a bit of a bore really, with rather old-fashioned ideas and not much sense of humour. But he was a good dancer. I actually preferred his friend Harry, who was full of fun and always larking about. However, I stuck with John for over a year, knowing that soon I'd be going away to live at teacher training college. At that point, I would chuck him and move on.

LOWER SIXTH FORM

The post arrived before I left for school. I was excited as soon as I saw my own name on the brown official-looking envelope. I took it into the living room where Mam was sitting by the fire, having a cup of tea. I tore it open, aware that she was watching my face, and scanned the contents with dismay. Unable to hold back my feelings I thrust it into her outstretched hand saying, 'They don't want me. Well, I'm leaving school anyway.' I was close to tears. It wasn't meant to be like this.

'What will you do?' Mam didn't argue or say you can't do that; she could see how upset I was.

'I'll still apply for Teacher Training College to start next year; in the meantime I'll get a job. Anything will do so I can earn some money for buying books and stuff. Whatever it is, it'll be better than school.' I could imagine Ann's delight when she heard the news. At least I'd not lose face if I could get a job. However, when I got home from school that afternoon I was even more steamed up.

'It's not fair,' I ranted. 'How come girls with fewer O levels than me have been accepted?' Mam listened carefully as I reeled off their names.

'It looks to me,' she said when I'd stopped raving,

'as though they were chosen not because of their own academic achievement but because of the merits of their fathers' position in society. There's a bank manager and a police superintendent to name a couple. And,' she paused, 'their wives don't need to go to work.'

'Yeah and my dad just works in a garage serving petrol,' I said bitterly. 'This is her fault; she never did like me. She's a lah-dee-dah snob.'

Mam knew full well who I was talking about and didn't disagree. She also hated the patronising manner of my headmistress, who regularly went into the milliner's shop where she worked. I was proud of my mam who'd had to leave school at fourteen. She'd grown up surrounded by adults and for her age was far ahead of the rest of her class. The school was in a poor area and a lot of the boys were illiterate. At the end of each day the teacher used to ask the class a question, usually relating to that day's work. The first person with a hand up giving the right answer could leave at once. It was always Christine McGuiness, my mam. She said she ran home as fast as she could because the other kids would chase her. On her fourteenth birthday she was apprenticed to a milliner and learned the skills of altering and adorning ladies' hats. The shop she worked in in Cleethorpes was well regarded locally and owned by a lady with the grand name of Madame Lomax.

The reason for my disappointment was that after finishing one year in the sixth form, I'd hoped to go into an infant school for a year. Grimsby Education Committee had the innovative idea of allowing girls who hoped to teach to be in a school environment for a year before they started college. It was a fantastic opportunity for seventeen-year-olds to find out whether they really were suited to working with children. At that time it wasn't necessary to have A levels for teacher training college. Interviews were based on aptitude, attitude and potential, rather than academic qualifications.

I went ahead and left school in July after completing the year in the lower sixth. I'd had a final interview with the head who asked me what I was going to do.

'I've no idea,' I told her, 'but I still want to teach and shall apply for Teacher Training College.'

'You'd stand more chance if you stayed for A levels, young lady,' she retorted. I didn't bother to answer. Thanks to her lousy reference I wasn't one of her golden girls who'd be starting in an infant school that September.

Every day I looked at the adverts in the Situations Vacant column of the *Grimsby Evening Telegraph*. I only went for one interview and was accepted immediately for an office job in the Bird's Eye frozen fish factory. I could stick it for a year, though I didn't tell them of my plan because nothing was going to wreck my dream of becoming a teacher.

About two months later Mam came home very excited, bursting to tell me her news. She'd been to Grimsby and by accident had bumped into Nell, a long-time friend, who was on the Grimsby Education Committee. Nell had asked after me and when Mam explained the situation, she was furious. She said she would take the matter to the next committee meeting.

The result was that I was offered a school to start in in the new term after Christmas. I was thrilled. I'd rather enjoyed the banter and fun in the office and receiving the little brown envelope each week containing my wages but the work was repetitive. I was on a machine called an addressograph, which printed the labels for boxes of frozen fish that went to the same destinations week after week. After only a short time I'd learned no end of towns along with the counties they were in and could quote Salisbury Wilts, Andover Hants, Mansfield Notts, St Albans Herts and Crewe Cheshire. It was like a party game; I'd never been to any of them or even heard of some but it sounded impressive to an audience of friends and family.

JANUARY, 1956

My dad is on his knees in front of a few faint embers glowing in the fireplace. He isn't praying because in his hands he is holding a large double sheet of The Daily Express. He puts it in front of the open grate resting his outstretched hands firmly against the fireplace surround. Like magic the embers turn into flames and the fire comes to life. Then a dark circle appears in the centre of the paper and a dragon's tongue of fire tries to lick his hand before "whoosh", he barely has time to scrunch it up before the paper's swept up the chimney. One or two blackened wisps float back down into the burning coal. Dad stands up, wipes his hands down his trousers, then picks up and finishes his cup of tea.

This was the sight that greeted me every morning when I got up at six o'clock to make the long journey to Yarborough Road School in Grimsby.

Dad was always up before six despite the fact that he only worked at a garage a five-minute walk round the corner. I think he liked the peace and quiet at that hour of the day. It must have been in his genes because it was passed on to me, Chris and Jon in later life. Early to bed, early to rise. Leave me alone and don't expect me to chat. The fire lighting became easier after he made a drawer-upper; an oblong sheet of metal with a handle welded on. It worked twice as fast and it didn't go up in flames; however, the handle got extremely hot and the noise of the fire drawing up the chimney sounded like a factory furnace. Sometimes he even set the chimney on fire and had to chuck a bucket of water on it before someone phoned the fire brigade. It wasn't very likely to be a neighbour because nobody near us had a phone and the nearest red phone box was about half a mile away.

Dad was definitely not a do-it-yourself man. Unfortunately, whatever he made, from bits that he found or was given, was so rough and ready it didn't last long. We had a few hens for a short while after the war and he made a run, quite rickety, with the usual second-hand chicken wire and wooden posts. One day a strange dog ran into the garden barking and the hens took off. They panicked and flapped, squawking and flying in all directions over the fence into next door, or down the passage behind the bottom of the garden.

Then he decided he wanted a pond so he dug it right in the middle of our little square of grass that passed for a lawn, where we had great fun jumping over it.

One exceptionally hot summer, the goldfish bred and there were scores of tiny brown fish. Dad's photo was in the *Grimsby Evening Telegraph,* showing him testing the temperature with a thermometer. We all laughed like mad because we'd never owned such a thing and knew that it was only a pencil. Mam was sick of his daft ideas and once when she was really mad, she tipped a teapot into the pond. She said he spent more time on his dozy ideas than doing things with his own family.

It was true he took no interest in us except to play the occasional game of draughts which he always won. We cottoned on to this as we got older after John, who was watching him play a game with Ann, saw him remove a piece from the board very sneakily with an outstretched finger, which he then concealed in the palm of his hand.

After that, no one would play with him again.

I left just after seven in the morning, when it was still dark in the winter months, to cycle the five or six miles – whatever the weather. For the first term I was observing and helping in the nursery with the four-year-olds. Margaret, the young teacher, was newly married. She was warm and enthusiastic, bursting with energy and ideas; a perfect role model for me. The children loved her. After only one term, to my surprise and delight, the headmistress asked me just before the Easter break whether I would like to have a small class for the summer term. I was over the moon. For ten weeks I was in my own classroom with twelve children all rising five. In educational jargon, they were what's called "summer born". These younger children often get a raw deal by virtue of their birthday. They're thrust into a class of boys and girls born between the previous nine months of September to May and expected to catch up. At the tender age of four this can be a big problem because, physically and emotionally, they are immature. I felt proud and privileged to be given the responsibility for these virtual babies and was able to give them much more individual attention. Initially I modelled myself on Margaret but quickly developed a style of my own as I became more confident. Those ten weeks were worth their weight in gold when six months later at college I did my first teaching practice. After being observed for an hour by a tutor her actual words were, "You've been in front of a class before, haven't you?"

In September that year, on the day I went to college, Mam went to the station with me. As I leaned out of the train window I saw tears in her eyes, but I don't think she was unhappy just pleased. Dad always said she lived her life through me and scoffed at her ambition for her kids. He wasn't a bad father really. He just showed no interest in any of us, which was fairly typical of the men of his time.

I'd just turned eighteen at the end of July and was so excited at the prospect of a room of my own and a bed all to myself. At last, I would no longer be subject to Ann's bullying and name-calling.

A ferry crossing on the paddle steamer called *Tattersall Castle,* which went back and forth daily over the Humber estuary between New Holland and Hull, followed the short train journey. I was travelling with Joan, who was in my class at the grammar school but up until that time we'd had nothing in common. An older girl called Anna had joined us in the same carriage. She'd already turned twenty and to me seemed to be much more worldly wise. We actually ended up together all on the same floor in Wilberforce Hall. There were nine bedrooms on our corridor, each containing a bed, a small wardrobe, a chair and a table to work at. In the corner there was a small handbasin but the bathroom and shower facilities were shared. There was also a separate common kitchen. Joan and I had a room that looked out over the big quadrangle, a pleasant area of flowerbeds and shrubs. On the far side we could see the sister building called Marvell Hall. Both William Wilberforce, well known for his involvement in Parliament for introducing the first anti-slavery bill, and Andrew Marvell, the poet, had close connections with Hull. Hence the names.

I made new friends and loved the freedom and the fact that we were treated as young ladies. We were expected to work hard, attend all lectures, and be good timekeepers and hand assignments in when requested. In fact, by Christmas, at the end of the first term, three girls had already been asked to leave.

Although all the students were female, we were situated right next door to Hull University which was bursting with a young, male population. A dance was held there every Saturday night, the only evening we could stay out till midnight. If we went out in the week, we had to sign out and on return sign in and be back by ten when the doors were locked. Because nine people were sharing a common kitchen it meant that at any time of day there was usually someone in there putting the kettle on. We spent hours sitting in nightclothes, often on someone else's bed, bunched up together, hugging knees and talking about boyfriends. We shared clothes and often swapped them to wear for the dances in the university.

It was amazing how flattering a dress could look on another girl with a different hairstyle and earrings. A large number of students came from the north-east; places such as Durham, Darlington, Stockton-On-Tees and the smaller mining communities. I loved their different accent, and the way they spoke seemed more melodic. When I went home for Christmas I wasn't aware that I'd picked up several expressions like, "Do you not like it?" or "Have you not been?" Ann immediately picked up on this.

'What're yer talking like that for, Maggie?' she mocked. After a couple of weeks at home, I couldn't wait to go back.

SHEFFIELD TRIP, 1957

In our haste, we practically fell off the train the minute it drew to a halt in Hull Paragon Station. As we were tearing up the platform with two shopping bags swinging wildly, Anna suddenly grabbed my arm. We both overbalanced, ending up on the ground and causing the folk behind us to sidestep and scurry round us, perhaps thinking we'd had too much to drink. There were no knights in shining armour at a quarter to midnight at a half-deserted station terminus.

'What the hell were you doing getting hold of me like that?' I grumbled as I scrambled to my feet and picked up the scattered bags.

'Sorry,' said Anna, who couldn't get up for laughing. 'My heel's snapped. Look!'

She held up the shoe with its four-inch stiletto broken in half.

'You'll just have to go barefoot. We'll have to run else we're going to be in big trouble.'

The man at the ticket barrier grinned at Anna in her stockinged feet but we didn't have time to catch his remark as we headed for an empty taxi. Once settled in the back of the cab, we had a fit of the giggles.

'Do you think Joan's ready with that rope and the basket?' I said. Anna looked at her watch.

'Hell, it's ten to twelve we should have been back ages ago. I bet she's been on the lookout since half past eleven; she'll be having kittens wondering where we are.' She leaned forward and asked the driver if he could put his foot down.

'Anything for you darlin',' came the answer, which set us off giggling again.

We'd been to see Janice who was doing domestic science at a college in Sheffield. We'd had a great time in the different shops and been to see her room in the hall of residence where we'd had tea. She'd even made a couple of dozen cakes and scones for us to take back and share. We weren't supposed to go anywhere out of Hull without permission, but because it was a Saturday when normal checking-in time was extended in order for girls to go to the uni dance we thought we'd have plenty of time. We'd checked the train times and would easily have been back had it not been late. It would have been obvious that we'd not been dancing next door if we'd walked in with armfuls of shopping, but we'd planned for that.

Joan, who never went out on a Saturday night because she had a boyfriend at Liverpool University, was our ally. Her bedroom on the third floor, which overlooked the drive, was not too close to the front door where she'd be noticed so she promised to be ready for us. She had a basket to lower on a piece of rope so that she could haul up our bits and pieces. It was five past twelve as we ran up the gravelled drive, Anna wincing as her stockinged feet touched the ground. We were just in time to see the front door being closed.

Joan was ready at the open window and the basket came down as planned. We rammed the stuff in, trying not to squash the precious cakes, and watched as it swayed back and forth with the uneven weight. I held my breath when we nearly lost the lot as it hit the wall and then a windowsill, which made the basket spin. Joan was leaning out as far as she dared in order to grab hold of the rope.

'Hell, I hope no one over there's looking,' said Anna, pointing to Marvell Hall where only one or two bedroom lights were still on.

'They'll think someone's committing hari – kari.'

'They won't see her, you daft bat, it's too dark,' I said, trying to smother a laugh.

'Quick, get back inside, there's someone coming,' she whispered to Joan. No way did we want her to be involved if we got into trouble. As we stood wondering what to do next, we heard voices and the sound of footsteps crunching up the drive. Three girls appeared, laughing and out of breath, apparently undaunted by the fact that the front door was shut.

'You locked out, too?' one said, eyeing us. 'Are you first years?' We both nodded.

'Don't look so worried, it happens to someone every week. Old Mother McCloud is used to it; she'll be looking at the names to see who's still missing. She's a good old stick under that outward harsh manner. I must say, though, it's usually the second years that get caught out.' Another girl who'd been listening turned to knock on the door. Miss McCloud, who was wearing a blue dressing gown, immediately opened it.

'Come along, girls, let's not make a habit of this,' she said in her soft Scottish accent. She shook her head as she noticed Anna's stockinged feet and the broken shoe in her left hand as she was bending over the book signing in.

'Well, you'll not be dancing in those shoes any longer, young lady,' she said as Anna turned to face her. Anna blushed but I swear there was a ghost of a smile on Miss McCloud's face. We said goodnight and walked sedately up the stairs until we reached the swing doors. Only then did I relax. From the way she'd looked at us when we'd walked in, I could swear Miss McCloud had rumbled something was afoot.

Joan had already boiled the kettle in the communal kitchen and made three drinks. She was dying to hear what went wrong and we couldn't wait to tell her.

'Bloody train was late, wasn't it?' said Anna, flopping on to the single bed. 'Here, have a shoe.' She tossed it to Joan. 'But Miss McCloud's a good sport; I've changed my mind about her.'

BRIEF ENCOUNTER, 1959

'I'll never marry anyone with ginger hair,' I remember saying to Janice with the arrogance of youth. Anyway, I wasn't ready to be tied down with domesticity the minute I left college and was at last earning a proper wage. Janice and I had resumed the weekly dancing but this time with money in our handbags. I'd moved on from drinking Babycham, the fizzy drink with a picture of Bambi on the bottle, to the more sophisticated gin and orange. If I'm honest, it took me a little time to actually enjoy the taste of gin but at least the orange modified it. I couldn't stand the smell of beer, never mind get it to my lips. Neither of us smoked, both thinking that hard-earned money was too precious to burn. We were in our first teaching post doing the required probationary year. She was working in a rough area of Grimsby with very challenging secondary-school children. I was in an infant school teaching a class of fifty children aged five, also in Grimsby but in a better area. We were both under obligation to return there, because they were the local education authority that had paid our grant and who also guaranteed to find us jobs when we qualified.

I had a very supportive headmistress who came into my classroom regularly that first year. She was like a mother hen to me, often making suggestions by showing not telling. She never criticised the way I worked but instead tried to make life easier for me with such a large number of young children to organise. I can remember her being horrified when one day I'd arrived on my bike as usual but with hair still wet having washed it that morning. It was my usual practice: wash, rub with a towel, scrunch up and leave to dry.

'You'll get your death of cold, my dear,' she said. 'You shouldn't come out of the house with wet hair.' I felt a bit like a little girl being told off but was grateful for her obvious concern. Like most of her generation in teaching she was unmarried and I guess I was a substitute daughter.

My favourite time of the year was the summer term, when during a spell of prolonged good weather she let me take the children outside in the afternoons. We had circle games and PE on the grass where they loved doing handstands and somersaults. I liked exploring the school grounds, showing them where to look for insects and beetles under stones and wood. We picked daisies for making daisy chains, and buttercups to see who liked butter by holding the yellow flowers under chins and looking for the reflection.

'You can pick the dandelions,' I once said, then trying to keep a straight face, added, 'but don't smell them because they'll make you wet the bed.' Some shook their heads and wrinkled their noses in disbelief while others were unsure. Then a few little lads immediately picked a flower and began to chase the believers.

'Here, smell this!' they shouted and laughed, making the little girls run screaming across the grass.

Each week in the classroom we had a nature table overflowing with bunches of wild flowers and sometimes garden flowers standing in vases or jam jars of water. We watched frogspawn turn into tadpoles and then tiny frogs in a shallow glass tank. We usually finished the session outside with the children sitting in the shade of a big horse chestnut tree, while I sat on a little chair that someone fetched for me and read them a story. They knew that after I'd finished, it would be home time. The youngest children who'd only started that term and who still hadn't had their fifth birthday found a whole day very tiring. By late morning, I was often asked, 'Have we had our dinner yet? When's my mummy coming?'

Boyfriends came and went with an alarming number, for me, who turned out to be called John. One of them was an identical twin but I swear on one occasion it was his brother I was with. The more they protested, the less I believed them.

Then I met Kerry. It wasn't love at first sight, not for me anyway, but definitely for him. He did all the chasing. So how did I fall for him and marry him, when after all, he had ginger hair? Well, for a start, it wasn't bright red like his sister who I met later. It was a more toned-down auburn, rusty colour. Then it was his name, so different from any that I'd ever come across. He was in RAF uniform, smoked a pipe, and bore a striking resemblance to Trevor

Howard, my favourite film star. Also he was thirty, ten years older than me, not a boy but a real man. To cap it all, he had a soft Welsh accent and a deep sexy voice.

We met at the Winter Gardens one Saturday night where I quickly discovered he was a very good dancer. Once we started going out regularly, I took him home to meet Mam. She loved him from the start.

He was intelligent, widely read, could talk about music, art and politics and most importantly was good at doing crosswords.

The fact that he was still married but awaiting a divorce didn't worry her. She'd already gone through the same set-up with Ann, who was happily wed to Ray and living in their first home in Grimsby.

Kerry was stationed at RAF North Cotes situated five or six miles further down the coast, where he worked with radar and radio communications. After seeing me home from the dance every week he carried on, walking back to camp. The route took him along unlit, narrow, twisting country lanes with ditches and high hedges on either side. He said that one night after hearing a deep throaty cough he'd stopped, expecting someone to appear out of the shadows. There was nobody there. Feeling uneasy and seeing nothing, he just had to find out. Then he heard it again, louder and very close. Quite alarmed by now he peered cautiously over a gate into a field. To his huge relief, it turned out to be a cow. When Mam heard the story, she said, 'I don't know how you can go to bed at night knowing that poor lad has to walk all the way back to camp.'

'Well, he quite often gets a lift. In fact, that road doesn't go anywhere else,' I said. I think she was more smitten than me or was it motherly concern? I was too young to know. Then he got posted to RAF North Luffenham in Rutland. By then we were a pair, and I felt ready to move on.

I'd seen an advert for a job at Bovingdon Primary School in Hertfordshire, so wrote to Anna who'd been at college with me. She was married with a new baby living in Beaconsfield, close enough to Bovingdon to drive over and see what the place was like. After her positive review, I decided to apply. Mam didn't believe me when I said that I was leaving and might be going down south. Nearly all the girls I'd been at school with were still living locally, settled down with a job and a regular boyfriend, a few even married.

I was the only applicant and after a brief, informal interview with the headmaster, who at the time was leaning casually against the big radiator in the school hall, I was offered the job on the spot.

I accepted to start the following September.

ARMY MATTERS

Although North Luffenham was a long way from Bovingdon it was very near to the A1, the major trunk road from north to south. Every weekend Kerry was able to hitch–hike quite easily on Friday teatime. At first he came and stayed where I was living, with the family of a colleague. This was temporary until I could find somewhere to rent. Pauline, who worked in the same school with me, was married to Keith who owned a chemist's shop. They lived in a large, detached house, set in its own grounds and had a cleaning lady called Nellie who came in every day.

She did the washing, ironing, general tidying up, and prepared the vegetables for a family of five people. It was very different from what I was used to but I was made welcome and so was Kerry. They had three lovely little girls: Catherine, eleven; Hilary, nine and Philippa, six, who all went to a private school.

They thought that I talked funny, like the people on *Coronation Street*, a television series set in the north. I could make them laugh with my accent when I told them a story and deliberately used words that they'd never heard of like "flitting", meaning moving house, or "faffing", meaning messing about. My class also commented on my use of vowels. Once I was telling them a story and used the word grass.

'Do you mean grahss?'

I laughed. 'You say grahss; where I come from we say grass.' Then I added, 'I also say past and fast and bath,' making sure they could hear the short "a". They thought it was really funny and went out of the door trying to mimic the way I spoke.

The school was lucky enough to have its own swimming pool and in the summer term, as well as lessons, it was used by the older children for sports day races. When someone suggested a teachers' race I was horrified. I'd only learned to swim at college when I was eighteen. The rest of the teachers weren't keen either apart from one very good swimmer called Margaret. When she wasn't around, we thought of an idea that wouldn't make us look so bad trailing behind. We all agreed it would be a laugh.

At the start we got into the water each in our own way, some diving, others like me lowering themselves into the water inch by inch. Margaret was already halfway down the pool by the time I even started swimming.

I made sure I was by one side, not confident enough to be far from something to grab onto. The plan was to let her race away while we kept together doing a slow breaststroke. The second she touched the far end we turned round and headed for the start. Naturally we got there first. The children and parents thought it was hilarious and Margaret took it all in good fun.

After three or four months of living in Bovingdon, I moved to a flat above a shop in Hemel Hempstead. The plumber's merchant who owned the property happened to be a friend of Mr Hamer, who knew that I was looking for somewhere, but it had to be on a bus route in order for me to get to work. I loved being independent for the first time in my life and would have been married were it possible, but Kerry was still going through a protracted divorce. He'd been married barely six months when he'd had to go on an unaccompanied posting to the island of Sylt. His wife, who was left behind in an unfamiliar market town in Lincolnshire, went back home to live with her parents. Then she was involved in a major car accident and amicable divorce proceedings had come to a sharp halt. Kerry had been honest from our first date but to both of us the normal time of three years for a divorce seemed to be dragging on and on. I was sick of people asking, 'When are you two getting married?' It wasn't common to be going out with a married man in the early sixties, let alone be living together every weekend. We didn't tell many people other than close friends, which included Mr Hamer and Pauline and Keith. I discovered early in our relationship that Kerry was able to get on with anyone and people warmed to him. We made lots of friends and were invited out for meals. Then, one weekend, he dropped a bombshell.

'I've got a posting to the Far East,' he said. 'Let's get engaged before I go.'

It softened the blow and we went on a bus to Watford where there was a better choice of jewellers. I chose a Victorian diamond cluster, with a large stone in the middle encircled by ten smaller ones. Because it was second-hand, there was no purchase tax and it cost £50. I was thrilled he could afford to spend so much on me.

A month later he'd gone and I lived day to day for his regular weekly letters, but I was unsettled, so without telling a soul except Mr Hamer I applied for another job to teach overseas.

I even went back to live with the family in Bovingdon, much to the girls' delight who regularly came to sit on my bed to chat. Then, things began to move. Halfway through a Monday morning, just before playtime, Mr Hamer burst into my classroom.

'Miss Gorbutt, the War Office is on the phone, they want to speak to you. I'll take your class.'

'Maybe it's my calling-up papers,' I joked as I left the room. I ran down the corridor, an act forbidden to children, but there was no one about. I raced into the office and picked up the phone lying on the desk.

'Miss Gorbutt here,' I said trying to catch my breath.

'Good morning Miss Gorbutt. I'm sorry to disturb you while you're with a class. My name is Major Benson, working for the British Forces Education Service. We would like to offer you a post, not in Singapore as you requested but in Germany.'

I paused, a bit taken aback; it wasn't what I wanted. When Kerry had been posted to the Far East for two years, I'd applied for a job in a service school in Singapore. I'd already been interviewed in London but as I was only twenty-three, the army in their wisdom had probably decided that I'd be safer and happier a bit nearer home. However, I had the cheek to ask if I could think about it.

'Certainly,' said the major, 'but let me know in a couple of days. Do you have a pen to hand? I'll give you my number.'

Disappointed and wondering what to do, I decided to talk to Mr Hamer. He was approaching retirement and was more of a father figure to me than a boss. He'd met Kerry and they got on well together. He knew how much I missed him but was able to see the bigger picture.

'You go to Germany', he said, 'and enjoy yourself; the Far East is bigger than you think.'

I liked him and respected his opinion; he was practical and hands-on, a man who never asked any member of staff to do anything he wouldn't do. On one such occasion, a small child in my class had had diarrhoea and sickness. He'd made a mess all down his legs and on his hands and trousers where he'd tried to wipe them. There was excrement and vomit all over the floor in the infants' toilets.

Mr Hamer had helped me by lighting a cigarette and puffing smoke into the confined area in an attempt to mask the smell. I had to close my mouth and try not to breathe in the fumes as I knelt and stripped the clothes off the little boy who stood crying. After I'd showered him Mr Hamer wrapped a big towel around him and I shot off to find some spare clothes. All infant schools had a box full of different sizes for such accidents. I passed the caretaker on the way armed with a bucket of sand, a brush and a mop and some disinfectant. When the little lad was dressed and ready to be picked up by his mum, Mr Hamer told me to go and get a coffee while he organised the children outside to have an extra-long playtime.

He was right with his advice. As it turned out, Kerry wasn't in Singapore for long. He was sent on active service to Borneo working on radio communications and living in a tent in the tropical jungle, sometimes waking up to discover his feet were in water. There were long periods when I didn't get any letters and I couldn't understand why. It didn't become plain until after I'd left Bovingdon and started the new job.

BERLIN HERE WE COME

When I left England I flew with other successful applicants to Hamm in Germany where we all stayed in a large boarding school that belonged to the British Forces. There must have been about sixty of us. On the second day we were interviewed again and asked about hobbies and interests. Some people had already expressed a preference for a specific part of the country, and listening to conversations, Berlin didn't seem to come too high on anybody's list. In fact, some categorically didn't want to be there. I didn't mind where I went; it would be an adventure wherever it was. On the third day after breakfast, all the postings, name of teacher and school address were pinned to a board outside the dining room. There was great excitement from the majority, all except a few assigned to Berlin who looked a bit shell-shocked. My name was on that list but at the time I was completely ignorant about the political settlement that was reached at the end of the war between the allies over the occupation of Germany.

At the end of World War II Germany was divided into east and west, the former controlled by Russian Forces and the latter by the Western Allied Forces of Britain,

France and America. Unfortunately, Berlin, the original capital, had to be divided also, so Bonn had become the new capital in the west.

Relations with the Russians in the early sixties were fragile, beginning with the blockade to stop supplies from the West being flown in and escalating into the erection of a wall overnight in 1961 that totally divided the city. When we arrived, it was September 1963.

I saw a gun for the first time in my life on the journey to Berlin. British soldiers who accompanied us on the military train were carrying arms when we travelled through the Soviet sector. We'd left Hamm in a small group comprising of seven young single women and about five male teachers, who would later send for their wives when accommodation became available. It was fortunate that we had the blokes with us. When we'd tried to get off the first train at Helmstedt on the border of the western occupied zone, German passengers, impatient to make the return journey, had swarmed onto our train as we tried to make our way with heavy cases down the corridor. We could go neither backwards nor forwards.

A heavyweight called Mike, not a chap to argue with, shouted at them and swore in English, making it obvious that we needed to get off.

They grudgingly stood still and we managed to squeeze past following the men in our group, who, perhaps deliberately, banged the legs of the unsmiling passengers with their bulky suitcases. This was just the beginning of seeing behaviour that was more than foreign but downright rude to us so-polite Brits.

We had no such problems getting on the military train that would take us onwards to Berlin. As soon as we were settled in the carriage, an army officer handed each one of us a large piece of card with safety and security instructions written in bold black capital letters. It read:

AT NO TIME OPEN THE WINDOWS

DO NOT LEAN OUT OF THE DOOR WHEN THE TRAIN STOPS

DO NOT GET OFF THE TRAIN EN ROUTE UNLESS INSTRUCTED TO BY AN ALLIED ARMY OFFICIAL

DO NOT WAVE TO OR FRATERNISE WITH THE RUSSIANS WHEN THE TRAIN IS STANDING IN THE STATION

I read it with disbelief and astonishment and laughed, then the girl sitting next to me laughed. The last phrase "do not fraternise with the Russians" had appealed to our sense of humour. Admittedly we might have done, had it not been strictly forbidden. What young girl isn't going to look at a man in uniform without flirting, irrespective of nationality? We introduced ourselves and when we got talking it turned out that she'd been at Hull training college at the same time as me, but had been in the other hall of residence. Her name was Judy and she came from Cheshire. We had a lot in common and would become close friends. From the train, the married men in our group all had private army-owned houses to go to but we were taken in a small military bus to RAF Gatow some way from the city. Our accommodation was in the teachers' mess where we each had our own room where we slept or worked, but we usually ate together in the dining room with meals provided. Later in the evening when the serving staff had left, we were allowed to go into the kitchen to make a drink or a sandwich. Although we had officer status by virtue of our profession, the best entertainment we soon discovered was in the sergeants' mess. When I got the chance to go there and play table tennis, Judy went with me to watch and was chatted up by a sergeant called Dennis. She started going out with him regularly but unfortunately because of his non-commissioned status he wasn't allowed in our mess or even to step into the garden. They always had to say their goodbyes at the gate. There was a weekly Saturday night dance that we went to and more formal dos like the Christmas Ball and a Valentine Special. I won a prize one night doing the best rock and roll with my partner. After all, I'd grown up with Bill Haley and the Comets and at home Kerry and I were always first on the floor.

I stood with Judy holding a cocktail glass in one hand, feeling very self-conscious and out of place in my cotton dress. Around us in the officers' mess, army wives with their coiffured hair and expensive elegant gowns were chatting and laughing together in groups.

We'd only been in Berlin a few weeks and already the job of teaching was becoming secondary to the social life we were thrown into.

We'd had an official invitation to attend a farewell cocktail party to mark the traditional Beating of the Retreat of the Welch Regiment who were about to leave the city at the end of their tour. The evening began at 6.45 p.m. with drinks. Neither of us had ever attended such a grand event but fortunately waiters came round with the drinks and the nibbles so we just helped ourselves every time one passed. I wasn't impressed with my first mouthful of caviar, black slimy fish eggs; they tasted like they looked, disgusting. I suspected that the young men serving us recognised our discomfort because they seemed to appear every time our glasses were empty and gave us a wink and a smile. The official ceremony followed outside in the barrack square. A trumpet fanfare introduced the arrival of a Welch guardsman, leading in the regimental mascot. It was a magnificent white goat with two enormous horns, its body draped in a ceremonial coloured blanket bearing the arms of the regiment. The pair stood quite still throughout the following noisy parade of marchers and drummers with the regimental sergeant major shouting instructions. As it ended with a final dramatic drum roll, I turned to Judy and whispered, 'Did you remember to order the carriage?' She had to stifle a laugh.

'No, but I've got a bus timetable in my handbag.' It was a reference to the final wording on our invitation: "Carriages at 2100".

We'd managed to afford a taxi to get there, not wanting anyone to see us arrive by public transport, but we fully expected to return by bus or tram. However, hoping no one was looking, we made our exit before the rest and walked towards the gate. An army lorry drew up alongside and stopped. A man leaned out of the window on the passenger side and, with a big grin on his face said, 'My name's Corporal Prosser, can we give you a lift girls?' It was too good to be true. Alas, he'd forgotten to tell us that we'd have to scramble into the back through the tarpaulin. It was easier for Judy with her long legs.

'Good job we didn't put our best evening clothes on,' I joked. I was feeling a bit dizzy as willing pairs of hands pulled us up into the lorry where we sat on the floor with a group of friendly young army lads. We talked and laughed all the way back to RAF Gatow feeling more relaxed and happier than we'd been for the whole evening. From then on, a "Prosser lorry" became part of our vocabulary and friends wondered why we laughed every time we saw one similar.

One day Dennis took us to see the Berlin wall right away from the city centre in order to tell us the history. It was erected overnight in 1961 to stop people fleeing to the West. Standing over three metres high and topped with barbed wire, it zigzagged through the heart of the city, even going through buildings in certain areas. To us it was shocking and quite frightening to be scrutinised through binoculars by the Russian sentries. Where the concrete ended on the outskirts of the city, a barbed-wire fence took its place. Behind this fence was a separation zone, mined and booby-trapped with a ditch, then another high barbed-wire fence on the far side. Dennis was classed as high security because he spoke Russian; it was part of his work, so he wasn't allowed into East Berlin.

However, as we posed no threat, we could go on an organised accompanied tour. The coach entered the East at Checkpoint Charlie, which was in the American sector. It was a depressing visit. The contrast between East and West Berlin was stark. Shabby shop fronts, dilapidated buildings, old cars and vehicles that were not really fit to be on the road emphasised the general drabness of the place and this was reflected in the posture and faces of the few people we saw. I began to understand why so many people risked their lives in order to escape to the West.

A NIGHT AT THE OPERA

On the 22 November I was sitting on the back row in the crowded opera house. With me were Judy and two more teachers. I was looking forward to seeing my very first live performance of the opera by Smetana, *Die verkaufte Braut (The Bartered Bride)*. We were surrounded by wealthy-looking couples. In front of us were seated two well-endowed ladies, each one clad in a thick fur coat. The husband sitting alongside his wife wore an expensive dark woollen overcoat. I had to resist an urge to lean over and stroke the soft animal fur, so instead nudged Judy and rolled my eyes as I pointed towards it. She grinned and, in reply, touched her nose, closed her mouth and wrinkled her upper lip before she lifted her head and sniffed the air. A heady mixture of perfume and cigar smoke pervaded the hall, adding to the opulence and grandeur of the occasion. It was a far cry from my working-class background in an east coast seaside resort. I thought about Mam. She would have loved the opportunity to do what I was doing. When she was growing up as an only child, surrounded by adults of family and friends, they were by virtue of their work strictly working class. However, she'd been immersed in art, classical literature and music that they listened to on the wireless or gramophone records. I used to wonder how she could recognise and name the music and the composers when we listened at home. It wasn't until I was much older that I realised how much I had retained that I'd learned from her.

I felt the buzz of anticipation as the orchestra tuned up, then the music carried me away as I sat enthralled by the scenery, the costumes and the singing. All too soon it was the end of the first act. There was a short ten-minute interval when everyone remained seated. Barely fifteen minutes into act two, without warning, the curtain came down and the musicians stopped playing. A man strode on to the stage and made an announcement in German, which no one in our group understood. There was a collective gasp; some women put a hand to their mouths as if in disbelief or horror. Then the whole audience stood up and began to leave. We were flabbergasted, having no idea what was going on.

Doreen, the only one among us who spoke German and who could actually understand a reply, grabbed the sleeve of a woman who was just about to leave.

'*Was ist los?*' (What's the matter?) she asked.

'*President Kennedy ist tot. Er wurde erschossen.*' (Kennedy is dead. He was shot.)

We left subdued, affected by the sombre faces and the hushed conversations of the German people standing in groups outside. After a long wait for a taxi to take us back to RAF Gatow, we travelled through the city centre where cinemas and other public places of entertainment also seemed to be closing. Out of town, in every shop, flat and house along the deserted streets, a single candle on a windowsill glimmered in the darkness. It was eerie. We didn't really understand the serious nature of the event or the possible implications.

That night, the Allies put Berlin on "Red Alert".

BERLIN END

For Judy and me, that Christmas in Germany seemed to be a round of non-stop food, drink and entertainment, with invitations out for meals and dancing and parties in the sergeants' mess, ending with the annual Christmas Ball in the officers' mess, which we enjoyed the least. Too posh, too stuffy we decided.

Every Saturday we caught a tram and went into the city centre to the biggest and best department store in Berlin, KaDeWe (pronounced phonically as "cardevay"). We always headed first to the toy floor where we spent a good ten minutes playing with the wind-up dogs, ducks and sheep, howling with laughter as they walked robot-like across the counter, quacking, baa-ing and barking. The locals stared at us with disapproval written all over their faces, then the girl assistant started giving us filthy looks until we produced our purses and waved some money at her. We each bought one, not really for a present but more to keep as a souvenir and make us laugh. From there we walked through the food hall, full of the delicious spicy smells of cooked sausages and cold meats, the like of which I'd never seen in my life. I loved the different German sausages, which we regularly bought as a snack to eat in the hand, and soon learned the difference between *Bockwurst*, *Bratwurst* and *Knockwurst*, even smothered in thick German mustard. The smell of gingerbread and marzipan always made my mouth water so I bought a tin of traditional Christmas biscuits to take home and some wooden tree decorations that I'd never seen anywhere in England. We only left the store after having a drink and a massive, scrumptious cream cake in the cafe, sitting alongside the German *Hausfrauen* clad in their familiar thick fur coats, matching hats and stout, knee-length, real leather boots. It was a far cry from the lives of most married women at home and gave me the idea of asking Mam and Dad to come over.

When I went home for Christmas, I suggested it. Straightaway Mam said yes, whereupon Dad's reply was, 'Definitely no, we've only just finished fighting the bloody Germans.'

'Arthur,' said Mam, glaring at him; she rarely called him by his name, except in bed when he was snoring. She paused, then added, 'Well, I'll go on my own then; you can look after your bloody self for a week.' So she did. She made all the arrangements herself; a ferry to France, then a long train journey to Berlin.

I had to apply at my end for what the army called movement orders, the pass that allowed her to cross the Russian-held eastern sector by military train. She arrived tired but elated, full of stories about her fellow travellers who expressed their admiration for doing the journey alone. We spent the week in a private house, a married quarter that an officer friend and his wife had kindly let me use while they were in England, so Judy and I could take her to see all the familiar sights. Mam revelled in the easy-going affluence of the Berlin society, the pavement cafes, the *Bierkellers*, and the *Weinstube* where we sat in the evening waiting for Dennis to join us before we each ordered half a chicken in a basket. All too soon she went back home, where she was asked to speak about her experiences to different branches of the Townswomen's Guild (the TG) and the Women's Institute (the WI). She was treated with admiration and in a letter told me that the most common remark made was, "Weren't you brave? My husband wouldn't have let me go on my own." Mam was fifty-three at the time, still working as a milliner and had never been out of the country. However, I think it sowed the seeds for future holidays abroad with Dad when they got older and could afford it.

My letters from Kerry had been infrequent for the six months he was in Borneo, often arriving in twos or threes. They were full of description of the Borneo landscape, the flora and fauna, and the Dayaks, the indigenous people who were so proud of their country. He wrote about the leeches that became attached to his legs when they were setting up camp in the jungle and even sent a photo of one he'd removed. When he sent photos of the huge butterflies placed next to a matchbox to show comparative size, it became a joke with Dennis.

"Have you had any more pictures of matchboxes,

Maggie?" he said, meaning 'Have you heard from Kerry?

In the early summer of 1964, Kerry's tour of the Far East was reduced from two years to one because he'd been engaged in active service. He flew back to Britain for a period of rest and relaxation (R & R) and after a short settling-in period, he came over to Berlin. I was shocked when I saw him after an absence of eighteen months. He was so thin, almost emaciated; he'd never been a hunky man to start with.

It took me a while to resume the warm relationship we'd enjoyed before he went away. I wondered whether I'd made a mistake and that I wasn't ready to settle down with him again. Then I felt guilty that I'd been enjoying myself, dancing, drinking and dating other men, while he'd been living and working in such harsh and sometimes dangerous conditions. I was confused. However, his feelings for me seemed to have become intensified by our separation and he was still the loving, caring, patient man ready to accept the fact that maybe I needed a little time to get used to his presence. It didn't take long. He and Dennis became great friends while he was living in the sergeants' mess and I soon forgot that despite his scrawny appearance he was the same man underneath who had the power to make my heart jump with his deep, Welsh, sexy voice. He'd been posted back to North Luffenham again so I decided to apply for a job in Rutland.

UPPINGHAM, 1964-65

Before leaving Germany, I'd applied for and got a post at Oakham Primary School but I needed a car to get there, so I bought it in Cleethorpes as soon as we were home. It was a white Triumph Herald and although I was next to the youngest of four, I was the first one in the family to own a car. Kerry and I were now living together. We were renting a downstairs' flat in a Victorian house on the High Street in Uppingham. It was a pretty run every day between Uppingham and Oakham, a distance of about six miles. Another young couple lived upstairs; he was also in the RAF but went into camp on his motorbike. The people who owned the property lived in a purpose-built extension at the back. To them and the few folk we knew outside of my job, we were married. I wore Kerry's mum's wedding ring on occasions depending on where we went, but never at school where I was known as Miss Gorbutt. Kerry's mam had died while he was in the Far East, though he'd been flown home some weeks before on compassionate leave. I'd only met her and his dad a couple of times; she was only in her early fifties; a small, kind, gentle little lady.

Once on the journey to school, I gave a lift to an old

man. I felt perfectly safe because the dog we'd recently acquired was sitting upright on the back seat. He was a large red and white boxer called Carlo who'd been advertised in a shop window. A farmer had bought him for a guard dog but he was too soft so he was "FREE TO GOOD HOME". He went to school with me every day, often sitting in the front seat, and I walked him through the town to the park at lunchtime where he got a good run around. Mam was afraid of him the first time I took him home but his looks belied his gentle nature and she soon learned to love him. Kerry, who didn't drive, went off to work one morning with my car keys in his pocket. At first I panicked, wondering how on earth I'd get to school as there was no bus service. Nothing ventured, nothing gained, I told myself, I'll just have to hitch like he does. I walked to the end of the road and planted myself, right thumb extended, pointing in the traditional way of someone who wants a lift. A lorry driver stopped.

'Where to, love?' he asked.

'Oakham; are you going that far?'

'Am going on to Melton; hop in.'

It was a climb up Mt. Everest to get into his cab, never mind hopping in. It reminded me of the incident when Judy and I climbed into the back of the Prosser lorry. Here we go again, I thought, I'll have to write and tell her.

That October I stood in the witness box in court in Oakham. I was giving evidence against a man who'd indecently exposed himself on a deserted country lane where I'd been horse riding one Sunday morning. I'd made a note of his car number, which was parked nearby on the grass verge, and had gone to the small police station in Uppingham to report it. A couple of days later, two officers came to see me to ask whether I'd be willing to testify as they thought they had strong evidence for a prosecution. Unfortunately the court hearing was on Wednesday, bang in the middle of the same week I'd gone home to Cleethorpes for half term. Mam and Ann, who was visiting with her first baby, David, were both keen to go with me. I was glad of their moral support.

The court appearance was unpleasant to say the least, especially when I was asked personal probing questions about the man's behaviour. For example,

'Where was he standing?', 'Which way was he facing?', 'Where were his hands?'

The police had been confident about his guilt and even provided photographs of the road, hedge, gate and field where it took place. His defence was that he'd been picking blackberries and then gone for a wee. He had a very good lawyer who'd cleverly swayed the verdict in favour of his client.

I was annoyed, but the police, though disappointed, said he would do it again and they would get him the next time. After the harrowing experience, we went for a coffee and snack, Ann fed the baby and then we started the journey home. As we were approaching a T-junction in Boston, all the traffic appeared to be turning left.

'We need to go right here,' I said and kept signalling, trying not to show any anxiety, but the policeman in the middle of the road madly waved his arms and directed me to go with the flow. My heart sank. At the first opportunity I pulled over.

'I don't know which way to go now and we haven't got a map.' I was a bit flummoxed. Mam spotted another policeman walking towards us on the pavement on her side. Before I could protest she'd already wound down her window.

'Wait, I'll ask this young lad.'

I gripped the steering wheel and stared at a wasp that had settled on the windscreen. When I glanced in the rear-view mirror I could see Ann clutching the baby, not uttering a word. Her face was a picture and reflected my own feelings of guilt and fear. I knew what she was thinking. Mam, meanwhile, was chatting and laughing with the policeman as if she'd known him all her life. Apparently he was from Grimsby so could tell us the easiest and quickest way to get back to the familiar A road. As she thanked him, he raised a hand and smiled to acknowledge Ann and me and wished us a safe journey.

I didn't speak for the next few minutes as I was too busy listening to Mam's instructions and concentrating on the traffic.

When we eventually got back on the A16 going north, I expelled a huge breath of air as though I'd been holding it for a long, long time.

'Phee—w,' I said. The relief was enormous. Ann broke the silence.

'God Maggie, if you don't pass your driving test tomorrow I'll jump in Grimsby dock.' Neither Mam nor Ann had ever driven a car.

I passed the test in Grimsby the following day in spite of the fact that Kerry, who accompanied me to the test centre, was also a non-driver. He went on to take his, after some lessons, a few months later.

'Put your collar up; it hides your face and the colour of your hair at the back,' I said to Kerry as he fastened his heavy blue overcoat over his RAF uniform.

'Miss Bird might be looking out of the bedroom window.'

He laughed before kissing me goodbye. I was terrified that Miss Bird who taught at the same school as me and lived a few doors up the road might suspect something if she recognised him going by each morning. I wasn't sure whether I could lose my job if our living arrangements were made public.

It was half past seven and he needed to get a lift in order to get back to camp. When a vacancy came up in the school in Uppingham it made sense to move from the job in Oakham, though I'd made some good friends whilst there and we kept in touch. I liked Miss Bird, a quiet, diminutive lady with grey hair who'd been teaching all her life, but I think she would have been shocked had she known I was living in sin! One other member of staff had guessed; an older lady married to an ex-serviceman, but she was more open-minded and well-travelled.

Kerry's decree nisi came through that September and at last we could plan to get married after the statutory period of three months when it would become absolute. Having waited for five years, we couldn't bear to wait for a day longer than necessary. It turned out to be 24 December 1965. The ceremony was held in Grimsby Registry Office on a bleak and foggy Christmas Eve.

There was only Mam and Dad, Auntie Alice and John and Ann present. I wore a grey and white flecked coat with a small black fur collar and Mam had a new hat. We went back to her bungalow where Kerry and John took photos. Despite the fact that there was no honeymoon and very few presents I really didn't care. At least I had a new wedding ring and was finally married to the man I loved.

We bought our first house in Uppingham, a newly-built bungalow on the edge of the village. The mortgage was for £2,500. Within a couple of months I was pregnant but was able to carry on working until I left school at the end of the summer term.

That August we went camping in a tent that was given to us, plus all the gear. It was uncomfortable, to say the least, sleeping on the floor on an air bed with an ever-growing baby bump. I managed without complaining until one night when we had the most tremendous thunderstorm. We were situated in an exposed position on the Llŷn peninsular in North Wales, not even on a campsite where there would have been other people. The force of the wind and the torrential rain combined with thunder and lightning frightened me to death. I wanted to move into the safety of the car but Kerry practically insisted we stayed put. We moved inland at dawn to Lake Bala, a pretty campsite surrounded by mountains and supposedly sheltered. However, they'd had it worse than us. Caravans were blown over and some tents were even flooded. We decided to go home.

Jonathan was born on 7 November and Kerry was present at the birth in Leicester Royal Infirmary. It wasn't common in those days but I'd had complications and he'd been at my bedside day and night for forty-eight hours. Jonathan was born with a shock of black hair that folk said would soon rub off. It never did. One of the first questions everyone asked was, *Has he got hair like Kerry?*

In May 1967 Kerry came home from work bursting with news. 'How would you like to go to Singapore?'

'Do you mean it? All of us?'

'Yeah, RAF Seletar, I've been posted there again. We leave in July.'

I was stunned, excited and over the moon. All my childhood dreams were coming true. I'd grown up listening to the words of songs that talked about faraway places and vowed that one day it would be my turn to go and find them. It was barely three years since we'd come home from Berlin and soon we'd be off again but this time to the Far East. What a coincidence I was going to where John had been stationed. Now Mam would be writing to me at the same place. She said she'd have to get a new address book because she was running out of space. It was my seventh move since leaving home.

JALAN TARI PIRING

June 1967

Dear Mam,

*The flight out was long and boring, broken only by two short stops
to refuel. In Istanbul we didn't disembark because it was the middle
of the night and most families were asleep. About nine hours later
we got off in Bombay where at first I thought the oppressive heat
came from the engine of the plane as we walked past. It was made
worse by the very high humidity. At least in the airport lounge all
the fans were going full blast but our stay was to be short-lived.
After only an hour and a half we had to take off early to avoid a
monsoon storm but in fact caught the edge of it. I was sick from
then on. Jonathan meantime slept blissfully in his sky-cot above us
unaware of the bumps and lurches. The stewardesses were brilliant*

and brought hot water for the half-dozen babies on board. Kerry fed and changed the babe while I lay back with my eyes closed wishing we were anywhere but three-thousand feet in the air in a tropical storm. By the time we'd landed and been transported to the hotel room, which resembled a third-rate holiday-camp chalet, we'd been travelling over twenty-four hours and were both shattered.

We've moved now into rented accommodation in a place called Jalan Kayu. It's like a small village on the outskirts of the camp where Kerry works. The road we live on, called Jalan Tari Piring, is uneven with potholes where after heavy rain large puddles remain until they slowly evaporate in the stinking heat. Flat-roofed, terraced, concrete bungalows line either side of the road, each one occupied by a service family. Like ours they all have windows with no glass, just bars and shutters, and a front yard guarded by a six-foot-high chain link fence. The metal security gate is always locked because windows are open all the time, except after dark to keep out the mosquitoes. Apparently families have had small things pinched by thieves getting over the gate and fishing between the bars with a long stick with a hook at the end.

The walls in our living room are painted turquoise green and the armchairs and settee are covered in pale blue plastic. You can imagine how this feels in a temperature constantly above 80 degrees Fahrenheit (28 Celsius). I sit on a cotton teacloth to stop it sticking to my legs. In the small kitchen there's a two-ring stove and a Formica-topped table with two stools, but no utensils or cleaning things whatever. We've had to buy a couple of pans and sweeping brushes, and have only bought two cups and saucers, two plates and dishes and two knives, forks and spoons. If we have any visitors it's hard luck; they'll have to *wait or bring their own. When we eventually move into married quarters on camp, everything will be provided.*

We bought a bamboo cot for Jonathan and an English Pedigree pushchair. You'd laugh if you could see me bathing him in the backyard in a small tin tub that the amah uses to do the washing in. I wonder if Mammam washed you in one. All service families are given an allowance for employing an amah; it provides much-needed work for the local girls and I know that in this climate I definitely couldn't do housework. Ours is a young local girl who was recommended, but quite honestly, I suppose because she's pregnant, she's so slow and not even thorough. Apparently they work right up until the day the baby is born, but I reckon I'd feel guilty watching her while I sat around so we've decided to keep her until we move.

The lavatory, which I hate using after dark, is outside off the kitchen. This is because as soon as I switch the light on huge cockroaches with a hard shell, bigger than oversized black beetles, scuttle across the floor. I had a worse scare last night when I put my hand on the switch and felt something move. When I screamed Kerry came running in; I was nearly in tears. He laughed and said,

"It's only a praying mantis, it won't hurt you."

"What do you mean only? It looks like a green alien with its popping-out eyes and feelers and great long dangly legs," I shouted.

I'm getting used to the lizards now. They're small and green and run up and down the walls and over the ceiling but they eat the mosquitoes. The nickname for them is chit-chats because of the clicking sound they make. Jonathan loves them; he points when he sees one, then sticks his tongue out and clicks trying to make a similar noise. I've been bitten to death at night when I'm asleep despite the fact that we burn incense coils in the bedroom. There are trillions of ants and I have to be so careful not to leave any crumbs on the floor from biscuits or bread. I accidentally left a bit of rusk in Jonathan's little chair and when I went back to use it, it was swarming. Sometimes in an evening you can sit and watch the ants literally marching in single file down the walls like a troop of invading soldiers. I suppose they have a use if only to encourage people to be scrupulously clean after a meal.

There are ceiling fans in two rooms both with great enormous blades as big as aeroplane propellers. If you put them on high it's lovely and cool but far too noisy and the wind it creates makes anything loose fly all over the place. In an effort to cheer up this dingy-looking place, I've sunk to the lowest. No, I'm not sitting here with a fag in me mouth wearing curlers in me 'air, but have actually bought some plastic flowers.

They're not as bad as you may imagine and normally what I loathe, probably because they're white orchids. Even Kerry says they look real and rather tasteful in the nice china vase we bought in the market.

There's constant noise outside from early morning till late at night. The sound of a car horn up the road at 8.00 a.m. announces the arrival of the grocer with delivery orders. He comes in an open-topped three-wheeler pick-up that's stacked high with boxes of food, and amahs rush out to unlock the gates. Indian traders from the village rattle the gates and shout, "Missee, missee, you want plastic flowers? Buckets, dry cleaning or pictures?" An ice-cream seller wielding a large handbell drives up and down on his custom-made tricycle. There's no shortage of customers here where most of the houses contain at least two or three young children. Every day a couple of pigs forage in the monsoon drains by the side of the road rooting out waste food and scraps. They run away squealing when the children chase them. Harassed mothers, stuck inside with a baby or a toddler, sit around on plastic-covered furniture complaining to each other about the humidity and shout at their fractious kids above the row of a radio or a television on full blast. Sometimes they have parties that can go on till three or four in the morning. If it's a Friday night we can often hear the voices of couples rowing from right down the street.

The smell of rotting vegetation combined with the lack of drainage and discarded food and household waste is disgusting. Now and again it's masked by cooking smells and spices depending on the time of day and in which direction you're going. I've already seen rats running up the monsoon drains, even in the daytime. Children from the nearby kampong come every day looking in the dustbins, which stand outside the gates, for discarded peelings and food for their livestock. They live in wooden huts with thatched roofs on the edge of the jungle-like plantation behind the main road that runs parallel to ours. The opposite side of the same road is lined with open-fronted shops, where old men and women with brown wrinkled faces squat on spindly legs resting their elbows on their bony knees.

Our grocer's shop is along there. His name is Chee Kow. It's painted big in bright red and yellow above the entrance. He always wears shorts and a white vest, which barely hides his big, fat belly. He's an easy-going and very wealthy man, a little fella who owns half of the rented RAF accommodation in Jalan Kayu including ours.

Looking forward to hearing your news
Love M K and J

EARLY DAYS AND
LEARNING CURVES

14 August 1967

Dear Mam,

Thanks for my birthday card. I bet you bought it in France; it's very unusual. On the actual day I went to the swimming pool in the morning. Jonathan loves it; he puts his face right in and comes up dripping wet, laughing like mad. In the evening we went to the amahs' market. It's held every Friday night all the way down the middle of the road in the village. It's buzzing with noise and people and has a good atmosphere because everyone's so friendly. All the stalls are lit with candles or hurricane lamps and the smell from these mixes with the spices on sale and the cooking aromas drifting over from the stalls that are selling hot food. The traders are vying with each other to get your attention but it's all good-natured. I learned in the first week not to trust in "what you see is what you get" after buying a large Johnson's baby talc. The top inch of the container was genuine but the remaining stuff was chalk dust. I also bought a pretty coloured transparent stone to be made into a pendant. When I took it to the jeweller's later he said it was only worth about seven shillings. I paid five times as much. Would you like a piece of yellow glass for your birthday? I've got a lot to learn! I love the wooden hand-carved ornaments and the Indian brassware that looks even more spectacular as it catches the light from the flickering candles. We'll probably get some later to bring home.

We went into a bar that was recommended for forces to use, having been advised not to buy any cooked food from the stalls no matter how good it smells. It was a grotty place compared to those in Berlin. Do you remember when I took you out? Didn't we laugh? Anyway, the steak and chips were excellent and we had Birds Eye eclairs instead of birthday cake for afters, which cost more than the steak. I bought some little cotton string vests in the market for Jonathan that he wears in his cot now with only a nappy. He's no longer wearing the rubber pants to sleep in because he sweats like mad and already has a rash called prickly heat all over his little body. In fact, I usually end up changing the bottom sheet because it's wet with perspiration when he wakes up in the night for a drink. His hair has gone really curly in this heat and no end of people think he's a girl.

"Too pretty for a boy," they say.

I've had a dress made in the village for a dance this week in the sergeants' mess. You choose the material, draw the style or *find a picture or photo in a magazine, then finally after being measured it's ready the next day. It only cost… wait for it… £1 for the lot. The materials on sale are lovely. They're a lightweight, poly/cotton mixture, non-iron in lots of colours and patterns and so cheap. In the daytime, like everyone else, I've started wearing flip-flops. They're the most comfortable footwear and cooler than traditional sandals or shoes in this heat. It resembles a sandal but has just a sole and a thong between the second and big toe.*

We went into Singapore for the first time, leaving the baby with a friend on camp. Taxis are cheap, it was only 9/6 for about twelve miles, but boy was it frightening. They drive on the left as in England but don't seem to have any rules or road sense regarding other drivers or pedestrians trying to cross over. We looked around four main stores. One was like Selfridges, one like Littlewoods, one like Woolworths and another had a department called the St Michael Shop. Apparently a lot of people go there to buy clothes when they're going home. The meal in the cafe was the best part of the day. It was quite a shock to find the city of Singapore as dirty as the village we live in. Although it has the bonus of pavements, they're sticky with chewing gum and citizens are allowed to spit in the street. It's revolting because you can actually hear them coughing up the phlegm beforehand and wonder where it's going to land. I realise now what it meant on the buses at home when it said NO SPITTING. When I was little I thought it referred to children. Stuff in the shops is also dearer than what we can buy it for in Jalan Kayu and I think now I've seen the mess they become, we're better off with no pavements.

We went out last night to the home of a chap who works with Kerry. He's coming to the end of his tour and the tradition is to have a boat party before you leave. There were about fifty people there but he rents a house much bigger than ours. We sat outside all evening drinking and eating and I pitied the neighbours while the record player inside was on at its highest volume for anyone who wanted to dance. Some of the women looked a bit tarty in their floral trouser suits and dangly earrings. There's a big fashion here for ladies' wigs at the moment because they're so cheap. Instead of having your hair done, you take the wig to be styled; a few women even have several, each one in a different colour. Blonde is the most popular. I don't think I'll bother.

Our amah finishes next week and one from across the road is starting. The family employing her is going home and has had the same girl since they arrived when their present three-year-old was just a baby. Someone told the new amah that she was bad taking the job away from our girl. It was similar to the grocer episode when we changed him after the first week. The old grocer sent someone to threaten the new one. It's a bit law of the jungle, isn't it? Here's something funny to end on. As Kerry was standing holding Jonathan, who'd been stripped ready for his bath, he wee-ed all down Kerry's belly and trousers. I laughed and said,

"C'est la vie."

"Non, c'est la pee!" he answered quick as a flash.

Lots of love M K and J

FROM THE SLUMS
TO MAYFAIR

12 September 1967

Dear Mam,

We're in quarters now on the camp and it's like moving from the slums to Mayfair. Not that I'm all that familiar with Mayfair apart from the fact that it's the most expensive property on a Monopoly board. Our new address is 13 Edgware Road but I'm not superstitious. Another crossing-out in your address book! It's a bungalow and the rooms are big and light, especially the living room, which has three picture windows and two glass doors opening out onto a balcony sitting area with two steps down into the garden. There's a dark green Indian carpet covering most of the floor, two comfortable chairs and a settee. A dining table and four chairs are at the end of the room where I'm sitting to write this letter. There are two bedrooms with a double bed in ours and two singles in the other. The big kitchen off the living room has a cooker, a fridge and a large table for food preparation. Out the back there's a washhouse that the amah uses and a small plot of land for a clothes line.

The cot provided for Jonathan doesn't half make the temporary bamboo one look small and shabby. It's so big he usually ends up with the pillow slung adrift and his feet where his head should be. There's far more mosquitoes on camp, probably because of all the trees, so we sleep under mosquito nets now. Once a week a man comes in with a smoke gun and goes into every room to kill them. Absolutely everything is provided, from all the linen, pots and pans, buckets, brushes etc. to a cheese grater, rolling pin and egg cups.

We pay for a gardener to come in for half an hour a day; the garden, which is at the front, is one of the best on this road. There's some flowers, don't know what they are, a coconut tree with fruit on it, a banana tree and a pineapple plant. There's a big expanse of grass, which will be nice for Jonathan when he's more mobile. He crawls in a funny way with one knee on the floor and the other leg just bent so that he can use his foot to push off.

There seem to be a lot of sparrows in the shrubs and I love the huge black and orange butterflies, which are as big as my hand with fingers outstretched.

Kerry was on leave last week and went to play golf a couple of times. The second time he tripped over a monsoon drain, or so he said. How he failed to see it when they're at least a foot wide *and eight or ten inches deep I don't know. Anyway he twisted his ankle and couldn't play any more; neither could we go out anywhere. He's managed to buy a small motorbike from a chap who's going home; it's more like a Vespa scooter.*

The top speed is only thirty-five miles an hour but it's ideal for going to work and means he can pop back at lunchtime.

I forgot to tell you that before we moved the landlord actually changed the grotty plastic furniture. The new stuff was bamboo with Dunlopillo cushions covered in blue sailcloth. It was nice until Jonathan christened it! Then I had to wash it myself as the amah had just gone home. That was a first; fortunately it dried in two hours.

I really enjoyed the summer ball in the sergeants' mess although it was hard work dancing on the concrete floor. The Chinese band and the singer were a bit crummy but it added to the fun of the occasion. On arrival the ladies were given an orchid to wear; wasn't that lovely? I heard one chap saying it was a bloody waste of money, they could charge less for the tickets instead. It surprises me how tight some people are because life here for Westerners is so much cheaper and everyone has a chance to save, whatever rank they are. Apparently even though we all get an allowance for an amah in the wage packet, some families choose not to have one or choose just part-time in order to keep the money. I think it's immoral when the young local girls depend on the people stationed here for their jobs and are able to contribute to the family income.

Our new amah is called Awah. She's four-foot-ten, twenty-two years old and knocks spots off the last one. She babysat with her sixteen-year-old sister last week while we went to the pictures on camp and when we got back they'd done half the washing for the next day. I popped over the road for a coffee today when Jonathan was asleep after dinner and came back to find Awah had already changed his nappy as soon as he woke up and was sitting on the floor talking and playing with him. She even prepares the vegetables for the evening meal before she goes home without being asked.

Another reason I'm glad we've moved is because of the alarming numbers of burglaries. Apparently there were twenty-seven break-ins in one week on an estate where only service families live. I suppose it would be easy to bribe or blackmail the amahs who know exactly the layout of the houses and where money or possessions are kept. Airmen are paid fortnightly in cash whereas senior NCOs like Kerry are paid monthly. We used to take the precaution of sharing his wages between us and carrying it with us whenever we went out. Hopefully security on camp will be different as all personnel, including officers, airmen, wives and any workers that enter are checked in at the gate and can't get past the guardroom without a pass.

I've finally found fresh milk after using powdered, tinned and sterilised.

A Malaysian dairy van delivers on camp every day, so now we can enjoy a decent cup of tea. Talking of which, I shall make one; wish you were here to share it with me.

Write soon.

Love M K and J

MOSQUITOES AND CREEPY CRAWLIES

1 October 1967

Dear Mam,

Had two letters from you this week; lovely. Don't ever think that what you say is trivial. I don't mind if you tell me what colour knickers you're wearing! Your letters make us laugh and we feel closer because it's like talking in the same room. Sometimes I feel that when I'm writing to you, all I do is moan about stuff like the weather, or the people we meet or the food. I'm still acclimatising and slowly it's getting easier. Kerry's so patient and seems to understand my ups and downs. You asked what the women do all day as no one does housework. Some play golf, whist or bingo while energetic folk play netball and badminton, though heaven knows how they can in this heat. You can also do voluntary work in the library or help to weigh babies in the clinic. I was twenty-fourth on the list for a typing class so have given up that idea and put my name down for supply work at the school on camp.

I've joined a choir called the Seletar Singers and we're practising songs from the musicals Oklahoma, South Pacific and My Fair Lady for a forthcoming concert. It's funny because one of the songs, "Some Enchanted Evening", always reminds me of John when he was going out with Pat before they were married. I can remember him singing it word for word. Another one we're doing, "I'm Gonna Wash That Man Right Out Of My Hair", reminds me of Ann. Knowing her, she'd probably just finished with a boyfriend. We all like singing, don't we? We get it from you. It's definitely not from Dad. I've never heard him sing. I've started listening to The Archers; it's broadcast on the radio late afternoon round teatime. Jonathan can recognise the signature tune and the minute it starts he jigs up and down in time to the music and gets quite excited. He loves the little budgie called Joey which we got from a chap who's going home. He points to it and says "Jo, Jo". When he hears the put-put noise of Kerry's bike, he shouts "dadadadad" and waves his arms in the air. He also says "doggie" and if he hears a door banging shut he goes "DANG!". Do you notice he doesn't say, "mum, mum, mum" yet?

On the day he got his first tooth he started to crawl properly. Then when he began to make a beeline for the table-lamp flex. I said in a quiet, warning voice, "No". He looked at me, paused and carried on. When I repeated it a bit louder he stopped, gritted his teeth (or should I say tooth) and with arms and legs stiff with rage shouted back in baby language. It took me all my time not to laugh.

We went to the pictures last week to see a Bond film: You Only Live Twice. I was enjoying it until I noticed there were loads of baby cockroaches running up and down the seats. Then, horror of horrors, halfway through the film, I saw one on the back of the chap's shirt who was sitting in front of me. I couldn't take my eyes off it and watched, waiting for it to go down his neck. It gave me the creeps and I began to imagine I had an itch, first on my leg, then on my arm. Kerry said if we go again we'll have to take some fly spray and have to make sure I wear a cardigan and trousers.

Jonathan had a dreadful rash from sleeping under a net so we've taken it away and bought a mozzie killer that plugs into the electricity. It releases a pleasant flowery perfume and seems to do the trick as the rash has gone. I got six free china cups and saucers after buying six boxes of wash powder. I know it sounds a lot but we soon get through a box. Awah washes every day, sometimes twice if there are a lot of nappies, because while Jonathan isn't wearing plastic pants we change him as soon as he's wet. She does the washing in bare feet on the washhouse floor, in cold water in a tin tub, then rinses it in buckets. If I have a second shower to cool down at midday, which is usual, she even takes the clothes that I was wearing that I've dropped on the bedroom floor and washes them straightaway. Of course everything dries so quickly here, unlike home.

We had the first monsoon rains this week and boy did it pour. It's so heavy you wouldn't go out in it if you didn't need to and the water soon fills up the monsoon drains. I bought some blue gingham material in the village and Awah has made some curtains for the kitchen and four seat pads for the dining chairs. She really is a talented girl and so willing; she'll do anything for me and adores the baby. I feel quite humble as it makes me think you are what you are by virtue of when and where you're born. I laughed at the graphic description of you "diving into your Double Diamond" at the pub. Have you dried off yet? Pity you haven't got an amah to wash your smelly clothes. I bet Dad didn't even notice and carried on drinking his pint of Tetley's.

I'm reading a book from the library called Lark Rise to Candleford by Flora Thompson. It's wonderful; have you read it? It's all about an area of rural England in the late 1800s; a social history of customs, work and country life. After another downpour it's a bit cooler this evening; the temperature's gone down to 80 so we've switched the fan off. The rain is short and sharp, only lasting about twenty minutes. Will stop now and have a cuppa and do a bit more of the jigsaw you sent for my birthday. It's a bit difficult with all the sea and sky but I've noticed that Kerry can't resist adding two or three pieces every time he walks past.

Lots of love from us all

M K and J

FIRST TASTE OF SCHOOL

6 November 1967

Dear Mam,

Thanks for only half the letter today! I can't wait to get the first page; where is it, woman? It was infuriating to start midway through a sentence and not know what the heck you were talking about. I'll put it down to your age; after all, if I was twenty-nine in July, you were fifty-nine in September. It's handy knowing you were born in 1908 and me in 1938 so I can always get your age right.

Guess what…? I did four days' teaching last week and two this week at very short notice. I was still in my nightie when the deputy head knocked on the door at 8 o'clock on Monday. School starts at 8.15 a.m. and finishes at 12 p.m. so I really enjoyed it because Jonathan didn't miss me. He greeted me with delight when I came home at dinnertime. The first class was a second year of eight-to nine-year-olds. The school's massive, just juniors from seven to eleven, with over a thousand children and thirty-five teachers. The classrooms therefore are quite scattered; mine was in what's called an ATAP. It's a tin hut affair with dried palm leaves on the roof, which apparently give rise to the funny name. Inside it looks like a barn with two wooden beams from floor to ceiling right in the middle of the room. When I'm talking to the children or showing them something I have to keep walking from side to side in order to see them all. It's supposed to be the coolest form of building and I must admit it wasn't bad. This will make you smile. I had a different class this week: third years, nine years old and to put it kindly not so bright. They were putting words of a similar spelling into sentences, namely moat, stoat, moan, toad, toast, etc. Half of them didn't have a clue what the words meant. Even after the lengthy explanation I gave before they began, some still couldn't remember. The choice one read, "I toad you so"! It's sad really because these children are constantly changing schools, teachers, methods and friends so it's pretty hard on them. There's no continuity. It was a great change for me to look forward to going out, seeing and talking to people and having something fresh to tell Kerry in the evening. The money's good too at thirty-nine dollars a day. They did ask me if I was interested in full-time and I said yes, knowing Jonathan's quite happy with Awah.

I've done what you suggested and bought a cheap pair of pyjamas off the market so that he can wear just the bottoms when he's crawling. His latest trick is shoving things down the lavatory if anyone forgets to shut the door. I know when he's *done it because I can hear him chuckling and when I go and look he's hanging on to the sides jigging up and down with glee. He's also learned to climb on a low shelf in the kitchen where the wash powder and Ajax are kept. Awah's removed them but he still gets up there, then kneels and can't back off. He loves flowers. What a hippy baby! But he generally ends up stuffing them into his mouth and laughing when I say "No". When I went in to him this morning he'd taken both of his nappies off. I don't know how. It could have been because Kerry got him ready for bed last night?*

I can't believe he'll be one tomorrow. He's already had lots of cards from England. I do wish you could see him. We've bought him a Chad Valley baby walker. It's a wooden truck filled with coloured bricks that he can push; they're supposed to be non-tippable. Is there such a word? Hopefully it will help to get him walking as he's started to walk sideways holding on to the settee from end to end. I wanted something made in England because the toys that I've seen here made in the Far East don't appear to have the same standards of safety. We did have a spectacular bonfire and firework display on camp on 5 November. I reckon it's the first one I've ever enjoyed. I used to be terrified when I was little watching Dad setting ours off outside the back door. I hated the bangers and only liked the Roman candles and Catherine wheels. And the sparklers of course. Ann said I was such a baby. Ask her if she can remember.

I've posted all the Christmas presents this week in one parcel addressed to you. I hope you don't mind giving them to the family when you see them. It was nice for a change to be able to afford something a bit more than the usual five shillings per present. On Wednesday morning I went to the ladies' church guild to watch some woman giving a demonstration on Xmas wrapping. It started off quite well but she got rather carried away and went on and on and on. I was getting bored and so were the girls sitting around me, then we all got the giggles. In the end the chairwoman had to stop the speaker else we'd have been there yet. I'm enclosing some more photos taken recently of the little lad. I hope you don't bore everyone with his pictures; if people start avoiding you, you'll know why. Does Dad ever read my letters or do you just tell him bits of it? I hear regularly from Ann; she said she's going to try and get a record played for us on family favourites. We only hear the last half-hour because the rest of the programme is mainly for troops stationed in Germany. Keep your fingers crossed.

Lots of love
M K and J

BIRTHDAY BUBBLES

10 November 1967

Dear Mam,

Thanks for the letter that started, "Dear Maggie, Jonathan and Sugarplum"! Kerry noticed it before me and says to tell you he's very flattered. Yes please, we'd love to have one of your homemade Christmas cakes. I'd ask for an apple pie as well but I guess it would be off by the time it arrived. I do miss your lovely pastry. They reckon that the dock strike at home will delay overseas Christmas parcels so I'm glad I got mine off last week.

I do wish you'd been here for Jonathan's first birthday. He's so gorgeous and I feel you and the family are all missing out. However, for this reason, we've bought a cine camera and have been keeping a record of him ever since we arrived. It'll be *lovely for you to watch it when we do come home. Mind you, the films aren't cheap and they only last about eight minutes. I'm sure it will be worth it because we've already caught some precious moments, like today when Kerry was sitting on the front doorstep blowing bubbles. Jonathan sat with his hands on his knees fascinated, trying to catch one if it floated near him. His face was a picture when he touched one and it disappeared. I've also taken a few minutes of him jumping up and down in the baby bouncer. He's trying to pick up a football between his bare feet that Kerry is rolling to him. Sometimes he can lift it and at other times he gives it a kick as the bouncer brings him down.*

On his birthday we spent the day in the garden with six baby boys all of a similar age. The mothers sat on the grass playing with the children and enjoying the cups of tea with fresh milk, while the dads took loads of photos and drank beer. Jonathan is the only one not walking yet but I think he'll soon be there. He just loves the baby walker and pushes it everywhere, inside and out. The trouble is he can't steer as he's so busy concentrating on his legs and feet that we have to watch him as he heads for the coconut palm or the little monsoon drain that runs round the edge of the garden.

Talking of monsoons, I got absolutely soaked cycling home from school today. The water was gushing along the drains like a stream in full flow. When it rains like that a lot of people just walk barefoot and carry their shoes; it seems the sensible thing to do. The small drains like gutters around the houses feed into bigger ones by the road and then even wider and much deeper ones in town. All the drains are open so they can easily be cleared if there's a blockage.

There are stories of children being swept away, though you never know how much to believe. We took the mosquito net off a couple of nights ago because I got too hot and kept waking up. Now I can feel the fan but we've had to change sides in bed because Kerry says it's too windy and he's cold. We're also using mozzie coils again because they burn right through the night and are much more effective. It's awful if a mosquito gets inside the net; you can hear it and not see it. "Oh to be in England now that winter's here" – my apologies to Robert Browning.

I've been teaching every day for two weeks, year three juniors who are nine to ten years old, but they're what Judy and I in Germany used to jokingly call the A level group. No concentration and limited reading and language skills, which is reflected in their writing. Trouble is there are sixteen boys and only five girls. However, one ray of sunshine is a little girl who has cerebral palsy but is the best reader in the class and uses a typewriter for her written work. She also has a wheelchair if we change classrooms or go into the hall. Despite her disabilities she's delightful, popular with the class and always smiling.

I didn't tell you before because I didn't want you to worry, but I'm going into hospital for a varicose vein operation during the last week of this month. The specialist who saw me in September said he could do injections if I'd prefer but they would probably be short-lived. Anyway I shall be done and dusted and hopefully on the mend by Christmas. We all had to have the six-monthly cholera injections last week including the baby, who never made a murmur. Did I mention that Kerry has decided to come out of the air force when we come home? He'll have done twenty-two years by then and says now that he has a family he doesn't want to do any more unaccompanied tours.

Jonathan has developed a sudden fascination for library books and will sit for ages just flicking the pages. I bought him a cardboard book with pictures but he's not interested as he can't flick it. He's also taken to looking in the floor-length mirror that's on the wardrobe in our room. He has a short conversation with himself then moves away for a minute. But he can't resist going back to have another look to see if the same boy is still there. It's so funny; I wish I could understand his gibberish.

We went to a dance at the yacht club on Friday evening and it was the best night I've had here. I think it was the magic of the atmosphere. We danced outside under the palm trees with the light of the full moon reflecting across the water. It was like being in a film. Please write soon, then I'll get it while I'm in hospital. Awah will look after the baby and a neighbour has offered to take him out in the pram every afternoon. So don't worry about anything.

Tons of love
M K and J

CHANGI HOSPITAL

30 November 1967

Dear Mam,

Thanks for the little lettercards which I've been receiving every day while I've been in here. You're the best mam in the world and I hope I turn out the same. I came in on Wednesday and had the operation on Thursday. I was first on a list of three; good job because I was quite nervous. Despite being cut in three places there's not as much discomfort as I was led to believe by some folks who'd already had the same operation. I had to stay in bed for the first couple of days before I was allowed to get up. Now that I am mobile I must wear the bandage when I'm on my feet but can take it off whilst lying down. I'm doing this pretty often because the leg gets so hot and itchy. It looks dead funny because it's bright pink with antiseptic from the foot to the groin. It looks like a case of excessive sunburn.

There are twelve beds in the ward but just five are occupied. There's a television but it's only been on once. I did bring my box of scrabble hoping that someone would like a game but unfortunately no one knows how to play. The girls are chatty and we all have a good laugh apart from one, a young schoolteacher in her thirties who ignores us completely. She sits outside on the balcony, reading all day. She seems to have a superiority complex and can hardly bring herself to say good morning so I haven't let on that I'm a teacher as well. She's such a creep when Sister does the rounds, gushing and friendly and actually smiling. The lasses who visit her are teachers, too. They're real mod types, done up to the nines, giggling and shrieking. It reminds me of when Judy and I were in Berlin. I'll be honest, most of the teachers who go abroad to work for the forces are husband hunting. Judy found Dennis and had I not had Kerry I might have done the same. There's certainly no lack of opportunity. I can tell that it amuses Kerry because he sits and listens to them with a smirk on his face.

The nurses are lovely; they're mostly wives of servicemen stationed here. They're not strict about petty things like smoking or getting out of bed and it doesn't seem to matter how many visitors arrive together. The food is brilliant. There's a good choice from about six things, which we order the previous day. We get three meals plus afternoon tea and the helpings are very generous. I suppose the catering staff is so used to preparing good food in huge quantities for the healthy appetites of servicemen. Suits me; think it was the way I was brought up.

Changi is a long way from Seletar but even though it's pretty expensive Kerry's coming in every night by taxi. There is a bus but it's a two-hour journey each way.

I have an end bed so I can see out over the balcony that looks on to the water and the islands beyond. It's very picturesque with the coconut palms, the banana trees and the tulip flower trees among a mass of jungle green. The submarine HMS Dreadnought went past yesterday. Kerry said it's on a test trip from Rosyth to Singapore and back. He bought me orchids and carnations, which I've put on the locker by the photo of Jonathan. I do miss him and lie and gaze at his little smiley face; everyone says what a gorgeous baby he is. Awah and her sister babysit every night so he's getting plenty of attention. Did you like the snaps taken at his birthday party? They'd be even better in colour, especially the one in the high chair. It was the first time he's ever eaten chocolate cake and he couldn't stuff it in his mouth quick enough. Can you see it all over his chops? Quite a few more presents arrived late. Kerry's sister Shelagh posted hers from south Wales on 5 October so it's taken over two months. I hope you've had a couple of my letters by now; you must have been on edge every time the post came. They say that no news is good news so you would have heard soon enough if anything was wrong. I laughed about you getting an artificial Christmas tree. Whatever next? You'll be buying plastic flowers like me. It's very boring being in bed all day. Someone has just put the TV on and it's Batman so I think I'll take my book and go and sit on the balcony with laughing girl.

Give my love to everyone and write soon.

Love M K and J

BACK TO THE NEST

10 December 1967

Dear Mam,

Kerry came to fetch me in a taxi with Awah and the baby. I cried when I saw him. It seemed such a long time and I'm sure he's grown in nine days. He came and sat on my knee for a little while but was a bit confused. Since I've been home he's been as right as rain with me but he's following Kerry everywhere and crying if he goes out. He's also going to him when he's upset. I'm sure he'll soon realise that I'm here to stay. Don't worry about me resting, Awah's doing everything, she's a real gem, bless her. Also Kerry starts his leave on Monday that will take him right up till Christmas. I have to keep the crêpe bandage on for a week, can walk and sit as much as I like but mustn't stand in one position. The surgeon said that 10 per cent need to have the treatment again so I'll have to take this opportunity of resting while I can. I was terrified when it came to taking out the stitches, particularly in the groin where there were seven, but it wasn't too bad. The latter were in an awkward place right on the knicker line. Now that the dressing has been taken off I've resurrected the huge cotton pants I wore when I was pregnant with Jonathan. They have no elastic in the legs and look like oversize underpants. Très élégante! I'll have to make sure I don't get run over. I wonder who made up that daft saying, Make sure you wear clean underclothes in case you have an accident.

Kerry's friend Ray and his wife Diane came this morning. They babysat a couple of times when he visited me. She doesn't like it a bit over here and I think they've applied to go home early. I thanked her for the get-well card that she'd sent and she asked me how many I got. When I said it was the only one she just raised her eyebrows and tutted.

Do you remember when we were little you used to say "Don't tut at me"? I always wondered how you heard. In my innocence I thought it was a silent protest. It's funny the little things that stick in your mind. Jonathan's almost walking. He takes one step while you're holding his hand, then when you let go his little legs give way and he plonks down with a bump. Then he laughs like mad. We practise on the grass so he doesn't hurt himself. He's such a happy little soul.

It's been a miserable, wet day, a bit like England but not so cold. Kerry's been trying to dry nappies on a clothes horse in the kitchen. He's placed them in front of a table fan switched to full speed. The trouble is if it's wet for a day or two with no form of heating and the high humidity, the washing just doesn't dry. I even put some nappies in the oven to finish them off this morning.

Last night I finished my Christmas cards and have enclosed a letter and snaps to family and best friends. We've been given a small, artificial tree from someone who's gone home so while Kerry's on leave he's going to put it up and decorate it. We found some lovely Christmas bits for it in the amahs' market. A jolly, fat Santa Claus, a couple of reindeer, some sparkly silver stars and a few baubles. I can't wait to see the little lad's face. I wonder if he'll try to pull them off.

Apart from not celebrating with you, there's another thing I'll be missing this year: we won't be able to go to the usual Xmas dance in the sergeants' mess. Kerry said we can go and sit and listen if I like. I know I'd hate to sit there tapping my foot to the rhythm, desperately wanting to be dancing. Also, he'd be such a gentleman he'd dance with someone else's wife because their husband doesn't enjoy it. I'd be dead jealous. There will be a big Xmas draw with very good prizes so we'll go to that. There's a buffet and music.

We've bought two LP records of Christmas carols on the amahs' market, Nina and Frederik and Andy Williams. I love them and play them over and over again. Jonathan's beginning to recognise some of the chorus'.

It sounds a bit odd though with the sun shining and all the windows wide open. It's like playing them in England in August. I've also bought some thick wool to start a chunky sweater for Kerry – wishful thinking. I'm not the world's best knitter but it will help to pass the time while I'm sitting around twiddling my thumbs.

Looking forward to hearing about your pre-Christmas shopping.
I bet you've already started receiving cards.
Much love from us all
M K and J

BOXING DAY, 1967

26 December 1967

Dear Mam,

We had a lovely day yesterday and toasted everyone back home when we had our Christmas dinner. I cooked the traditional chicken, roast spuds, etc., with lots of help from our visitors. Awah in fact prepared all the vegetables for me the night before, bless her. We're giving her a week off with full pay as a thank you for all the extra work she's done while I've been laid up. Diane and Ray came and so they were able to film us helping Jonathan to open his parcels. When the nesting cups that you sent fell out of the box he picked up the biggest and tried to drink from it. It's the same size as his little blue beaker. I love the two pairs of colourful rompers; they make him look much older. Although they'll be too hot to wear all the time, they're fine with just a nappy underneath as they'll protect his knees when he's crawling at speed. He still prefers to be on the floor if he's on a mission because he can get there quicker. His favourite toy seems to be a wobbly dachshund-type dog on four big yellow wheels. It has large floppy ears and a long tail attached to a spring. He hasn't cottoned on to pulling the lead but sits and whacks the tail, which vibrates and makes him laugh. We also bought him a big rocking horse mounted on springs but he's a bit too small to rock it on his own. However, he likes to sit on the seat looking around, enjoying seeing things from a different eye level. He's pointing to pictures on the walls and ornaments on the window ledges, smiling and saying "wassat", imitating what we say to him.

We had an awful fright last week. He was crying and grizzling constantly, which isn't a bit like him, so Kerry picked him up and walked around singing quietly as he tried to comfort him. Suddenly his little body went rigid on Kerry's shoulder. His eyes rolled up and back then he flopped like a rag doll. We were terrified. We dashed across the road to a neighbour who had a car. It took less than two minutes to sick quarters where the MO gave him an injection. He opened his eyes immediately. The doctor said it was a convulsion caused by a combination of the baby's high body temperature due to teething and the constant ambient temperature. He told us that if he gets hot and flushed again to either stick him in a bath of cold water or wipe him down with a cold flannel.

On a brighter note we took him in a taxi to Singapore to show him the toys in one of the big stores and to visit Father Christmas. Not a good idea. He clung on to Kerry looking the other way and wouldn't go anywhere near him.

29 December 1967

I'm beginning to wonder if anything is amiss, as we haven't heard from you since your last letter on 15 December. I feel sure you'd have written two or three times since then. I've written at least three letters and waited and waited, thinking there'll be one from you tomorrow. We know it's not the postal service because we've been getting Christmas cards for the past four weeks; we must have had over sixty from every man and his dog. Did you get the recorded tape we sent? I'm longing for you to send one back with the whole family talking to us. It's chucked it down with rain for the past four days and everything smells damp. We've been invited to a party for New Year's Eve, probably out of courtesy, as we hardly know them. It's a chap who Kerry works with. I'm still wearing the bandage so I doubt that we will go as we've never really made a big thing of that night. I do remember you taking us to the back door to listen to the trawlers and ships hooting in the Humber on New Year's Eve. One of the best nights I ever had was up in Hartlepool when I was eighteen. I was staying at your cousin's and went out with her lad and a crowd of his friends first-footing. It amounted to knocking on anyone's door after midnight to wish them good luck. At every house we got invited in for a drink and food. I don't think we rolled home till six in the morning.

If we don't hear from you by next week I'm going to phone. Blow the money; I don't care what it costs. I really miss your chatty letters.

Tons of love
M K and J

RAIN! RAIN! RAIN!

New Year, January 1968

Dear Mam,

Have you got over the surprise of the phone call? I felt all fluttery inside when I heard your voice. We were so relieved to hear that you were all right. That was the chief purpose of ringing, having not had a word since your last letter that was written well before Christmas. I hope you're over the flu. We saw in the papers that there'd been a big epidemic but now it's on the decline. I wonder which is worse; foot and mouth disease, flu, then snow; or mosquito bites, cockroaches, monsoons and too much sun. I suppose the grass is always greener in the other field. It's easy to forget which month it is over here because the days and seasons are all alike. It gets light in the morning at half six and dark in the evening at seven. You'd expect to be able

171

to go into the garden at that time like a summer evening at home when it's cooler. However, it gets dark quite abruptly and with the dusk come the mosquitoes. That's also when we have to close all the windows. Last week it rained non-stop for four days, then was blisteringly hot and humid until this morning when it started again. When the sun does shine I have to put all the cushions outside on the veranda to air because everything including the bedding feels damp. Even the suitcases being stored in the cupboard smell musty, so Awah puts those out too.

Jonathan's still grizzly with his teeth and the humidity and I'm on constant alert since he had that fit. He used to go through the night no problem but lately he's been waking every hour. I think I've aged ten years with the sleep I've lost. Last night we put him in his cot about seven and he was asleep in ten minutes. Half an hour later he was wide awake shouting, "Daddy, Awah, no!" I gave him another bottle with some medicine in from the MO and he slept through till six. I think it's a mild sedative that seems to cool and calm him.

I'm teaching first-year juniors this term. It's a nice little class and we have some good laughs. After Easter I might be transferring to the infants because a lot of families are going home early and numbers are dropping. Rumours are rife that Seletar will be closed by this time next year. I must admit, though, that the days are going quicker now that I'm working. When I get home from school Awah always has something ready for me to eat.

After being at school from eight in the morning till one o'clock, I have a rest in the afternoon. I know it sounds pathetic but it really is just too hot and sticky to move. I lie on the settee and watch Jonathan play. Sometimes I shut my eyes and pretend to sleep and he comes up and bashes me with a soft toy.

Next week is Chinese New Year so using your recipe I made some Lincolnshire plum bread for Awah. It's a public holiday that goes on for a week apparently, with lots of food, noise and fireworks. I'm glad we're not still living down in the village; it'll be hell let loose going on all night.

We were so disappointed that you can't come and visit next summer so instead have spent the money that we put aside for your airfare. We decided to go ahead and get a car so that we can go up to the forces leave centre for ten days at Easter. It's in Penang on the west coast of Malaya. We splashed out and really got a smasher. It cost £300 from a garage on the camp so at least we can go back if there's a problem. If you buy one privately and it lets you down, it's hard luck, because it's likely that the previous owner will have gone back to England. We've chosen a white Ford Taurus (German), a bit like a Corsair, with black leather upholstery that can seat six adults. It has a radio and a fan cooler. We even thought if we really like it we might drive it home; it's only 9,000 miles. Ha! Ha! Ha! They say it's a lot cleaner when you get off this island to go north. It needs to be as I reckon this is the stinkiest place on earth. It'll be a two-day journey so we'll stay one night en route in Kuala Lumpur.

I've just finished a book you might like by Rowena Farre called A Time from the World. It's a true story about how she joined up with a band of gypsies and travelled with them. I reckon she's crackers because she describes in one chapter where she walked alone in the middle of the night, through a wood, and through a churchyard where she lay down to rest on a tombstone. Just like you do, eh?

I'm going to finish now and put some anti-mozzie stuff on before I get bitten to death. We bought a new brand by Johnson's that also kills chiggers, if you know what they are. We don't either but we keep talking about them because we like the sound of the word.

Hope you're keeping warm

Love M K and J

WATER, WATER, EVERYWHERE

February 1968

Dear Mam,

Thank you for the pressed snowdrops; what a lovely thought and a touch of home. I could send you some orchid seeds but I doubt they'd come to much in Cleethorpes. Did you like the colour photos? I wanted to give you more of an idea of what our grocer's shop, Chee Kow, looks like and the state of the road and the grot everywhere in the village. Mind you, a picture doesn't bring the smell with it. The only trouble with colour photos is the price. We think it's expensive because the printing is extra, not included, as in the normal black and white film processing.

I think I prefer black and white anyway because Kerry can develop it himself.

We had a long spell of rain and now it's stinking hot again. When it's not moving it's like being in a greenhouse sitting in the car. We were going to do a practice run to Johore Bahru, the first place on the Malaya side of the peninsula over the causeway. Then we remembered you have to take Paludrin anti-malaria tablets from the day before, all the time you're there and for twenty-eight days after. Instead we drove to the outskirts of Singapore where we parked the car and took a taxi for the rest of the journey. The traffic in the city is frightening. There's a mixture of battered, clapped-out cars with the occasional posh one, and loads of laden, ramshackle lorries that look as though the axle has gone. They're weighed down on soft, almost flat, tyres, causing them to tilt to one side. Hundreds of bicycles wobble dangerously, ridden by skinny old men wearing wide, straw, coolie hats. They have difficulty keeping their balance as the two panniers strapped each side behind the saddle are overflowing with vegetables and stuff that they'll sell at the roadside. A lot of the side streets were flooded and up above, rows and rows of washing fluttered, pegged to hundreds of bamboo canes attached to the windows of the buildings. People were paddling barefoot in the dirty water amongst the debris of peelings, discarded boxes and paper and who knows what else that was floating in it. The monsoon drains in the city are as wide as a canal and it's actually frightening to watch the frothy, muddy brown water as it swirls and gushes towards the harbour.

You asked me what words Jonathan can say; I could fill half a page, which I reckon for sixteen months is pretty good. The distinct ones that you would recognise include Daddy, Awah,

Mummy (at last), teddy, talcum, chair, get down, I see you, chit-chat where?, cheese and moon.

There's a load more that we understand and he's repeating the last word of any sentence spoken to him. Yesterday he came out of the kitchen with the remains of a cucumber, biting the end, waving it and saying "nana". (Banana) The funniest thing happened in the garden today as he was helping the gardener.

Every morning when he hears him arrive on his bike he's out the door as fast as his little legs will allow, following him everywhere. The man has given him an old can that Jonathan fills with water from the bigger bucket, which he then carries, spilling most, to tip what's left onto the flowers. Leaving him to carry on, the chap disappeared round the corner for a minute, but Jonathan noticed straightaway and started to follow. However, he couldn't manage to get over the monsoon drain. I was watching from inside as he stood there, and I waited to see what he'd do next. Sure enough, he suddenly yelled, "Nardner! Nardner!". I laughed like mad when "nardner" came back, swept him up under one arm and carried him off. I'd love to be able to chat to the man. We've managed to establish, through sign language and the few English words he uses, that he has a wife and young children in India. He talks to Jonathan constantly and I'm now sure that the child understands him as he will often repeat the last word in Malay.

Please ask Dad from me just how can it be possible, or even common sense, that Jonathan is your favourite grandchild? You have five more living in England whom you've seen regularly since they were born and you haven't seen my baby for nine months. Tell Dad, if you dare, that he talks out of the back of his neck. What a stupid remark. I'm longing for you all to see him; that's what I most regret – you not being able to enjoy his progress with me. I had a long letter from Ann; she enjoyed your visit and seems to be more settled in Ormskirk now that David and Anna have started school. I bet you miss seeing her and the children regularly. I suppose it was harder for her to move to Lancashire away from family and friends when she's always lived and worked in Cleethorpes or Grimsby. She'll soon get to know other parents, though, through the children. They're great icebreakers. Is David's new girlfriend a teacher like him? I must admit I did like the other girl Elsa that he was going out with. She was well travelled and always sent me a postcard from her trips while I was working in Germany.

I'm trying to keep the snowdrops pressed, in a safe place, though I know from past experience that eventually they'll become too fragile to keep. Perhaps I could send you a flower but the snag is, like the butterflies and the creepy-crawlies, they are excessively large. Glad you're keeping warm; at least Dad is fond of a roaring fire so no worries there.

Lots of love
M K and J

MARKET IN SERANGOON

March 1968

Dear Mam,

Excuse the rotten writing; I've been doing school reports for almost three hours and my hand is about dropping off. We had to give the children tests last week. It upset my class. They're all children that are struggling; yet they were expected to do the same paper as the more able pupils. It seems stupid to me because it undermines their confidence, which I've been attempting to build all this term. I took them on a boat trip round Singapore harbour last Monday. We were on the water for an hour and a half and I actually enjoyed it. Like you, I'm not a very good sailor and I was going to opt out but I'm glad I went. Four mums accompanied us and the children loved it. They listened to everything the guide told them as he pointed to the sampans and the bigger ships. They've done some lovely pictures and writing about it.

We went to Serangoon market yesterday so that Jonathan could see the ducks and chickens. It's a much bigger one than ours in the village and is held in the morning and as well as food they sell livestock. The poultry is in cages or running about scratching in the dust. You can choose the one you want and they will kill it and dress it there and then. Just right for a toddler's eyes – what? The fruit and vegetables are displayed on the floor on paper or sacks. It's very colourful with the red and yellow peppers, the scarlet chillies and the lighter and darker green leafy stuff that I can't even recognise, let alone name. The sellers are mostly old or middle-aged women who sit on the floor, their legs splayed apart, with one knee up supporting an elbow and feet sticking out at right angles. They look bored or half asleep.

I was watching a chap who, wearing only shorts and sandals, was frying food in a huge black cast-iron wok. How he didn't get splattered with hot fat I don't know. He had a cigarette in his mouth, oblivious to the fact that the ash was about to drop in. Tasty, don't you think? We wouldn't dream of buying anything to eat in the street.

I almost forgot to tell you about the wedding party held by Chee Kow to celebrate his brother's marriage. All his English customers were invited and, with Chinese family and friends, there must have been nearly a thousand people sitting down. It was held last Saturday evening in a massive marquee set up in the village street right outside the camp. The catering was done there and then and the mouthwatering smell of young suckling roasting over the charcoal fires hit you the minute you walked in. It was fabulous. There were eleven courses, accompanied by as much wine or beer as you wanted. Waitresses were hovering between tables waiting to fill empty glasses. The meal for the English people, although basically Chinese, was cooked to European taste, while the Asians of course had proper Chinese food. Kerry didn't eat much, no surprise there, as he doesn't like his food "messed about". He said he enjoyed it though and spent more time talking than eating while yours truly tucked in. You'd have laughed to see me using chopsticks; as there were no knives and forks, it was a case of learn or go hungry. I think I used my fingers a lot when no one was looking. I'm sending you the invitation; even that's worth keeping. The event really was quite different from anything we've ever been to.

We're still waiting to hear about Kerry's application to finish with the RAF; they reckon it should come through soon. You never know, we could be home for Christmas. I've decided that I won't transfer to the infants after Easter, I'll just continue to do supply where I am. Anyway, I'm enjoying the change teaching older children because the staff in the junior school is a good mixture of men and women. You don't get that in an infant school; even one bloke would be unusual. There's a lot more laughter and joking in this staffroom.

When we had another heavy downpour this afternoon Awah called out "BIG RAIN missee" and shot out the back to get the washing in. Jonathan went mad and wearing only his little pants ran after her shouting, "Rain, rain, Awah!" He then dashed into the front garden and ran round and round getting drenched before he sat in the monsoon drain where he let water drip off the veranda, onto his head and down his back. He looked so funny that we took a couple of photos.

We've decided to take Awah and her sister to Penang with

us. There's plenty of room in the car and she's never been off the island before. I said we'd help them to find accommodation and pay for their bed and breakfast if they pay for their own food. They're both so excited. We'll be leaving this Thursday, really early, in order to go as far as we can before it gets too hot. I'll write to you while we're away and will look forward to one of your letters waiting when we get back. Thanks for Jonathan's Easter card. He pointed to the rabbit and said teddy. I shall miss your hot cross buns this year and your lovely simnel cake. I had the oven on airing some clothes this morning, so thinking I wouldn't waste the heat I made some meringues. They were rotten; I couldn't even get them out of the tin.

Happy Easter
Love M K and J

PENANG

April 1968

Dear Mam,

We've just got back from Penang and your lovely, long letter arrived today. The postman comes round on a bike and when he stops outside, he rings a bell. Jonathan has just cottoned on to this so runs out to get the letter. He also hears the van every morning that brings the fresh milk, and he insists on carrying it in and putting it in the fridge. It's in a carton by the way, not in a bottle like at home.

It was a long and interesting drive through Malaya. I expected it to be a bit cooler and less humid but it felt just as sticky to me. There were certainly far more mosquitoes. I can see why it's so important to take the anti-malaria tablets. Jonathan was extremely good on the journey and Awah and her sister chatted to him, sang and played games when he got a bit fed up towards the end.

As we were travelling in the car we passed flooded fields where there were buffalo or oxen, I'm not sure which, lying down in the water. All you could see was the big black head and an ear or a tail that flicked every time a mosquito landed on it. Behind stood a cluster of wooden houses on stilts; all so large I imagine there would have been two or maybe three generations living together in each one. Some distance further there was another buffalo straining through the sticky, wet mud as it pulled a very basic wooden plough. It looked as though it was handmade from a long, thick s-shaped branch. A little man in a wide coolie hat was trying to guide it while he struggled through the quagmire of wet clay. Two blokes were standing watching him. It quite amused me the fact that no matter where in the world you are, you see people watching someone else doing hard physical work. From there it was miles and miles of rubber plantations neatly planted row after row, and only widely scattered, mucky-looking towns where I was dying to stop and find a nice clean cafe. Ha ha, no chance. However, I took rolls and plenty to drink and we did stop once for an ice cream. We stayed the night in a posh hotel in Kuala Lumpur, paying far more than we anticipated. I was disgusted when I realised it didn't include an evening meal or even breakfast. For the same price in England, we could have stayed at the Hilton. We had a fright early next morning when we were rudely awakened about half past four by a voice on a megaphone coming from the temple nearby. It was apparently calling the faithful to prayer.

We stopped for breakfast outside of Kuala Lumpur in one of the recommended rest houses that are usually full, so before we left Kerry booked a night for the return journey. We had to make a lavatory stop later in the morning and found a reasonable coffee place, but the lav was awful. There was no pedestal, just a hole in the floor over which you had to stand or squat praying it wasn't going to spray your legs. It felt so unladylike and the smell was horrendous. Never again. You can only find western type lavs in the posh places or the decent shops in Singapore.

After another six hours driving, Kerry finally dropped me off with the baby before he took the girls and found them a suitable Chinese place in town. We were all hot, sweaty and exhausted. We had a large room with four single beds, a double and a cot. That night Jonathan slept like a log and we didn't wake up until there was a knock on the door about 8 o'clock. There stood a young man carrying a pot of tea for us with an orange juice for Jonathan. This happened every morning. The food was good English cooking; bearing in mind it is a leave centre for servicemen. There were cereals and toast for breakfast and homemade soup, mixed grill, steak and chips or chicken pie, for dinner. Jonathan ate everything he was offered, he takes after me, and had his first go at drinking juice with a straw. As he's under two, there was no charge for him and he loved sleeping with us in the same room. Because he was out all day, either on the sands or in the sea with Kerry, or playing in the paddling pool, by evening he was so whacked that he slept right through the night. It was bliss. He preferred going in the sea to playing with the sand and I filmed him toddling unsteadily to the water's edge where he sat down and let the waves lap over his feet and little legs. The sand was clean and soft, real sand, and palm trees grew right along the shoreline. It was beautiful, *just like you see at the pictures when it's a love story like South Pacific. I'll be able to show you when we come home. We spent every single day down there.*

Awah and her friend had a marvellous holiday. They were talking about it all the way back. She met her penfriend who lives there and apparently a crowd of them went out every day and each evening. I'm so pleased because it helped to soften the blow when we told her that we would be coming home earlier than first expected. It was a bit of a shock because amahs' jobs are becoming fewer now and even a couple of Chinese grocers locally are closing their shops already. Now that Kerry's application to leave the RAF has officially been accepted, he will apply to have any leave owing to be taken in the UK. That would bring us to next January. Roll on.

Much love from us all

M K and J

COOKING DISASTERS

May 1968

Dear Mam,

Thank you for the Lincolnshire Life magazine and the brochure about Germany. I bet you are looking forward to your holiday. It will bring back memories of your visit to see me in Berlin. I thought you were brave to travel alone by train all that way, including through the occupied Eastern sector. I can't imagine any of my friends' mothers doing the same; I reckon you were born before your time Chrissie McGuinness! I have to take Jonathan for his booster diphtheria vaccination today, bless him; it was only last week when we both had to have the six-monthly cholera jab.

I've had a couple of cooking disasters lately and am beginning to wonder if it's the electric oven. I much prefer gas. Now that I've stopped teaching and have plenty of time, I'm trying to make the dinners a bit more interesting. Kerry has lost a lot of weight and is down to nine stone, as he was when he returned from Borneo. Anyway, I bought a lovely piece of Australian pork for a change, put it in the oven for what should have been ample time but when I started to carve it, it was seriously underdone. I shoved it back in and quickly opened a tin of soup for Kerry. Nearly an hour later it still wasn't done properly. I know you can eat beef rare but not pork. The same afternoon I clarted about making a lemon meringue pie with real lemons. I did the meringue in my new Kenwood mixer and it looked great. Then the damn thing didn't set properly. In the end I made some shortbread; it was dead quick to make and tasted lovely. I actually found some fresh mint in the NAAFI shop. It was a bit scabby-looking, though good enough to go in with the potatoes and now I'm trying to root a bit in a plant pot.

As we know that we are definitely coming home in the winter, I'm beginning to think about the clothes we'll need. I can rig Jonathan out in Ladybird and Marks stuff, both available in town, and am knitting for him already. I might have to ask you to send me something warm, like long-legged underwear and flannelette pyjamas. Kerry wrote letters to a few different firms about job prospects for next year. Most have replied saying write again nearer the time, but two were actually offering work as a technical author, which is what he used to do at North Luffenham. One firm is EMI which has branches all over the country; the other is a publishing firm operating in Reading. It's good to have that reassurance of something positive.

I was interested to hear that you'd had a letter from Dora

saying she's in love with her doctor. The same week I read a book by A. J. Cronin called A Song of Sixpence. I think he was a doctor, wasn't he? There was a paragraph that explained how spinsters often go through this stage of being in love with their priest or doctor or similar and there is a special word for it medically. In her case, though, it's been going on for a long time, hasn't it?

Last week we went out with a couple we met in Penang to Bugis Street, a renowned place in Singapore. I know you wouldn't approve of your younger daughter visiting such places but I am nearly thirty! What an experience; I couldn't believe my eyes. There were these chaps dressed as women, so beautifully made up with mascara, lipstick, etc. and wearing fantastic blonde wigs and exotic-looking earrings. One was in a gold lamé dress complete with jewellery and high heels. He even walked exactly like a woman. Kerry kept whispering "there's one" because I honestly couldn't tell the difference. It's in a little side street thronging with people, where you can sit outside drinking as long as you like. It's all very open and there were even children as young as seven or eight going round the tables begging from the visitors.

Jonathan got two more teeth last week; I wish you could see him. He tries to provoke us now and deliberately does something again when you say no. I say stop it or don't and he repeats what I've said, then shakes his finger at me. I have to try not to laugh. He also says, "One two", followed by a big pause before three, and then chucks something; not always a ball, it may be a cushion or a toy. It seems incredible that he wasn't even sitting up unaided when we arrived and his hair that was very dark is now a mixture of silver and auburn, quite fair.

Well, I've saved the big news till the end. I didn't tell you before as I didn't want you to worry. I am having a baby in October. We are thrilled of course and now that I am halfway, twenty weeks, there isn't long to go. I didn't tell you straightaway because out here miscarriages are quite usual and I wanted to be really sure. I'm going to the clinic this afternoon for a check-up. I hope you are as pleased as we are; it's a cheerful note to end on for a change!

Tons of love from

M K and J

VISIT TO AWAH'S

June 1968

Dear Mam,

I've been dying to hear from you to see what your reaction was to the news about the baby. I knew you would be pleased but not surprised, in fact I said to Kerry I bet she writes and says she knew. I would love you to knit for Jonathan; he will need a woolly hat, scarf and mittens for sure. If you do a jumper I suggest you make it to fit a three-year-old please. He picked up one of my knitting needles this week, looked at me knowingly, then proceeded to press the point into his hand and said "Prick – ow" then he laughed. Thanks for the cigarette cards you sent for him. He loves the pictures and sits on the floor with his legs outstretched, sorting them and chuntering in a mixture of languages. When Awah was talking to the grocer in Chinese Jonathan was repeating everything she said, much to the chap's amusement. He's also started saying Kerry instead of daddy; it sounds really funny.

On Monday there was a knock at the door at 9.30 a.m. and there stood the deputy from school. He's a rather dishy bloke, tall, dark and handsome in his tropical shorts and short-sleeved white polo shirt. I was just about to go out and knit squares for the leper colony! Honest, there's a group of us at the church guild. We watched a flight sergeant from catering giving a demonstration on cake icing the other week. He was good but it's difficult with the climate to get it right as it takes so long to set. Anyway, I digress, and I ended up going into school for the whole week.

It was a class of ten-and eleven-year-olds and my goodness what a change from when I was that age. Miss Jackson would turn in her grave. The boys were fine; I think they enjoyed the attention of a female for a change. They even crowded around my desk to chat at the end of the lesson. A group of girls, though, really annoyed me. They were answering back whilst brushing their hair and one even started eating an apple when I was talking to her. They're far more mature than we ever were at eleven. I expect each generation thinks the same.

We were invited to visit Awah's home as she wanted us to meet her family. What an education, making me realise yet again how lucky I am.

They live in a kampong, which I think means village or community. It's just a cluster of wooden shacks all very close together in a clearing at the edge of what would previously have been jungle. Some roofs are tin, others are coconut palm and because there isn't a window the only light comes from the entrance where there's no door either. Inside there are no rugs or carpet and very little furniture; only the bare essentials for sitting, eating and sleeping. There's no oven because they cook on an open fire and only a few shacks have electric light. Water comes from a communal tap and has to be carried by the children in great tins. The women do their washing at the taps and take the young ones there to wash. You often see them by the roadside having a bath. All the aunties, uncles, cousins, grannies, etc. stay at home and look after the babies and toddlers. I don't know how many live in Awah's place; they have their own shack and Grandma lives next door. Her cousin, who is twenty-one, lives there with three children; the youngest is four weeks old. They're all girls and apparently when the last one was born she tried to give it to Awah's mother. This is quite common out here because they prefer boys and will give or even sell baby girls if they can. We saw the baby; it was an ugly little thing wrapped in a piece of torn cotton, probably an old dress or something similar. It was pathetic. I'd have taken it myself if the law had let me.

At the moment there's a big exercise on involving a lot of blokes from Seletar, which means they go off up to Malaya or Thailand to "play war" for about twelve days. This happens regularly and some of the wives spend half the tour on their own. I remember when we first arrived; Christine, who was only recently twenty-one, was left the first weekend. I was horrified and am glad that Kerry doesn't go. The woman next door always has her amah to sleep in when her husband goes away.

Thanks for the photo of Gillian and David; at least now I will be able to picture her when they get married. It was a posh invitation we received; bit far to travel, though, so I think we'll decline and anyway Kerry hasn't got a top hat or tails! It's lovely for you to have a big church ceremony at last, both Ann and John and I did you out of one, didn't we? I'm looking forward to seeing your wedding outfit and a stunning new hat. Where's dad getting his new suit from; the Army and Navy store? Actually, he's not bad-looking for his age. Tell him from me he has to do you justice now his son will soon be related to a major.

I made some of your plum bread this afternoon and Kerry ate a piece before it had even cooled. I'm really into cake-making since I got the Kenwood; am also doing real fruit juice for Jonathan in the liquidiser. He loves it.

Seemed to be lots to tell you this time. We look forward to your letters.

Love M K and J

ELASTIC STOCKINGS

July/August 1968

Dear Mam,

Thanks for you lovely, long letter about David's wedding. It quite upset me that we were missing such a grand event; I've never been to a posh do like that. I shall look forward to the photos. Did they get our telegram? I hope so because it was terribly expensive. We've found out since that we can send one much cheaper through the services but are restricted to only two. We shall save those for when the baby is born, one for you so you can then tell family and friends and the other for Kerry's dad in Wales.

I've been teaching far more than I'd expected having left the permanent staff at Easter. However, what with illness and folks going home they're so grateful that I can go in at such short notice. I even got paid for the whole day when I'd only been in from 1.30 p.m. till 3.30 p.m. I've earned over sixty pounds this term, enough to buy Kerry some new golf clubs and to stock up on bed linen, tablecloths and tea towels to bring home. The cotton stuff here is lovely; there's such a wide choice and it's much cheaper. Kerry asked me if I was stocking up for the next twenty years.

Talking about bedclothes, I went to lie down for an hour yesterday afternoon while Awah was still around to keep an eye on Jonathan. He was popping in and out to check on me, then appeared carrying his little wicker chair and a book whereupon he sat by the bed and read to me. Then he disappeared again, came back with a copy of Reader's Digest, climbed up beside me and, after making himself comfortable by leaning on the headboard, proceeded to read aloud. Soon bored with that he began his trampoline act! It frightens me to death. He's fallen off a couple of times but it doesn't stop him.

I went for my monthly check-up to Changi on the special bus which leaves Seletar at 8.15 a.m. and gets to the hospital at 9ish. It's not a good road and coming home the sweat was pouring off me. I could feel it running down my back. When I got off the bus the back of my dress was wet and the part where I was sitting clung to my legs and my knickers. There was a damp patch on the seat, which looked as if I'd wet myself. It's probably exacerbated by the fact that the doctors have recommended that I wear elastic stockings. It's murder putting them on leaning forward over the bump so I get Kerry to take them off.

Actually, I had a nice compliment from a girl at a do when we went to the naval base. She said she wished she'd look like me at nearly seven months because she was as big as I am at three. I'm pleased with my weight as I'm only ten stone. I think the heat has a lot to do with it. I don't stuff like I do at home. The naval base is called HMS Terror and I really thought the social was going to be on a ship! It's like our camp, though, and is a base for visiting Royal Navy personnel who are on leave. They can be at sea for a year or even two when they are on manoeuvres. They refer to the grassy areas as "overboard" and all the words they used were in naval lingo; it sounded very peculiar.

The church guild organised a boat trip to an island so I took Jonathan, of course, and went with a friend who has two little girls. It was better than I thought because the islands near here are not in any way like the ones in the film South Pacific. Generally they're mucky little places with dirty sand and water. However, this tiny beach was lovely with a few palm trees and it was pleasantly cool sitting on the sands in a light breeze. Jonathan really enjoyed the boat ride so every time we go to the pool now we also visit the yacht club next to it. He loves the brightly coloured flags flapping on the masts and if we see one elsewhere he immediately says "boat".

I took him to sick quarters on Monday because the cold he's had has left his poor little nose red raw and his spotty face looks a mess. They gave me four different things including medicine, cleansing lotion, nasal cream and cream for the spots. That's apart from the special talcum for the prickly heat round his neck where he sweats a lot and another cream for the monsoon blisters that keep appearing on his hands. He's such a darling and never complains. Bloody climate, I can't wait to get back to the cold of England. We're in the middle of a storm. A minute ago, there was a flash of lightning accompanied by a terrific bang. It made us jump. While I'm writing, "best friend" from across the road has just come over. Her house has been struck and all the electricity is off. That was obviously the bang we heard. Kerry was in the middle of writing a letter to his sister on the typewriter that we bought. He's only been at it for six hours! Now he's gone to find the woman's husband, who's at the golf course. The house next door to them was struck last year in exactly the same way. I think it must be the trees nearby. Glad I don't live over there.

Don't ever think your letters are boring; they're the highlight of our week. They cheer me up even when you are being horrible, reference "you know who and the deckchair". Rotten bitch! May God forgive you for such thoughts.

Lots of love

M K J and the 'bump'!

CRATES AND CREEPY CRAWLIES

September 1968

Dear Mam,

I'm just recovering from a chit-chat leaping out from the typewriter as I was about to start. They're harmless but it didn't half make me jump. I've decided handwritten is quicker anyway. We've enrolled for twelve lessons with an Indian chap in Serangoon, the next village; it's only eight dollars per session, which is roughly one and three pence. Staying on the creepy crawly theme, Jonathan had a tantrum this week when he heard the ice cream man outside and we said, "No, not before dinner." As he lay on the veranda kicking and screaming, no tears mind you, I shouted, "Get up, the ants will bite you!" I've never seen him move so fast in his life; it was comical. The postman makes a point of ringing his bell and waving every time he cycles past, so with the baker Mr Foo, the bus driver Sim who pips his hooter, and Chee Kow the grocer, not forgetting "nardener", he has quite a fan club.

Have you seen these teenage dolls called Sindy? I don't like them but they're all the rage here with little girls. They're made by Pedigree, manufactured in Hong Kong, sell for less than ten shillings locally but apparently are three times as much in England. I wrote to Ann and said I was going to buy a crateful and she can help me set up a stall on Grimsby market. We're already thinking about what to pack in the crates to send home, which will probably be dispatched during November. We've started sitting Jonathan at the table on a proper chair instead of his high chair, hoping that if he makes the break now he won't miss it later. Something he will not give up is his safety pram-pillow. He takes it everywhere. Good job it's completely washable since he's spilled juice and tea on it, wee-weed on it and even sat on it in the monsoon drain. It's usually damp with sweat every morning when he wakes up and Awah has to unobtrusively peg it out to air.

He went to a party on Friday. Deborah, the little Welsh girl who came out with us when she was two had her fourth birthday. A local lemonade firm does parties for children, providing swings, a slide, a see-saw, bikes and scooters and even little tables and chairs. The kids amuse themselves and all you have to do is stop the arguments and get the food.

I was really annoyed the other afternoon. I've mentioned to you previously that the woman across the road is never off our doorstep. She's usually pleading poverty and wanting to borrow something or other.

Well, I was lying on the bed resting, which I do every day now from two till four. Jonathan is quite happy playing on the floor nearby or running between Awah and me. Without any warning, round about three, this woman walked straight into my bedroom. I'd purposely locked the veranda door but she'd gone round the back and nipped in before Awah could stop her. I deliberately stayed where I was and made it obvious that I resented the intrusion. It means now that I'll have to lock the bedroom door and Jonathan will have to play in the amah's room.

Kerry's section arranged an evening to a place called House of Shells. Two Australians who do sub-aqua diving around Malaya and Singapore own it. They gave an interesting talk with slides about all the shells that are on display. There was also a dining room, a bar and a swimming pool. It was a great evening and we didn't get home till after one in the morning. I gave Awah the next day off as she'd stayed over. I reckon that if I treat her with respect, she will do favours for me when the time comes. I feel sorry for the girl next door who has to catch two buses and must arrive by 8.30 a.m. She never leaves before 6.30 p.m. because she cooks the evening meal and washes up. I know she gets the same money as Awah who arrives at 8.00 a.m. but is leaving by four o'clock and she only lives a five-minute walk to the village. The other poor lass must literally eat, sleep and travel to work.

We went to the amahs' market Friday evening, although we don't often go now because some of them are such twisters. Anyway, it worked out more than we had bargained for because we've had two parking tickets for using exactly the same place, but with a gap of six weeks between offences. It seems unfair that we weren't informed after the first time because obviously we wouldn't have done it again. Kerry says it's no good appealing; we'll just pay the fine. We'll sell the car after the baby is born but Kerry will need it for visiting me in Changi because it cost him a fortune in taxi fares last year.

We're going to another do at the naval base so I've had my hair done in the village. When she'd finished I was desperate for the loo so I asked the girl if I could use theirs. Never again. I followed her rather apprehensively through the back kitchen, which was too grotty to describe, to where she pushed open another door. It revealed nothing but the floor and a hole in the wall. Do it on the floor, she said, and obligingly shut the door behind her. As you can imagine with my present shape I couldn't even squat and, feeling most unladylike, just stood. I could write a book about this place in years to come if I could come up with a suitable title.

Not long to wait now, Grandma!

Lots of love

M K J and a bigger bump!

ANOTHER LITTLE BOY

LONDON TELEX GORBUTT 22 PARKER STREET CLEETHORPES LINCS

3.47 a.m. 4 October 1968

BOY ARRIVED SAFELY NO PROBLEMS

KERRY

Dear Mam,

It was amazing that you received the telegram at 8 a.m. on the fourth when the baby was born round midnight on Friday the other side of the world. Silly as it seems, Kerry didn't even send it until 10ish our time so you seemed to get it before it was sent. In fact, there was such a panic during labour that no one looked at the clock until shortly after the birth. Then one of the nurses said, "We didn't note the time; do you want the third or the fourth?" Kerry chose the latter and the baby's arrival was officially recorded as 00.01 a.m. I had the same palaver as when Jonathan was born and again lost a lot of blood without any warning, just as we were about to go in the library on camp. I was so embarrassed but fortunately it was seven in the evening and already dark. We went straight to sick quarters only two minutes away, where I'd been that afternoon and told the doctor on duty that I thought it was imminent. Then I went again at 6.30 p.m. with backache and saw the same bloke. He didn't even examine me and said, "I doubt it is the real thing, it's not due for three weeks. Go home and wait till the contractions start."

When we arrived half an hour later with me in a bloody mess, literally, he had to eat his words. While I was sitting on the veranda waiting for an ambulance I thought I'd peed myself, then realised that the waters had broken. A little Chinese man with a big smile on his face arrived with a bucket and mop and cleaned up around me. He was beaming and chattering all the time; I think he was trying to reassure me, bless him. Kerry went off to fetch Awah, who, he told me later, was at the pictures. Good job we'd visited her house so recently and met her mum so he knew exactly where to go even in the dark. He must have had that feeling of déjà vu as he followed the ambulance. It had happened in exactly the same manner when Jonathan was on the way, and they'd hastily transferred me from the cottage hospital in Oakham to a larger maternity unit in Leicester. The journey to Changi, however, was an entirely different matter. This time *he narrowly escaped hitting a cyclist, who was weaving from side to side laden with all his worldly goods.*

He had no lights and on the unlit road was almost invisible in the pitch black caused by the tall jungle trees and undergrowth that line every road across the island.

As we both arrived at the hospital, minutes apart, a tall efficient-looking doctor in a white coat was already waiting on the steps. His very first words to me were, "You've done it again, Mrs Silk." I was immediately reassured as he'd obviously been reading my medical records. After an examination they said the baby was well on the way but if I lost any more blood they would operate. However, following an injection to kill the pain, I can't remember much more. I was too far-gone to cooperate and in fact had this weird out-of-body experience. I had the sensation of hovering up above, looking down at someone else lying on the delivery bed. I could hear everything being said, but felt as an onlooker, it didn't apply to me. Then I heard a nurse say, "I can't get through to her; we'd better fetch the husband."

This is not normal in maternity in the services. From my vantage point high above, I watched Kerry come in masked and dressed in a green gown. As soon as he took my hand and spoke, I was back into my own body. Apparently I kept saying "I'm dreaming, it's a dream" but within fifteen minutes the baby was born. Kerry said later that when they wrapped up the babe and put him on my chest to hold, I couldn't have cared less. He also told me much later that the doctor in charge was rather annoyed with him because he left it so late to bring me in. When he explained about the MO's attitude on camp, the doctor apologised and said he would follow it up.

The baby weighed 6lbs at birth and has since lost three but like Jonathan he hasn't cottoned on to sucking properly. I'm trying to feed him myself; you should see my bust, move over Marilyn Monroe. His hair is black, thick at the back and lightly covering his head. He has really long fingers with lovely nails and his arms and legs seem long, but I don't know whether that's because he's so skinny. I think he looks like Kerry's dad, not a pretty baby by any means, more like a little old man. I keep laughing at the comical expressions on his face. The babies are by the bed all day, wearing only a muslin nappy covered by a cotton sheet. The first two nights they let you sleep but on the third they fetch you in the night if the baby wakes and you go down to the nursery to feed. We bath and feed them during the day, change our own beds twice a day and what with showers, meals and endless cups of tea and visitors, the time just flies. Conversation overheard as I'm writing.

"Sharon likes Coca-cola; it costs us a fortune. She looks at the colour to make sure it's coke (Sharon is not yet two). You should see her drink beer; she loves it, not from her daddy's glass but in her own plastic mug." Oh well, it takes all sorts.

Kerry and Jonathan are being well looked after by friends and neighbours, invited out for Sunday dinner and somewhere else for tea. I've got white orchids and pink carnations on my locker and the carnations smell just like England. Kerry also brought a little koala bear for the baby that's sitting at the end of his cot. Today we had a visit from a group captain and everyone sat up in bed, trying to look intelligent as he spoke to each mother in turn. As he stood at the end of my bed, he glanced at the koala and said, "Are you Australian?" Silly sod.

I said, "No, we couldn't find a bull dog." I was joking, of course, but he sort of half laughed. Maybe one doesn't talk to a *group captain in that familiar manner. What? Normally after a second baby they let you go home after five days, but they're keeping me in because they think the baby swallowed some blood before he was born. Each day they're testing his motions and as soon as it's negative we can go. I worry about Kerry driving the twelve miles each way every night. I hope you like the name Matthew; we changed our minds about Christopher.*

At the moment he has a Singapore birth certificate but we have to register him soon as a British citizen in order to include him on my passport. Bless his little heart.

I think I shall be out of hospital very soon now.

Tons of love

M K Jonathan and Baby Matthew

DANCING IN THE RAIN

November 1968

Dear Mam,

I still can't believe we have two boys. I've just said to Kerry, what shall I tell Mam we've done this week?

"Fed the baby" was his instant reply. Matthew is eating well and now weighs 8lbs 2ozs; he's having six feeds daily with added baby rice morning and evening. The monsoon season is in full swing and he is already showing signs of prickly heat. He's such a wriggly baby for only six weeks and can actually move to the top of the crib where I find him lying sideways on. You'll see on the first photos taken with Jonathan he looks like a skinned rabbit, bless him. Jonathan can say Matt-ew quite clearly and likes to hold the bottle when I'm feeding him. He also fetches a

nappy or five or six if he's feeling generous. Instead of a party on his second birthday I invited a few friends all with children to come here after the fireworks and camp bonfire. I did soup and hot dogs; much easier than faffing around with party food. The older girls played with the little ones while the adults sat around eating crisps and nuts and drinking beer.

Thank you for my winter coat and the extras you enclosed that arrived this week. Awah was thrilled with the fancy coat hangers. It's her birthday soon and when I told her it was a present from you she was surprised and said how did your mother know. The coat feels long and heavy after wearing short, thin cotton dresses for what seems all my life. Kerry has written to English Electric in Leicester regarding an advert he's seen. It would be smashing if it's suitable because we'd like to stay in or around Uppingham.

We had a fright a couple of days ago when next door discovered a family of rats in the bushes right outside their house. We'd found mysterious droppings in the kitchen and on our veranda only the day before. Traps were set by a couple of chaps who came out immediately and three were caught in half an hour. We've stuffed paper under the kitchen door where there was quite a gap and also the door into the living room. Touch wood they've stopped coming inside but we're still finding droppings outside. I'm getting very jumpy at night and imagining all kinds of noises. When I walked to the clinic yesterday, Jonathan was able to sit on a seat Kerry had rigged up on the front of the pram. I got so hot pushing the extra weight, although it was only a mile each way. Honestly Mam, in this heat it felt as though I was walking through a Turkish bath.

This afternoon I was sitting knitting while the baby was

asleep, when suddenly I realised how quiet it was. Jonathan wasn't around. I found him in the garden dancing barefoot in the pouring rain. His hair was soaked, as were his little T-shirt and cotton pants. The look on his face was sheer delight as water dripped off his nose and ran down his face. He's going to find it so different in England muffled up in fleecy trousers and thick cardigans, let alone shoes which are totally alien. All he owns is a tiny pair of flip-flops. You'd have laughed to see him last night when we put him in bed hoping to have him established before we come to Cleethorpes. He went in at seven without comment, gave a big grin, pulled up the sheet and said night night. Three or four minutes later he marched into the living room with his pillow under his arm and said, "I've finished now". Only last week when he'd had a tantrum a couple of times I'd put him in his bedroom and told him he could come out when he'd finished. He obviously thought he was in for the same reason. Kerry had to put him back several times before he settled. The trouble is since he's learned how to drop the side he's discovered he can climb out of the cot.

The grass maintenance team were cutting the grass around camp this week. It's a real eye-opener. Two chaps work side by side each wielding a scythe about five-foot long. They swing it in a circular motion above their head, then down to the ground, cutting grass with each sweep. After five or six swings they change hands in mid-air without even stopping; it's fascinating to watch. It's almost as good as the two blokes who came to fell the lightning tree over the road. One climbed up barefoot with his axe swinging on a rope from his waist and proceeded to take off the branches. That done, he climbed down and the pair of them soon hacked through the trunk. We've seen them picking coconuts just by shinning up the tree and chucking them down. We have a coconut tree on the front. I keep asking Kerry to have a go but he's somewhat reluctant to try.

I can't believe it's soon Christmas.

Lots of love M K J and baby M

PIERCED EARS
AND PRESENTS

CHRISTMAS, 1968

Dear Mam,

*It's four in the afternoon and all the boys are asleep including
Kerry so I'm starting this and will see how far I get without
interruption. I'm actually wearing a cardigan because it's cooled
down to 80 degrees since we had torrential rain earlier. When it
clouded over Jonathan looked out of the window and said, "Sky
black now, going to rain Awah." She loves him to bits and I
know it will break her heart when we finally leave. We had a
low-profile Christmas with just a small, decorated tree but lots
of cards are brightening up the living room. Kerry invited two*

single lads from his section to come for Christmas dinner and the evening. I made a lovely Christmas cake but didn't ice it. I would have liked to put marzipan on but I couldn't find any. We'd been invited to eat with friends but as they cook everything in a pressure cooker and do no home baking at all we politely declined. One of Jonathan's presents is a little plastic tea set. When Kerry asks him for a cup of tea he says, "Okay Daddy". It sounds hilarious from such a toddler. His favourite present, though, is the red plastic telephone set which works between two rooms. He lifts the receiver, says hello and laughs like mad. Then he puts it under his arm and marches into the bedroom where I'm sitting waiting patiently, because he likes to see who he's talking to.

For the annual ball in the sergeants' mess, I wore a long blue dress in Thai cotton that was made to measure in the village. Don't laugh, I also wore my wig but I'll probably never wear it again unless we go to a fancy dress party. We took a photo: it doesn't look like me; I don't like it. It seemed that I'm the only woman on camp without pierced ears so I decided to have mine done. I went to a Chinese chap in the village jewellers expecting him to freeze the area. However, much to my surprise and shock, he didn't. Holding the needle in his right hand he plunged it straight through the fleshy lobe into a cork that he was holding in the other hand behind the ear. I was so taken aback he'd done the other while I was still thinking about it. I only need false eyelashes now and a tattoo to be completely up to date.

Good job I've got big lobes. Once when I was showing a friend a photo taken at college, they commented on my nice earrings. I wasn't even wearing any! The bags under my eyes have disappeared now that Matthew is sleeping through the night. He sleeps very little during the day but is quite happy lying on the floor kicking without his nappy for half an hour. Jonathan sometimes lies beside him and talks and kisses him, but when I stopped to watch he said, "Go away, Mummy, and make a pot of tea."

Did I tell you we've sold the car back to the garage from where we bought it? It's been a good runner and has never let us down. It was also a blessing for Kerry when I was kept in hospital with Matthew for so long. We've both got used to driving a bigger car, too, so will ask Dad for some advice and see whether he can get us one through his work.

We've finally got the date when we leave. Do you ever notice I always save the best till last just like I used to with my dinner when I was little? It's Saturday 1 February, arriving in England Sunday morning. It's later than we thought. Kerry is quite annoyed because he has to report to RAF Innsworth on the fifth. I suppose from the weather point of view it is to our advantage but everyone is saying it's an awful time to go home. Fancy you keeping all my letters. I read yours about ten times before I throw them away but always hang on to the last three or four. I've kept all the little lettercards, though, that you sent each day when the baby was born. I read them over and over while I was still in bed. It makes me laugh how you flit from one topic to another in almost the same breath. I can imagine you writing, then remembering something else and thinking, I must get that in before I forget.

Not long now.

Love M K Jonathan and baby Matthew

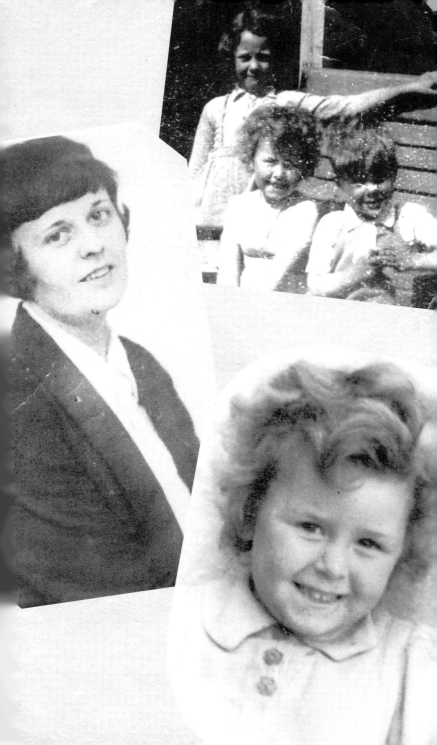

DEUTSCHE OPER BERLIN

FREITAG, DEN 22. NOVEMBER 1963

Beginn: 19.00 Uhr   Ende: 22.00 Uhr

BIRTH REGISTRATION NO.

68-32599

Nº 87427

REPUBLIC OF SINGAPORE

CERTIFICATE OF REGISTRATION OF BIRTH

Birth registered at **ROYAL AIR FORCE HOSPITAL, CHANGI**

CHILD'S PARTICULARS		
Full name (surname first) **SILK MATTHEW JAMES**		Hour of birth **00.02am**
Sex **MALE**	Date of birth **4 OCTOBER 1968**	
Place and Address of birth **ROYAL AIR FORCE HOSPITAL, CHANGI**		

MOTHER'S PARTICULARS		
Maiden name **GORBUTT MARGARET CHRISTINE**		County of birth **ENGLAND**
S'pore Identity Card No. **ENGLISH**	Nationality/Citizenship **BRITISH**	
Date of birth **28.7.38**	Address **13 EDGWARE ROAD, RAF SELETAR, SINGAPORE 28**	

FATHER'S PARTICULARS		
Name **SILK KERRY GEORGE**		County of birth **WALES**
S'pore Identity Card No. **WELSH**	Nationality/Citizenship **BRITISH**	Name and Address **AS ABOVE**

INFORMANT'S PARTICULARS	
State relationship (see Father, Mother, etc.) **MOTHER**	
Singapore Identity Card No.	

I certify that the above information given by me is correct.

M. C. Silk   **5.10.68**

Informant's signature or
Thumb impression

Part B   Date

Registrar of births and deaths **(J E ABBOT) W.O.**   **5.10.68**

Date

Charges to pay

s.   d.

RECEIVED

POST OFFICE

TELEGRAM

15

Prefix. Time handed in. Office of Origin and Service Instructions. Words.

No.

OFFICE STAMP

GRIMSBY LINCS
4 OC 68

At   m

From

By   ED   VR 62 3.47 AM LONDON TELEX   11/12

At 15
To
By

CSN GORBUTT 22 PARKER STREET CLEETHORPES - LINCS

= BOY ARRIVED SAFELY NO PROBLEMS = KERRY +

GORBUTT 22   ÷Ŧ   YO O

51-5695 J.P.Ltd. 11/66

at office of delivery. Other enquiries should be accompanied by this form   RAMS ENQUIRY" or call, with this form
and, if possible, the envelope. B or C

CRATES AND CLOTHES

January 1969

Dear Mam,

The crates are finally full and waiting on the veranda to be picked up. Jonathan went mad when we started to pack his favourite toys especially the walker/truck. He uses it every day either to help the gardener or to just tear madly round the garden at full speed spilling the contents en route. We had floods of tears even though we assured him it was all going to England, so we stopped packing the first time and carried on while he was in bed. He was so funny the next day because, after realising it had disappeared, he marched into the bedroom with a doll and pronounced, "Doll NOT going to England." I had to laugh. It was one of three that I'd bought to dress for the church fair and he'd taken a fancy to so we'd let him keep it. We didn't pack it but I can give it to the little girl down the road or to Awah for her niece's baby. It took Kerry four days to pack the boxes. He's filled eleven and we only came over here with one. We'll probably have to pay customs on some things like the photographic stuff and the Kenwood mixer.

Do you remember last Christmas we had a present from our grocer, Chee Kow? Well, this year he brought me practically the same stuff, Pyrex, which we have loads of because Shelagh, Kerry's sister, gave us a lot for a wedding present. I was really cheeky and asked him if we could have a tea set. We knew from talking to friends that not everyone gets the same. He didn't mind me asking; I think it's because he loves the children. He brought instead a beautiful china Harlequin set, which includes cups and saucers, plates, sugar bowl, milk jug and teapot. I'm thrilled with the swap. Do you think I'm awful? It seems the more we get the more we want.

We bought Jonathan his first pair of proper shoes and it was hilarious watching him in the shop as he walked across the floor looking at his feet. He picked up each foot so slowly before carefully putting it down, as though it weighed a ton or as if he was walking through deep snow. He's not at all impressed and hasn't looked at them since but loves the red hand-knitted woolly hat I bought at the church fair. He's taken to wearing that round the house. "Ready for England" he says. Obviously he hasn't a clue what England means, it's just a new word to him.

I can't believe we'll be on our way in a couple of weeks and I'm dying for you to see the boys. Matthew is 13lbs now and is such a good-natured baby he laughs whenever anyone *talks to him. He's lost all his hair but his head and little ears are a perfect shape and size and everyone comments on his big brown eyes.*

The poor little soul had to have a smallpox jab yesterday so I have to keep his arm dry for two or three weeks. I thought he was too young, as Jonathan had it at nine months, but apparently there could be a hold-up either at this end or when we arrive in England. I suppose it's natural because a lot of these diseases seem to start in the Far East, like the Hong Kong flu that is spreading worldwide at the moment. Jonathan's measles vaccination last year must have been effective because nearly every child on camp has had it. The one-year-old next door was extremely poorly.

We came out on a Britannia but they're no longer in service, so we'll be coming home on a VC 10. Apparently they're much faster and it will knock six hours off the flight. Despite the time of year we're coming back, I don't care if there is still snow. We've shown Jonathan what it looks like on the Christmas cards and I've never met a child in my life that doesn't like it. To young children in all the schools where I've taught, the two words "Christmas" and "snow" always go together. I remember when I was little we rarely got snow; it was a huge event. I didn't realise until I grew up that it was because we lived near the coast. I never thought I'd ever be sick of the sun, though it's more the humidity that gets to me. Again, I never experienced that where I grew up. I know we'll feel the cold especially as you have no central heating. Tell Dad I hope he's got plenty of coal in. This will be our last letter from Singapore.

See you soon Chrissie McG xxx
Love from us all
Kerry, Maggie, Jonathan and Matthew.

GOODBYE RAF SELETAR, FEBRUARY 1969

The thrill of going home was overshadowed by a sense of loss as we said goodbye to Awah. We hugged each other, both of us struggling to hold back the tears, not wanting to upset the children. Jonathan was jiggling up and down excited at the prospect of going on a coach to the airport, then on a big aeroplane. He didn't realise the significance of our departure; England to him was just another name like Changi or Malaya. In his little mind, he probably thought we'd be coming back after a couple of days.

'Awah not coming,' he said, very matter-of-fact. 'England too cold.' She squeezed him hard, then had to turn away to hide her tears that she could no longer contain. She'd played such a significant part in his young life and shared our highs and lows as a family. She wasn't just an amah whom we happened to employ, but a friend who was devoted to the boys and who proved to be a rock in the times of a crisis. We would never forget her.

The plane landed in Cyprus for refuelling and

everyone got off to change into warmer clothes. Jonathan looked like a different child dressed in his blue gingham shirt, a hand-knitted jumper and short pants with long woollen socks. Matthew slept for most of the flight but the stewardesses were very good and regularly brought the warmed milk for his feeds. They also kept Jonathan supplied with water and juice whenever he needed it. We landed eventually at Brize Norton in Oxfordshire and were taken to the train in order to get to London where we would be meeting Mam, who was waiting at David and Gill's flat. Mam was overjoyed to finally hold her new grandson and to hug Jonathan, who'd only been seven months old when she last saw him. He was overawed to say the least after the coach, plane and train journey, followed by a taxi ride through London traffic. For the first time in his little life he was awkward and shy, refusing to speak to anyone except the baby. When Matthew began to whimper because he was hungry, Jonathan looking directly at me said, 'Matt-ew want some milk Mummy; go home to Awah now.'

Like magic Kerry appeared from the kitchen, bottle at the ready, and quickly handed it to me. Scooping up Jonathan he carried him over to the big sash window which looked down onto the busy street.

'Let's count the red London buses,' he said and Jonathan's attention was immediately diverted.

We took the train again next day from Kings Cross to Cleethorpes where we could only stay for a couple of nights before Kerry had to report for his discharge at RAF Innsworth near Gloucester. I loved the warmth of the bungalow where I'd grown up with the same books, pictures and ornaments; everything was so familiar, stirring memories from childhood. Dad had hardly changed; a man of few words, unless he'd had a drink or two, but he made an impression on Jonathan with his magic. He held a coin in his hand and made it disappear, finding it elsewhere. We'd grown up on his card tricks and sleight-of-hand games; no wonder he always beat us playing draughts. Mam cooked a delicious Sunday dinner of roast beef, Yorkshire pudding, vegetables and potatoes roasted round the meat in dripping fat. We barely had room for the homemade apple and blackberry pie with pastry to die for. Halfway through the meal, Dad put on the television where in black and white two boxers were prancing about in the boxing ring. To Mam's consternation and Kerry's embarrassment, I exploded. 'We've just come 7,000 miles after two years away and you want to watch bloody television,' I said.

He looked at me, astonished that I'd dared to challenge his routine. Ann was normally the forthright outspoken one, not this easy-going younger daughter. He switched the set off, then grinning, turned to face Kerry. 'When are you going back?' he asked. We had to laugh.

MOVING AGAIN

Barely able to see through my tears, I stood with Kerry in the hospital corridor looking through a glass window that separated us from the cots of tiny babies in the isolation ward. As I heard the doctor's voice telling us the symptoms and the expected progress of meningitis, I was either unable or unwilling to accept what he was trying to explain or what could happen to our baby. I only knew the word because a girl in our class had had it when we were all thirteen years old. She had been absent for months and when she came back, her hair was only just beginning to grow again; it was fair and spiky. At that age, not one of us was aware that it was a life-threatening illness. Now my precious baby was having tests for this very disease. He'd begun two days previously by constantly crying, which in itself was unusual, and then he started refusing the bottle and vomiting, becoming dehydrated very quickly. His big brown eyes were glazed and sunk into the sockets of his little face. He spent that night in Oakham Cottage Hospital on a drip and was transferred early next morning in an emergency to Leicester General. We were told that they were going to do a lumbar puncture and further tests, so we returned to Uppingham where we'd left Jonathan with a next-door neighbour.

That evening, unable to settle and focus, I was standing in the kitchen ironing; I was so close to crying that I daren't speak. The thoughts going round and round in my head were impossible to voice aloud. As I picked up a baby bib and placed it on the ironing board, smoothing it flat with the side of my hand, the tears began to flow. They dropped onto the little piece of towelling with the picture of a teddy and the word "Monday" written above. The most terrible thought flashed through my head: *Would he ever wear it again?*

I turned to look at Kerry who was sitting in the adjacent room, equally silent and too stunned to speak. Then, out of the blue, I remembered that I'd taken Matthew for his triple vaccination ten days previously. He should have had it at three months before we left Singapore but they'd run out of vaccine. I stopped short. Could this have anything to do with it? Kerry went next door to use their phone and rang the hospital. They acted immediately. Apparently, the cause of Matthew's distress and worsening condition *was* a violent reaction to the whooping cough part of the vaccination.

After the right treatment, our baby soon recovered and there were no lasting effects. It took us a bit longer to get over the trauma.

A few weeks later, much to the delight of the boys, we bought a new boxer puppy. Back in the Far East, Jonathan had become almost hysterical when he realised that Awah wasn't coming back to England with us. A fact made more obvious because we were all upset and crying as we said goodbye. One of the bribes to placate him was the promise of a real live puppy and now he was over the moon. When we'd gone overseas I'd had to rehome Carlo, which broke my heart, the only consolation being I knew he'd gone to a boxer-loving family. The new puppy was brindle and white and we called him Jason. We were back living in our first home. It had been let to the RAF while we were away and the tenants had been good.

However, as Kerry was travelling twenty miles each way to work every day, we soon realised that we'd have to move house. We put the bungalow on the market and started buying the Saturday edition of the *Leicester Mercury* to study house prices and suitable locations. Neither of us knew the Leicestershire area at all. As the evenings grew lighter and we already had a potential buyer, as soon as Kerry had eaten when he got home, we started to go and look seriously. We packed the boys into their pyjamas and put them on blankets in the back of the car prepared for a late homecoming. After a number of viewings and some that we didn't even bother to look at because the descriptions were so wildly inaccurate and exaggerated, we usually returned disappointed. Then en route for home from the far side of the county, well after nine o'clock one night, we called in to look at one Kerry had seen that lunchtime that wasn't even in the paper. It was perfect; at the right price, in the right place not far from his work, in fact within walking distance. It was meant to be. In July 1969, we moved to Cosby. Quite by coincidence, when I wrote to Judy with our new address, she revealed that she and Dennis had lived in the same village after he came out of the RAF before they moved to Shrewsbury.

24 ELMTREE ROAD, JULY 1969

I couldn't get used to the stairs at first. I seemed to be forever running up and down looking for stuff or putting it away. We'd moved from a ground-floor flat to our first home, which was a bungalow, then spent two years overseas living in another one. To make things worse we'd put up a safety gate to stop the puppy from going upstairs and it was quicker to step over it, albeit a big step for my short legs, than to faff about with the opening. June gave me the solution. "Why don't you leave the stuff at the bottom until you go up later?" Such a simple idea; why hadn't I thought of that?

On the day we moved, when I arrived with the boys and the dog in the car, June was the first person I spoke to. She lived in the corner of the cul-de-sac across the road and saw us, my young friend Sarah from Uppingham and me as we struggled with Matthew and all the paraphernalia of young children and a dog basket whilst trying to keep an eye on Jonathan who wanted to help. Kerry was following with the dog and the furniture lorry. June came over and introduced herself then left saying, "When you're ready, come and have a cup of tea; you can use my phone if you like and I'll tell you anything about the village you might need to know." It was the start of a lifelong friendship; we became almost like sisters.

The position of the house and size of the garden, which faced west, was beyond our expectations of what we might be able to afford. We'd saved enough whilst abroad for a deposit and having made a small profit from the sale of the bungalow we were able to raise a mortgage for the sum of £4,000, the house costing £5,500. There was a third of an acre, mostly grass, with an apple, a pear and a plum tree. At the far end, a low hedge separated us from the field where a herd of forty or fifty cows grazed. Beyond that, in the distance, the land rose to a small spinney that acted as a windbreak for the main farmhouse and gave rise to its name. On the left-hand side of the garden stood a long row of young poplar trees and a low, scrappy hawthorn hedge that would need barricading measures. Unfortunately the opposite side was open straight through to next door, so one of Kerry's first jobs had to be rigging up a temporary wooden fence backed with chicken wire to keep one boisterous boxer puppy enclosed.

Until that could happen, he had to be tethered by a long piece of rope. It was a good time of year to move as throughout July the weather was warm and sunny so the boys played outside most of the day. Jonathan had space again to tear up and down with his beloved wooden truck, this time transporting Matthew, followed by Jason bouncing on his long ungainly legs and barking at his heels. Matthew at this stage was still crawling though beginning to walk with help, so I decided to get him his own truck to push in order to avoid tears or arguments later.

Now that Kerry was working for English Electric I was the proud owner of an automatic washing machine, which he bought through the firm at less than shop price. I'd given my twin tub to Mam when we'd gone abroad. He tied a rope washing line between two of the trees where every day I loved to see white nappies and baby clothes dancing in the wind. As Jason grew bigger he would jump up and try to reach them as they flapped on a gusty day and later when the plums ripened, he even picked some from the lower branches. Jonathan who'd been dry in Singapore had reverted on our return to England, however, he soon learned again that summer. Once, dressed in shorts and T- shirt, he found it quicker to wee in the hedge than to interrupt his game by running inside.

We went camping in Tenby, south Wales, for a week in August, meeting up with Judy and Dennis and Alison, who was about Jonathan's age. It was good to see them again and to catch up on everything we'd both done since we were in Berlin together. I took the cine camera that we'd bought in the Far East and filmed the men, both smoking cigarettes, with Dennis carrying Matthew in the crook of his arm, as he kicked the black and white ball to Kerry who in turn passed it to the two young ones.

'Look at Jason, look at Jason!' Jonathan suddenly shouted and left the game. The puppy, head down, was digging furiously to Australia, sending showers of sand in all directions in his frustration at being tied to the pushchair unable to join in the fun.

COSBY COTTAGES

June introduced us to the neighbours and it felt good to be living amongst people with whom we had more in common. Peter, her husband, also an ex-serviceman, was a keen gardener and like Kerry was interested in art. June had met him when she was in the Women's Air Force and she told me that when she left to get married she was asked whether she was pregnant. She said no. Had it been the case, her papers on leaving would have said "discharged" instead of giving the right reason. They had one little girl, Louise, who was ten months older than Matthew. Their garden, even bigger than ours, was like that of a stately home with beautiful lawns showing no trace of moss or a single daisy, and no weeds amongst the colour-coordinated azaleas and rhododendrons. Peter worked at English Electric, as did our new neighbour Mike who moved in next door with his family shortly after us. In fact, we discovered that a big percentage of families in the village were connected to the same business.

We learned from Peter that the estate we lived on had a chequered history. The forty-eight houses, each with a plot of land with at least a third of an acre, were built by the Land Settlement Association (sponsored by the government) in 1938. The purpose-built estate at first housed a mixture of unemployed families relocated from the depressed areas of south Wales and Tyneside, then later evacuees from war-torn London.

Each home, built with a steep Dutch-style roof and weatherboard gable ends, was a basic two-up and two-down. It came complete with a large shed adjoining, which contained a wheelbarrow and the necessary gardening tools for the owners to grow vegetables and keep chickens. It must have been difficult for those former coal miners and shipyard workers to adapt to rural life. Some villagers, fearing the worst, shunned them and made it clear that they were not welcome. They resented the mothers with three or four children using their ration books in the village butchers and taking "our share of meat". One lady who asked to join the library housed in the little school was told firmly, "No, we don't want your lot coming in here." During the war when American troops were based at Bruntingthorpe, girls from "up the settlement", as it was known in the village, regularly went out with GIs and this gave the area a bad name, even disgust if the serviceman was coloured.

By the time we arrived in Elmtree Road, it had become a desirable place to live and although some houses remained looking the same, many, like ours, had been totally transformed and were three or four times bigger than the original cottage. When we'd been looking to move, I wanted a house where there was the potential to start a home playgroup. I couldn't imagine going back to teaching and once Matthew was past his first birthday, Kerry and I talked about adoption. After two births fraught with difficulties and with the return of my vein problems, we still wanted more children. We decided we'd like a girl if possible so wrote to a couple of agencies, one in Leicester and the other in London. We had no idea whether we would be eligible; Kerry had turned forty and we already had two little boys. The Leicester Diocesan Board was quick to reply and we went for an interview. They made it clear that we would not get a healthy, blonde, blue-eyed baby, if that was our choice, but if we were willing to accept a baby of mixed race or with a minor health problem we could go on a waiting list. We said yes and left feeling elated, though we had no idea how long we might have to wait. It could be one, two, or even three years.

In early 1970, I applied for planning permission to start a playgroup. There followed inspection visits from the district council, a health visitor and a member of the fire brigade before permission was granted. I began collecting cast-off toys from jumble sales and advertised in the village post office. In April we finally had a reply from the adoption agency in London, asking us to go down for an interview. That same week, I discovered I was pregnant again. We cancelled the visit and I put the playgroup plans on hold until further notice.

In July, Marion who lived opposite us invited the boys and me to go to Ingoldmells for a week. We stayed in a caravan and her two lads, Ian and Paul, ten and nine, were brilliant with the little ones. They played chasing, paddled, dug holes and made sandcastles and generally made them giggle. Matthew's attempt to make us laugh happened in the caravan and nearly resulted in disaster. He was walking around unable to see where he was going with a bucket on his head. We all sat laughing as we watched him bumping into things, then he turned completely round and walked straight towards the open door with three steps down. Ian leapt up and grabbed him just in time.

NEW BABY, 1970

'I've seen you before,' said the midwife to Kerry.

'Have you? I don't think so. We haven't lived here long.'

'Definitely, I remember the colour of your hair and your lovely Welsh accent.'

She bustled out of the room and was back a minute or two later. 'I knew I was right, I've just checked your name against the records. I delivered your baby four years ago.'

It seemed a remarkable coincidence after two years abroad and another baby in between that here was the same nurse on duty again. We were back in Bond Street hospital where Jonathan had been born, after I was transferred from Oakham Cottage Hospital in a panic.

When I was expecting Jonathan, we'd done the old trick of tying my wedding ring onto a thread and letting it swing over my distended tummy. We knew it was an old wives' tale but it made us laugh anyway because we couldn't remember whether it was a boy when it swung clockwise, or up and down.

Christopher, the third boy, was born with no panic in October 1970. This time, there was no accompanying nurse being sick in the ambulance and no little Chinese man with a bucket and mop. Such were the indignities I'd been through previously. In case it was a girl we'd chosen Christine after Mam, but it was not to be. He weighed a hefty 9lbs, 3lbs more than Matthew, and because everything was so straightforward I was back home the next day. Funnily enough June was pregnant at exactly the same time as me, but her baby, Jeremy, arrived three days before mine. He'd weighed in at 8lbs 13ozs and June had joked, saying beat that if you can.

The first week home, I sat in bed each morning and bottle-fed the baby while Kerry went down to make a cup of tea. I smiled as I watched the bedroom door slowly open and two little pyjama-clad boys crept in and slid between the warm sheets at the side of me. The baby's tiny hands and fingernails fascinated them. They measured them against their own and stroked his little head. As he leant against the pillow for support I let Jonathan cradle him, while Matthew went to fetch his own favourite toy. It was a rather large, plastic owl, aptly named Owly, which rocked on its base and made a melodic jingling noise. I was so happy. Blimey, I thought, one day these three little boys will be teenagers. I just couldn't imagine it.

By the time Christopher was four months old he was in a good routine, sleeping each morning from after his breakfast till his next feed at 12.30 p.m.

I was itching to get the playgroup started and already had a list of prospective four-year-olds, so felt confident to go ahead and opened in late February.

Initially I had permission for twelve children and

the number of boys far outweighed the girls until the following September, when some of them would start school. Each session began at 9.30 a.m. and finished at 12 p.m. Every day a young mum in the village who had twins came to help me. It was a good working arrangement since she couldn't afford to pay for two, so no money exchanged hands. By the time the warmer weather arrived I could afford to buy a decent outdoor climbing frame that could accommodate up to a dozen small children. It was like the one in the nursery where I'd worked in Grimsby before going to college. Play outside was not structured. The children flitted between ball games, chasing, having races and playing hide-and-seek. Our big garden was ideal as they could make as much noise as they liked and no one complained. We usually went inside about 10.30 a.m. for a quiet session with a story and some singing. They all drank a small bottle of milk that was a government allowance, exactly the same as in primary schools. I had to apply for it and it was delivered every day. When the local schools broke up at the end of June, I also stopped for the holidays.

It was a good summer and when the boys played outside which was most of the time, Christopher in his little blue cotton overalls crawled down the slope from the kitchen onto the grass to join in the fun with Jason never far away. Matthew, who, whatever the weather, always seemed to be wearing his little red wellies, found the shears one day. When he started cutting the long grass around the willow tree, Christopher grasped handfuls and tried to stuff them into the dog's mouth.

I removed the shears so Matthew fetched his wooden truck, whereupon the baby managed to climb in and then sat waiting for a ride. Matthew, who was not yet three, pushed him, gradually building up speed while Jason danced and leapt from side to side, barking and enjoying the fun. All of a sudden the truck hit an obstacle and stopped abruptly. Christopher tumbled out head first. Matthew, no doubt thinking he would be told off, immediately started slapping Jason.

'Naughty boy, bad dog,' he said, while Christopher unhurt, stood up and joined in. I'd been watching all the time and couldn't help laughing. Poor Jason, he would have laid down his life for that baby.

ENTER KATHRYN

'She's a bit of a live wire,' said Boo.

'Mmm,' I agreed and couldn't help smiling. I could think of several other words to describe her and placid wasn't one of them.

I was standing in the nursery of the small private school with the owner Mrs Chamberlain, known to friends and staff as Boo. We were watching Kathryn, who was dashing round like a whirlwind, up the steps, down the slide non-stop. As she elbowed bigger children out of the way, they were so surprised they stepped to one side. At the top she lay on her tummy and whooshed down head first, landed on the mat, scrambled to her feet and repeated the process. One by one, the children drifted away from the slide and this human tornado.

'I'm sorry,' I apologised. 'She doesn't get her own way with the three lads.'

'Don't worry, they won't let her have her own way for long,' said Boo. 'Look, she's fed up now and looking for company; she'll soon learn.'

Kathryn came into our life in May 1972 when Christopher was still only seventeen months. Before we took her home we were invited to see the baby at the Diocesan Adoption Board's offices in Leicester to decide whether she was right for us and the family. They left us alone in the room and we held our daughter for the first time: A brown-skinned, chubby baby, her dark eyes framed with long black eyelashes, wearing a pretty blue dress sprigged with tiny white flowers. Her head was a mass of black corkscrew curls. We knew instantly that she was perfect and more than we could have wished for.

Because the society was funded by the church, we'd had to have a reference from our local vicar. He was an amiable old chap close to retirement and although neither of us were churchgoers, he was willing to oblige. We met with him in his book-lined study at the vicarage, where his wife, a rather bossy woman, was also present. After listening to Kerry, she chipped in with the words, 'You want to be careful with those darkies; you don't know what you're getting.' I raised my eyebrows and glanced at Kerry. The vicar looked at his wife with a face like thunder. 'Please go and make a pot of tea for our *visitors*,' he said, stressing the last word. I felt sorry for him but Kerry with his usual diplomacy stepped in and steered the conversation to a particular book that he'd spotted on the shelf. The little man visibly relaxed.

A few weeks later, when all the paperwork was completed and Kathryn was finally home with us, we had a charming letter from the vicar wishing us and the family well. The following January, when Kathryn was nine months old, we all had to go to the Leicester County Court to see the judge in order to make the adoption official. Kerry and I had had qualms beforehand, wondering whether the man might be formally dressed in his robes complete with wig. At that time, four-year-old Matthew, for some reason we couldn't fathom, was terrified of shop models. If we went into a particular department store, Kerry was forced to pick him up. If we walked by one, his whole body tensed and he buried his head into Kerry's shoulder, screwing his eyes tightly shut. We needn't have worried. The gentleman in question was wearing a suit and tie and he greeted the boys with a big smile. He spoke to them in turn and asked how they liked their little sister. Two-year-old Christopher, always shy in unfamiliar situations, held back and clung to my leg while Kathryn was asleep in my arms. Jonathan and Matthew chattered away telling him about Jason and we felt proud of them especially, when they shook his hand as we left.

As Jonathan had been christened at St Peter's Church in Cleethorpes before we went to Singapore, we decided to have the other three children done together. A new vicar and his wife had moved into the vicarage, a lovely couple with whom we became friends. John and Pat, David and Gill, and Ann and Rae all came with their children. Mam was so thrilled to have us altogether, probably the first time since John went into the RAF at eighteen. Even Kerry's sister Shelagh, with her husband Ron, and Andrew their son, came from south Wales. It was a perfect day in August and the nine grandchildren, aged between one and twelve, played outside, the two girls keeping tabs on Kathryn while the boys had a game of football. At tea time, Gill, David's wife, offered to feed the baby, but Kathryn, as was her way, turned her head and refused to open her mouth. Gill, who was totally unused to children and the contrary behaviour of babies and tots, had even forgotten her name. 'What's her name, Maggie?'

'Griselda, she's a bit of a grizzler,' I said jokingly.

'Come along, Griselda, eat your lovely baby rice,' said Gill, holding up the plastic spoon.

That summer, with advice and assistance from two of his little boys, Kerry made a huge sandpit. He dug a rectangle about twelve foot by seven foot and they both helped to chuck rubble in to form a solid base for the wooden structure. Matthew used a mallet to bash the bricks flat while Jonathan measured the planks of wood lying ready-cut to line the bottom and the sides. Kerry had all the patience in the world with the lads. The sandpit was in continual use long after I gave up the playgroup when I was offered a teaching job at the small private school in the next village. It was a bonus that I could take Kathryn and also Christopher until he was five. Kerry's salary at English Electric was poor compared to what he'd been earning in the services and a bit more money coming in with my wages was a godsend.

NEVER WORK WITH
CHILDREN OR ANIMALS

'Does that parrot bite?' she said, pointing to the two birds in the cage.

I smiled at the little five-year-old girl who was standing looking up at me.

'No, of course not; anyway, they're not parrots they're budgies. Do you like them?'

She nodded and ran back to stick her finger through the bars as if to test my point. I was thrilled; it was a breakthrough. After a few weeks in reception, Patricia, although she listened and did as she was told, had not uttered a word. All the communication I'd had was a nod or a shake of her head. The difference was amazing. She began each day by going straight to the birds to talk before she came to tell me what secrets she'd shared with them. It was September 1976 when I went back into mainstream education. The boys were all at school and Kathryn, due to go after her fifth birthday the following March, was happily established in the nursery department of the school where I was teaching. She was much better behaved, having had the rough edges knocked off by the two years in Boo's nursery.

The school was in an area of social deprivation in the city on a large post-war council-house estate, where over 90 per cent of the children were eligible for free meals. It was an old building with high windows and not a blade of grass for the children to play on. Unemployment, financial difficulties, the absence of a father in prison, drug and alcohol-fuelled problems often resulted in a home background of neglect, obscene language and physical abuse. School and an understanding teacher provided the only security, love and routine that was missing in the lives of many of those young children. Behaviour problems were manifest. This made straightforward teaching harder and took second place to the learning of manners and the realisation that what was acceptable and normal at home would not be in a school situation. When a parent came into the school using foul language to the head or the class teacher, what chance did these children have? When two women had a brawl round the Christmas tree in the nursery, swearing and punching each other, watched by horrified staff and frightened three-and four-year-olds the police were called to come and remove them. Once I made the mistake of glancing up at the clock when a dad turned up with his little boy at five to twelve, just before we stopped for dinner. The look on his face and the stream of verbal abuse that followed really scared me and I was careful not to cross him again. Despite the difficulties, I was very happy teaching there. I loved the children in my class and I faced challenges so unlike anything I'd met before.

The confidence and success of every little boy and girl despite their background was my first priority and to this end I used a variety of out-of-school activities to enhance what went on in the classroom. We visited Leicester market; thirty excited children going upstairs on a double-decker. In the town hall square, where we watched the pigeons drinking and paddling in the fountains, one child exclaimed, "Phwoor, look at them chickens, Missilk."

"What's that stink?" was the comment from them all when we went to the farm in Cosby, but the memory of the smells disappeared when they stroked the calves and touched the lambs. Two little girls were even allowed to hold the bottle of milk for the cade lamb that had no mother, before everyone climbed on to the bales of straw in the barn to sit and have their own drink and sandwiches. The pictures they drew and the thank you letters they wrote later were touching. During the summer term I took the class on a train from Leicester station to Narborough, helped by friends and two reliable parents. We visited the village school, which had its own swimming pool, and the children who wanted could have a swim before we had the picnic and played games on their big playing field. The *Leicester Mercury* later published an account of the trip with a photo of all the children waiting on the station platform and another picture of the engine driver showing a small group the controls in his cab.

"I didn't realise you let the birds out," a parent said one morning. I spun round, almost shutting the door in her face. There they were, two little green budgies unaccustomed to their freedom, fluttering and flying in the vast open space of a big classroom. The children sat transfixed while I took the register, the only sound in the room coming from the beating of tiny wings. The high ceiling was an area to be explored; the water pipes and window ledges provided secure resting points. After my feeble attempts to catch them, I decided to leave the cage with the door open on top of a cupboard and we carried on working. The birds, by then unafraid, began to dive-bomb the children, skimming over their heads as they were trying to write. They loved it and laughed as they ducked. An hour and a half later, the birds were still free. I was beginning to worry. While the class went out to play, a colleague came in to help me. By then the errant pair were tired and had sought refuge on a curtain rail. One of us climbed on to a table and held the cage on high while the other tried to coax them in with the long window pole. At last the female, having had enough, flew in, followed by the brother. A few days later a little boy said, "When are you going to let the birds out again, Misssilk?"

As well as the birds in the classroom, I introduced a rough-haired guinea pig called Olga. She had to go home with me every weekend where she became friends with Jason and shared his blanket in the kitchen when she came inside for the winter. We bought a rabbit the following summer that Jonathan named Argonaut after the mythical Greek heroes who accompanied Jason in his search for the Golden Fleece. Christopher, who became Chris after he started school, mispronounced the name and called him Argomort, so the name stuck.

THREE BOYS, A GIRL AND
A DOG CALLED JASON

The only time I came close to rowing with Kerry was each year when we went camping. I've never been one to write lists but there's always an exception. With four children, two adults and a dog, it was like preparing for an expedition to Everest. Two cardboard boxes were full to the brim. One contained tins of beans, soup, spaghetti hoops, tomatoes, fruit, tins of mince, meatballs and hot dogs in brine. The other was packed with teabags, coffee, cereals, biscuits, cream crackers, cheese, milk, potatoes and vegetables; the list went on and on. As we had no cold storage in the tent, we had food that was quick and easy to prepare. The pressure cooker that I'd scoffed at in Singapore was brilliant for the whole evening meal that I cooked on a two-burner Campingaz stove.

The food was really the easy part; it was the clothes and the gear for the children that I needed the list. Wellies were always at the top and second came disposable nappies, the only time I ever used them. I ticked off clothes for hot weather, cold weather and rainy days. Clothes for going in the sea and plenty of towels, buckets and spades, card games, pencils and crayons, books and yards of used computer paper for drawing on that Kerry used to bring home from work. Washing-up bowl, cloths, small washing line, and plastic water carrier, binoculars, sunglasses and suncream. I put the boxes in the porch for Kerry to organise and he methodically packed them into our white Hillman Minx estate car. The tent was strapped onto the roof rack. What really annoyed me were the same expected questions.

'Have you remembered the toilet rolls?'

'Have I ever forgotten?'

'Did you put the kettle in?'

'Yes dear.'

'Pegs?' he asked, spotting the washing line.

'Of course,' I snapped.

'What about the suncream?' I'd had enough.

'You get on with your bloody job and trust me to do mine!' I shouted, going back into the house and slamming the door behind me. Not only was packing the stuff an art but seating four children and a large dog needed a degree of finesse. Matthew had to sit near the door on the verge side as he was always carsick. Kathryn could not sit by Christopher because they argued, but neither could she sit near a door. Poor old Jason was squashed in the back with the boxes and bedding. The duvets and pillows were covered by a green and black tartan car rug and often Christopher would scramble over and lie down with the dog. When the children were under ten, we went south to Devon or Pembrokeshire. Kathryn was only two when we went to Pentewan in Cornwall, a place recommended by our neighbours. It was a disaster. The beach was stony and too rough to walk on and the water was a funny milky colour from the china clay works. Kathryn spent the whole day trying to follow the boys stumbling and whining, 'Pick me up, pick me up.' Whereupon Kerry scooped her up like a bundle of dirty washing and and tucked her under his arm. When the boys played hide-and-seek in the sandhills she sat down and cried with a pair of spare pants draped on her head. Like Jonathan and his T-shirts, she loved the silky feel of the label on her knickers. Unorthodox but funny to onlookers. She was so cute with her dark skin and curly hair I often saw folk nudge one another and turn to look at her with admiring smiles. *If you only knew,* I thought. To her credit, she was dry in the daytime at sixteen months from the time I caught sight of her weeing in the garden. She was standing facing the hedge, nappy round her feet, with her little, fat legs thrust apart and her lower body tipped forward, copying her brothers.

We decided to go to north Wales one year and after finding Shell Island, we were hooked. It was cut off from the mainland for a couple of hours or more each day when the causeway over was covered by the incoming tide. The soft sand on the west coast backed by dunes as big as a two-storey house and close to the safe, warm waters of Cardigan Bay was a dream. There were no official campsites so we set up tent on a flat grassy area behind the dunes. The children loved it and disappeared into the sandhills straight after breakfast every morning. It was safe and unspoiled. No proper roads so no traffic, caravans were not allowed and no jangling ice cream vans. There was a small shop that stocked basic necessities so we had fresh milk and bread on hand. We were there in 1976, the long, hot summer when the sand was too hot to walk on in bare feet, and we carried on going there until Jonathan was twelve and Kathryn at six was better behaved and much more amenable. Then we tried the Lake District, different terrain and different challenges for the lads. Jason, by then grey around the chops, still accompanied us.

One day, when Kerry, the boys and the dog were climbing and scrambling up the fells with Kathryn and me in tow, Jason collapsed, probably due to his age, the altitude and the heat. We revived him with the spring water that was cascading down the mountainside, leaving little pools among the boulders. It scared us so much that for the rest of the week Kerry went off with the lads and left me with Kathryn and the dog to walk around the lake.

SOMEWHERE IN THE MIDDLE OF NOWHERE

Children travelled for a pound. It was an offer by British Rail so we'd booked a holiday in Cumbria. Although we all loved camping we'd graduated from a tent to a caravan, then to the luxury we hoped for, a stone cottage. We'd no longer be sleeping on the ground or eating off a plate balanced on a lap or a table with legs sawn down to children's size. And best of all, no more going outside with a torch to use a chemical toilet. The Duddon Valley where we'd be staying happened to be the setting for a book called *The Plague Dogs* that I'd recently read by Richard Adams. It was about two dogs that escaped from an animal testing laboratory. We decided that Kerry and Matthew, now shortened to Matt, would go ahead in the car with the luggage, clothes and food, and we fixed a time for them to pick us up at Oxenholme, the nearest station. Kathryn's best friend, Sally, who lived next door came too, after we realised that she stopped annoying the boys and was better behaved if she had other company.

The journey north was scenic, especially where the railway ran parallel to Morecombe Bay. The mountains on the right provided a spectacular backdrop to the flat expanse of sea, sand and muddy estuary. As our station drew near, we gathered together anoraks and rucksacks. When the train stopped, Jonathan put both hands to the window on the door and tried to lower it. It wouldn't budge. The doors could only be opened from the outside so we all moved to try and open another window. No luck. The platform was deserted and time was ticking by. Just as I succeeded and had reached out to push down the door handle, the train began to move again. I hesitated.

'Jump,' said a voice, but the train was picking up speed and common sense prevailed. I grabbed the swinging door and pulled it to. What now? At that moment, a guard strolled into the carriage. I was furious.

'We needed to get off,' I stormed. 'My husband is meeting us and won't know where we are.' His sympathy with our plight was lukewarm.

'Sorry, you'll have to get off at the next station and come back when this train returns in an hour.' Five minutes later, we stood on an empty, nameless platform in the middle of nowhere and watched the train disappearing in the distance along the single track. A narrow road crossed the line and by my reckoning one way led to the coast and the other inland. I could have been wrong but as we urgently needed a phone and no one disagreed, I opted for inland. The children thought it was all a good laugh and raced ahead down the traffic-free lane.

They shouted back from a bend in the road, after spotting a solitary wooden bungalow. We trooped through the wide-open gate up to the front door that was ajar. I knocked and called,

'Hello.' There was no answer so I paused. 'Hello, is anyone there?' I pushed the door open.

A gentleman in a wheelchair appeared. He was wearing a dark suit with an immaculate white shirt and a black bow tie. The children gaped as he propelled himself forward, his hand outstretched in greeting and with a broad smile of welcome on his face. As I explained our strange situation, he shook everyone's hand in turn much to the discomfiture of the children. I'd never seen them so put out. The man seemed unaware, only delighted to have our company.

'Come in, come in, you can use my phone. Would you all like a drink?' Not waiting for a reply, he manoeuvred the chair down the dimly lit hallway and waved us in the direction of the living room. He disappeared for a few minutes, then returned with a jug of lemonade. As he handed each child a glass, they thanked him then perched in silence on the edge of the huge old-fashioned settee. I'd never seen them so subdued. He poured himself a whisky and offered me one, but I shook my head.

'There's a pub right by your station,' he said, picking up the phone directory and flicking through. 'Ah yes, The Prince of Wales, here we are.' He passed me the number and the handset and beamed at the children. I dialled and waited.

'Prince of Wales,' said a man's voice. I suppressed a laugh; this was getting more and more bizarre.

'You won't know me but I'm ringing from…' I

stopped and mouthed, "Where are we?" After a lengthy explanation punctuated by the publican's jokes and me laughing, I finished by describing Kerry and Matt. He promised to look out for them and I relaxed.

Our host was sorry to see us go. The children were in high spirits as we got back to the station and started fooling about on the track by putting an ear to the rails in an attempt to hear any vibrations of an approaching train. We were ready long before it finally appeared as a speck in the distance. Some ten minutes later, we got off again to cheers and applause from a small crowd of locals who'd been drinking and playing snooker with Kerry and Matt. It turned out to be a great holiday. The cottage was perfect, the weather was good, we enjoyed long walks in wonderful scenery and had the satisfaction of climbing the Old Man of Coniston.

A BAD YEAR

Kerry's first heart attack in 1989 happened as a result of the enormous stress we'd been going through during the previous couple of years. His dad, Ivor, had come to live with us after the death of his second wife. He'd also lost Shelagh, Kerry's sister, some years before, who was only in her fifties. I said it would make sense for us to have him living locally rather than Kerry having to make a long trip to south Wales should he become ill. Initially we'd moved Kathryn downstairs to accommodate Ivor, after Kerry, who would have a go at anything, partitioned off the playroom, turning it into a bedsit with French doors leading straight into the garden. She was nearly fifteen by then and we were beginning to have problems. Her school phoned me at work one day and said she was constantly playing truant and asked us whether we were willing to go in with her in order to talk to a counsellor. Kerry and I went along with Kathryn, who insisted that Chris went too, much to his discomfort. We went through an awkward session, first with a social worker and a psychologist, who was actually sitting behind a window made of one-way glass, observing us as a family. Kathryn was defiant and nonchalant as she sat cross-legged with a cigarette dangling between her fingers. Chris answered questions briefly and I could tell he was uncomfortable, torn between loyalty to his sister and his parents. When asked about her bad behaviour and why she did it, Kathryn waved a hand towards her dad saying, "Because he hits me". I went home and cried and refused to go again. We'd both been made to feel as though it was our fault. As soon as she was sixteen, Kathryn left school with a single certificate for typing and no further qualifications. She hadn't even bothered to turn up for the exams. She also left home and went to live in a squat in London with the girl next door.

That summer, things went from bad to worse. After being kicked in the left hip by a horse the previous day, I discovered a lump next morning when I was in the shower. I was looking for a bruise and as my right hand held back the opposite breast in order for me to see, I felt something with my middle finger. I didn't tell Kerry until I'd been to see the doctor, who immediately referred me to the cancer specialist at the Royal Infirmary. After a lumpectomy, which left a scar about five inches long and the nipple on the left breast pointing to the sky while the right one was definitely losing to gravity, I underwent several weeks of radiotherapy and was put on the relatively new drug called Tamoxifen. The treatment centre was a forbidding place in the bowels of the hospital. There were no windows and hideous pipes for the water and heating came down the walls and across the low ceiling. However, the nursing staff and the volunteers who made tea and brought biscuits worked down there day after day. Their cheerfulness and positive attitude was uplifting and distracted the patients from the dismal surroundings. During my first visit I was tattooed with three blue spots, while the nurse explained that they were for lining up the rays and once done would remain forever. The next day as I lay on the bed naked to the waist, I shivered with the cold and a little apprehension as a technician twiddled with the machine next door. The young male nurse holding my hand said, 'Are you cold or just scared?'

'Both.'

He put a sheet over my lower half and asked me whether I'd like to hear some music. I nodded and he switched on a cassette of carols. The nurse who operated the machine returned.

'Right, we're ready. Lie very still and don't move.' They both disappeared from the room with the comforting words, 'Don't worry, we can see you all the time.'

Blimey, I thought, *what if I want to sneeze or scratch my nose?* I heard a buzz as the machine was switched on so closed my eyes and listened to the carols softly playing. In no time at all I was done. This procedure was a daily event for five weeks in the run-up to Christmas. I drove myself in each morning, the only side effects being an increasing itchy redness of the skin. I had to fight the overwhelming desire to scratch.

Ivor had company when we fetched Mam for the half-term holiday. They could both talk for England and Wales. When I took Mam's case upstairs and opened it I found a nightie, a pair of tights and a jumper. No knickers and no wash things. I was horrified something was very wrong. I'd had misgivings in Cleethorpes when she'd made no comment about me not working in term time. We hadn't told her about the cancer, although the rest of the family knew. By January, after she had had a spell in hospital for investigation, my suspicions were confirmed and she was moved to a residential nursing home. Meanwhile, I went back into the Royal Infirmary for further treatment where I had a radioactive rod inserted on the scar line of my breast just under the skin. After the operation, I came round, lying on a trolley, to see a man hovering over me with a Polaroid instant camera. Only half awake I said, 'What you doing?'

'Taking a photo for your records,' he said.

'Can I have one?'

'Here, don't tell anyone.' He stuffed one under my pillow and quickly took another. I was in isolation with one other lady for four days. We were both highly radioactive and if we as much as put a hand out of the door a warning orange light flashed and an alarm went off. We were only allowed one adult visitor for twenty minutes a day. However, we did have the bonus of our own television and video player with a good selection of films, but, best of all, each evening we had a glass of sherry. I was quite nervous on the day that the rod was due to be removed and waited anxiously. A nurse came in wearing what to me looked like riot gear, holding in her gloved hands a pair of surgical tweezers and a silver-coloured canister. She placed the canister on the bed and as she took off the lid, a cloud of white vapour rose into the air. Holding the tweezers she pulled out the rod in seconds, dropped it into the container, rammed on the lid and ran out of the room. Moments later, she came back with a Geiger counter and ran it over me to see whether I was still radioactive.

'You can go home when your husband comes after dinner. And your sherry,' she added as she left.

Mam died in February and Ann and Pat, John's wife, cleared the bungalow. Mam had few worldly goods of any value so I asked the girls to give me a couple of her hats. I also asked for some snowdrops from her garden to plant in my own. It was an emotional time for me losing her while I was still recovering from the cancer treatment. We went to Cleethorpes for the funeral and as we sat in the car I noticed that Kerry looked very pale, but put it down to the cold weather and the occasion.

The following month we lost Bramble, the boxer we'd come to love after Jason had died at thirteen. She was only seven. Chris, who was in the sixth form, was the only person at home with me and I sobbed in his arms.

'Bad things come in threes,' I snivelled. 'Hopefully that's the last.'

Barely a few weeks later, just when I'd gone back to school after an absence of six months, Kerry collapsed at work and was rushed into hospital for possible heart surgery.

AT THE BOXING DAY RACES

'A cruise?' Kerry's face was a picture. 'But you hate water.'

'I'll give it a go and see; apparently you can stuff yourself with food all day and night if you like.'

After the hell we'd gone through during the previous year, we both needed a tonic. Kerry was sixty when he had his heart scare so he'd retired on health grounds. We could survive on my salary, as I'd always been the higher wage earner anyway. Although he was still pretty fragile, we'd managed to go to Jonathan's graduation in June. It was such a proud moment for us and for once I wore a hat. In September, we were thrilled when he married Katharine; it was a fairly low-key affair with family and a few friends at the registry office in Loughborough. Our own Kathryn was back in the area, still not living at home but at least she went to the wedding.

So, there we were in one of the cheapest cabins on the *SS Canberra*, on the lowest passenger deck where only the crew and the engine rooms were beneath us. It was Christmas 1990 and we were celebrating our silver wedding anniversary. Having had no experience of on-board dining, we'd opted for the second sitting for dinner at a table for eight. Each evening ours was the noisiest as we laughed and joked and we were always the last to leave the dining room. We'd left Southampton to a fanfare from the band of the Royal Marines playing on the quayside and sailed south towards the Canaries. In Las Palmas we visited the Columbus museum, which was actually the house where the explorer stayed while his ships were being repaired and revictualled. We drove through a fertile valley of subtropical orchards, then climbed and descended through vineyards. The contrast between the holiday islands of the Canaries and the Republics of Senegal and Sierra Leone on the West African coast was manifest. Large cruise ships rarely visited Freetown where there were no sophisticated European-style services. We were shuttled ashore by the ship's motor launches and herded on to an old bus with wooden slatted seats. Our guide asked us to refrain from taking photos from the bus because there could be objections and repercussions from the locals. We bumped along dry, sandy orange roads, passing shacks made up of sheets of tin, which reminded me of the old air-raid shelter I'd slept in. Small children were playing in the dust or helping the women who manned the rickety old trestle tables at the roadside selling fruit, eggs and cooking pots. Young girls carrying rusty bowls of bright green vegetables on their heads walked alongside boys balancing trays of cake or bread.

Only the multicoloured clothes of the women and the vivid orange or yellow T-shirts of the young men relieved the drab surroundings. In the middle of a road island on our way back, a blue traffic sign with a white arrow was pointing incongruously to what appeared to be a white bundle of rags but, in fact, was a man asleep. We went back to the ship in a sombre mood.

It would have been silly not to enjoy the Christmas atmosphere and the endless activities planned. We sang in the choir on Christmas Eve and even took a major role in the highlight of the Boxing Night Ascot Race Meeting. In a workshop, all materials provided, Kerry as ever the practical one made a jockey hat for me with red and black crêpe paper and a racing sash and rosette. For his own outfit as the trainer, he made a tall top hat lavishly decorated in the same colours. Five jockeys sat side by side poised ready to turn the handle of the contraption, which moved a wooden horse along a length of wire to the finishing post. There were five qualifying races and the winner of each then competed in the final for the Canberra Cup. The room was packed and folk were betting on the tote in 50p and £1 units. We were in the last heat, which I won. As we sat waiting for the final with people madly placing bets, a little boy sitting on the floor near me whispered, 'I've put all my money on you,' and when I discovered that I was the favourite my tummy churned.

I turned to Kerry behind me. 'Blimey, did you hear that?'

He grinned. 'Go on, you can do it.'

'S'alright for you,' I said. The entertainments manager then appeared onto the racetrack mic in hand.

'Ladies and gentlemen, before we start the final

race, unfortunately we've been informed that one of the horses has been nobbled.' The room went quiet but we were unable to see any faces in the dark as the spotlight swung round on to us. 'Would number three step down please for a vet's examination?' There was uproar as I walked into the middle of the floor. I've never been so mortified in my life as the man ran his hand down my lower leg before picking up each foot and inspecting my "fetlocks". I'd somehow changed from a jockey to a horse. To boos and cheers from the crowd, he patted me on the head and declared me clean. My heart was pounding as I sat waiting for the start. I was really fired up; it was win or bust. The encouragement from the floor was deafening and when I was first past the post, they went wild. Again I went into the centre of the floor, this time with Kerry to receive the cup and have a glass of champagne with the captain. The next day I felt like royalty as people smiled and acknowledged me often with the words, 'I won a tenner on you last night.'

They say everyone has five minutes of fame.

WASHINGTON DC, 1991

It was hot and humid, the temperature in the upper eighties. I was glad my bedroom was air-conditioned. I'd fallen into bed the previous evening exhausted after the journey to Gatwick with Kerry, Matt and Chris, whom I'd left as I checked in to board the flight with at least seventy more teachers all bound for America. At that point I knew nobody and as I sat on the plane, I sensed the familiar feeling of excitement mixed with an element of doubt and apprehension. Shortly after we returned from the cruise, with Kerry's approval I'd applied, been interviewed and accepted on a Fulbright exchange. I was going to teach for a year in the United States. I learned later from my American partner, Louise, that it was a highly competitive and prestigious honour to be accepted for a Fulbright. This had been her third attempt whereas I'd seen the advert in *The Times Education Supplement* and being fed up at school had applied on a whim. We were all staying in Washington University for four days, where on the first morning I was surprised to read the notice on the bedroom wall. No drugs, no alcohol and no smoking, it said. *Oh, sex is ok then,* I thought. The second shock was the bewildering mix of self-service food at breakfast. Apart from cereal and fruit, there were donuts, muffins, iced cakes, pancakes, waffles, eggs, frankfurters, hash browns and thin crispy strips of fat streaky bacon. I found a place to sit and couldn't help but compare my meagre portion with the piled plates of my companions. The man on my left introduced himself:

'Are you excited about the Channel Tunnel?' I had to stop myself laughing. 'I'm more concerned about the possibility of rabies entering the country.' 'Gee, that's common over here in skunks, foxes, racoons, bats and possums. Most folk have their animals vaccinated and keep dogs on a leash in the back yard.' He then went on to ask me about the Royal Family, a topic more widely talked about in America than at home. The vexing question of familiar words and phrases was addressed during a lecture we had on the cultural differences. I encountered this early on after using the word "fortnight", when it was apparent by the puzzled look on her face that the woman I was talking to had no idea what I meant.

The hectic four days of sightseeing by coach, when we visited the major monuments, memorials and state offices, came to a climax with the *'farewell banquet'*. What a disappointment. It turned out to be a picnic on the grass with hot dogs and beef burgers. Early next day, we all left escorted by our exchange partners to destinations as far apart as California and Vermont or Texas and Oregon. I was bound for Connecticut, which I initially pronounced with a strong British accent until, after constant teasing, I changed it to the American sound of Coneddycut.

Torrential rain greeted us on arrival and, to my dismay, instead of going straight to where I'd be staying, Louise first called in at the school. She introduced me to the head, then insisted on taking me to see the perfect home she'd found that I could rent. It was isolated and totally unsuitable, miles from any shops up a long, tree-lined drive, too dark and spooky for me to even consider. Eventually, wet and hungry, I was dropped off at Sharon and Carl's bungalow in Quinnetuk Circle, Longmeadow, just over the state border in Massachusetts.

The following day I was picked up again by Louise and taken to her home, where displayed on the outside of the bungalow was a huge, hand-painted banner bearing the words WELCOME MARGARET in large capital letters. She still lived with her parents who'd organised a party for me to meet the whole family. There was masses of food and drink on trestle tables outside and I stood chatting, with wine glass in hand, which never seemed to be empty, to the numerous cousins, aunties and uncles who all just lurved little old England.

Barely a week after arriving in the country, I was then on my way to Cape Cod with Sharon and Carl and their two friends who owned a holiday home. Cape Cod is a sandy peninsula in south-eastern Massachusetts, forming a wide curve enclosing Cape Cod Bay where the Pilgrim Fathers landed on the northern tip in 1620. On our first day, with the temperature in the nineties, we sat in the shade, eating and drinking, then as it got dark we lay on loungers under a brilliant clear sky watching shooting stars. Early next morning, I walked alone on the deserted beach feeling like Robinson Crusoe until I came across two twentieth-century notices, one saying TERN NESTING AREA KEEP OFF; the other NO ALCOHOL ON THE BEACH. After a swim in the ocean, Carl and David caught a huge bluefish, more than two-foot long, that they barbecued for supper.

The following week was a whirl of a lifestyle I'd never imagined. I went to an auction and numerous tag sales where people sat in their front yard selling any old things from toys to skis or furniture. I drank as much wine as I normally did in six months, wallowed in the hot tub and then the pool every evening, and ate more pizza and barbecued steak than I'd had in my life.

By the end of August I was beginning to feel homesick and was desperately missing Kerry. Originally we'd decided he would just come over for a holiday, because he couldn't leave his dad and our little dog Ben. Then, my sister Ann offered to have Ben and Ivor's lady friend said he was welcome to live with her if it meant Kerry could join me. I was over the moon and began seriously to look for somewhere to live. The first was a condo, short for condominium which we call a flat. I hated it with its chandelier and glass table and blousy curtains. The bigger houses all had basements with enough space in which to play a game of tennis or put a full-size snooker table and bar. Some even had a home movie theatre with tiered seating. Many were set back among trees like Hansel and Gretel cottages. They all had screens at doors and windows to keep out the mozzies, but at night I liked listening to the crickets in the trees.

My first week at school was dreadful with the temperature in the nineties, no fans and no air conditioning and a noisy class of over-confident children with no manners. It made me sick the way the staff talked to them. Even the youngest of five and six had rules that were gone over every day. If they broke the rules, they were counselled instead of being "told off". There were nearly as many counsellors and psychologists as actual teachers. Because of the different set-up from ours, I didn't meet the rest of the staff until the first staff meeting. It was an elementary school catering for children aged from three to eleven. However, because there were four classes in each year group, the play times and lunch times were staggered so you only mixed with your own set of teachers. Also, there was additional staff who took PE, art and library. At the meeting, I was introduced by the principal. 'This is Margaret; Louise has gone to live with her husband.'

Everyone roared with laughter. I made the biggest faux pas a week later when he came into my classroom. He asked me how I was settling in and then went on to ask where I came from. I told him that it was a small village in the Midlands called Cosby that dated back to the *Domesday Book*. He gave me a puzzled look.

'Pardon me?' he said.

'Oh, come on,' I replied, 'every intelligent person has heard of the *Domesday Book*.' The minute those words were out of my mouth, I wished the ground would swallow me up. However, he got his own back in the weekly staff bulletin when he posed the question to the teachers. He instructed them to write it down and give it to Margaret who will make them a proper English cup of tea. The word proper is not in the American vocabulary and I hadn't realised till then how often we use it. I knew I was forgiven when he appeared, bringing me a real teapot. I'd been looking for one ever since I'd arrived. Everyone there seemed to drink coffee and the percolators were permanently plugged in.

Sharon's dad died in September and it was a baptism of fire for me when I had to drive myself to school in the van. It was big and black, very similar to the one in the American comedy *The A-Team*. I nearly died when the sliding door flew open on the interstate, but worse was to come when I realised I was going north instead of south.

PIZZAS AND PUMPKINS

'Where is your honey?' asked one of the twins. I couldn't help smiling at her cute turn of phrase.

'He's in England but you'll see him soon.' It felt good to be saying that, I could hardly wait. I was visiting Sara's home where I met her husband, her honey, as she referred to him, and the five-year-old girls. Kathy, the other first grade teacher, had driven us there; as we worked and planned together it was fortunate that we all shared the same sense of humour, though I sometimes got the impression that they thought some of my methods were a bit wacky. The American curriculum, unlike ours, was highly structured and teacher-centred with regular testing geared to the attainment of certain skills. The staff all worked from the same manual on the same page on the same day, and asked the same questions; even expected responses were written on the page. Children were used to sitting and listening for long periods and all written stuff was recorded on worksheets. I was dismayed when I saw the room where the aids, classroom helpers, did all the photocopying. It contained several machines, which they hammered every day preparing hundreds of sheets of paper for the children to either tick a box or underline the right answer. At six and seven years old, this is no guarantee that a child has understood or retained the relevant information. By contrast, in my own room the emphasis was more child-centred where children learned through play and firsthand experience. I encouraged them to work in pairs and small groups of four or five and they began writing in books, so that over a period of time they could see their own progress. I introduced personal word dictionaries and showed them how to use a picture dictionary, a skill that was not taught in other first grade rooms. The effect was almost instant and the class began to take more pride in their work and the feedback from parents was most encouraging.

At the end of September, the British teachers working in the five states of New England all met in Windsor for an official feedback of first impressions. It was a relief to me when most people voiced the same concerns about the attitude of the children and the huge differences in methods. Everyone had suffered from homesickness and the feelings of "Is it really me?" or "What am I doing here?" Many of them who lived alone felt isolated. I could understand this because I'd noticed that no one knew their neighbours or even had a desire to do so where I was living at Sharon's. When I'd been for a walk or a bike ride nobody had spoken or even acknowledged me, and I realised how lucky I was because by then I was counting the days to Kerry's arrival and at last had found somewhere to rent.

The house belonged to a retired couple who went to Florida every winter; such folk are called "snowbirds", because they would be away from October till the end of April. It was a typical clapboard New England home dating back to the late 1800s with five bedrooms, a large living room with separate dining area, a library, a big kitchen and, added at some unknown date, three garages. The floors, walls and window frames were uneven and the antique radiators made such alarming noises in the night that Kerry frequently leaned out of bed and hurled a shoe at the offending piece of iron.

I'd not been scrumping since I was ten years old, so it was quite a shock when Sharon suggested it as we approached Halloween. Not gooseberries from someone's allotment, but pumpkins from a farmer's field. The real harvesting was finished, however, and what remained were a few scabby-looking specimens. I felt akin to the gleaners from the Middle Ages, the peasant women who were allowed to pick up the fallen seeds of corn from the field edges like Ruth in the Old Testament. In the build-up to Halloween, pumpkins were on sale stacked high upon trailers, or displayed on the ground outside the tobacco barns. Around one large house in Suffield, we counted more than twenty decorating the fence, windows and doors. In school on the 31 October, the teachers in first grade dressed appropriately, one as a witch, another as a ghost and the third as a gorilla. The relevance of that I couldn't imagine or dare ask. All the children wore masks and ate suitably decorated fairy cakes baked by their devoted moms. Unfortunately, after a communication from the school office about the possible contamination of M&M's (sweets that resembled Smarties), the parents were notified and asked to be vigilant if their offspring went door–to-door trick or treating. The next day I actually saw a notice, locally, advertising free X-ray for candy.

These inter-office communications with regard to incidents arrived frequently, something that I'd never experienced in my whole teaching career. The next one was based on information the police had received about a homicide and a subsequent incident involving a woman getting stabbed on route 75. As a precaution, a third person was to be on duty outside during lunch recess. After the children came back, teachers were asked to take attendance. That was common practice at the start of the afternoon in the UK. Then, there was a letter to the school and parents from the Health Department about an epidemic of racoon rabies that had spread to two family cats. We were given posters and brochures full of information. There was a class lesson pointing out the dangers to boys and girls of petting stray cats and dogs, and advice on what to do should they be bitten.

I found it both sad and disturbing that we had to follow a set "Say no to drugs" programme with such young children. Before they filled in the interminable photocopied sheet of questions, we had a discussion with pre-set questions for me to ask. These included: What is alcohol? What can it do to you? There followed a story I had to read about a recovering alcoholic. I thought it was distasteful and by their answers it was apparent that they hadn't a clue what it was all about.

I hadn't realised how much I'd miss Kerry and

mistakenly believed I could manage without him. One Sunday when I was alone in the house and Ann phoned I had to eat my words. I burst into tears. She immediately offered to have Ben for the year and Kerry's dad decided that he could go and live with the widowed lady he'd met at an afternoon club in the village. Louise's father took me to the airport to meet Kerry on 3 October and I flung my arms around him as soon as he walked through reception. We had to stay with Sharon before the big house was vacated and she later admitted to me that she'd thought our marriage was on the rocks and I'd gone over to escape. Kerry was able to tell everyone how quickly Louise had adapted and been accepted into village life. Her initial experience of the exchange had been smoother and easier than mine. I was looking forward to moving into our own house where I'd be doing some plain English cooking. Although I did enjoy pizza when I arrived, it was so unlike any we had in England. After two months, however, when it was offered four times a week, it was beginning to pall and I had withdrawal symptoms for vegetables. I also noticed that the Americans I met used an enormous amount of cheese, adding it to most cooked dishes. After a couple of weeks Kerry diplomatically told me that I'd put on weight. I wasn't surprised after the daily wine, crisps, dips and cheese-laden dishes I'd consumed.

We eventually bought a second-hand car, only after the salesman dropped the price again by $200 when we nearly cancelled. We told him that our insurance was so high that we might have to forget about even having one. It cost almost as much as the vehicle.

Every Saturday morning, our favourite supermarket was Stop 'n Shop. We enjoyed choosing stuff more suited to our taste from a huge variety of fruit and vegetables that were not available at home. As I'd learned to appreciate the merits of Californian wine whilst living with Sharon, we also added a box to our weekly shop. Having finished, we sat in the car eating an enormous warm blueberry muffin each. It was going to be hard to lose that weight.

HAVE CAR, WILL TRAVEL

'Do you know about the American phenomenon of the clocks going back at the end of October?' asked the lady sitting next to Kerry. He glanced across at me and subtly raised one eyebrow before he told her that we'd adopted it during the war in Britain in order to give the farmers more daylight hours. It hadn't occurred to me until I began to speak to groups of people, either formally or at a meal in someone's home, how naïve and ill-informed the average American was about Europe and the UK. That particular women's group was a prime example with further questions like; Do you have microwaves? Do you have fitted carpets? Have you ever seen snow? Do all your houses have thatched roofs? I found it hard not to laugh; these were classic chocolate box or Christmas card depictions. In fairness, although Kerry and I were familiar with the history and the politics of the United States, we were ignorant about the geography and the diversity of that massive country. The more we travelled the more we enjoyed the experience of meeting different people and listening to their views.

It was impossible to get to know the fifty-odd members of staff at school other than the people involved with first grade. The only time we crossed paths was at a once-a-term staff meeting or fighting for cakes every morning in December, when the teachers in all grades took a turn in providing home-baked cakes. After seeing the scrum when people were bagging platefuls to put on one side before school had even begun, I didn't bother to go in again. It was like children let loose at a birthday party. Apart from this, the teachers in first grade also started every Friday in a classroom with a donut breakfast at 8 o'clock. I loved the jam donuts at home but found the American versions far too sweet, smothered in icing and coloured sprinkles. I didn't join them, as I couldn't face the sickly smell at that hour of the day.

We found the highway patrol and the police in general to be most courteous on the numerous occasions when we got lost. I loved the old-fashioned way they addressed me as ma'am; it was suitable for a lady of any age from twenty to ninety years old. In early November, when we went for Kerry's first visit to stay in Helen's bungalow in Cape Cod, I misjudged the distance and the time it would take. It was dark before we reached the peninsula and after miles of looking for a familiar sign or landmark, we had to pull over. As we huddled in the pitch black peering over the map with a torch, we jumped at a sudden rap on the driver's window. It was a state policeman who soon reassured us that we weren't that far from our destination and he actually showed us the way.

I think our accents worked to our advantage as people were keen to chat and wanted to know exactly where we were from in case it was close to where their own family originated. Although they were proud to be American, they loved to acknowledge their British or Irish roots. On a warm weekend in late November, we travelled to Pennsylvania to see the Amish people, fulfilling for me a long-held ambition ever since I'd seen the film *Witness*. Needless to say, I realised we were on the wrong interstate when I saw a road sign saying New Jersey. We could have ended up in New York. I took the next exit and we eventually found somewhere to stop and have a drink. As we sat in the deserted diner with the map spread out covering the whole table, a young girl came to take our order.

'Can you tell me exactly where we are?' asked Kerry, pointing vaguely to where he thought we should be. The girl was speechless for a couple of seconds before she managed to tell us, then struggled to find it on the map. It wasn't a diner where they had many customers who weren't local, she later explained when she brought the coffee. I guessed it must have made her day. We enjoyed the weekend and were impressed with the guide on the coach tour who was well informed about the traditions and the day-to-day life of the Amish. It was interesting to hear how they lived together in a close-knit community, sharing the work, the needs, and the ups and downs of their friends and neighbours. From the coach, we saw a young lad farming in the age-old manner of walking behind the horse guiding the plough. No engines or mechanical aids were allowed, hence the absence of tractors and motor driven vehicles. Inside a typical home, it was plain, unadorned, no wall hangings and no pictures – not even a mirror. Just the bare necessities. There was no phone or anything powered by electricity and they still used a horse and buggy for going to town. Amish children went to their own school, a one-room wooden structure, but were expected to help with the harvesting and homemaking from a very early age when schooling stopped for the summer. It was not regarded as a holiday for messing about. Visitors were not allowed to take photos but I confess that I broke this rule. I stood at the door of our bed and breakfast early on Sunday morning, filming the procession of buggies with their huge wheels and equally large hoods raised to obscure the faces of any occupants. Only the shadowy shapes of the drivers could be glimpsed as the long-legged black horses clattered down the road to church in the pouring rain.

CHRISTMAS, 1991

The first snow fell in early December and school opened late every day. The children were as high as kites and because they all wore a one-piece snowsuit and boots, we seemed to spend half the day dressing and undressing them. The first time was when they arrived, then before and after morning recess and later before and after the lunch recess, not counting home time. There was also the faff of putting soaking mittens and gloves to dry on the radiators.

Through an inter-school staff meeting, I'd met an English lady, Miriam, who worked in the office at the middle school. I went to stay with her and her husband David several times when I was homesick. She took me to her church where I started going regularly and by the time Kerry came over I'd made some really good friends and he even went, too; something he'd never done at home. In mid-December we had our first visit to New York on a coach trip organised by the church. My vision of the city from the film *White Christmas*, with snow-covered streets and rosy-cheeked Santas greeting smiling shoppers was instantly dispelled by the drizzle that greeted us. People scurried along the wet sidewalk, heads down, some with umbrellas, all intent on getting out of the rain. Despite this, there was a festive feel and we followed the crowds to Macy's, the world's largest store, according to the massive sign painted on the wall outside. It was thrilling to walk down Broadway, home of entertainment, and to be able to recognise the familiar names of Fifth Avenue, Carnegie Hall and Madison Square Gardens, even if I wasn't sure why they were famous. It was nearly dark when we reached the ice rink in front of the Rockefeller Centre and I felt a touch of magic in the air. We stood for ages by the huge Christmas tree that twinkled with hundreds of coloured lights and watched the skaters weaving in and out rhythmically, in time to the music. It was such a shame I had to go to work the next day.

In sharp contrast, there was no such Christmas atmosphere in school where any religion is not allowed. The corridors were wide and empty because of health and safety regulations, nothing to impede a quick escape in event of emergency. To me it made the place look more like a hospital but even they had pictures on the walls, while here they were devoid of any decoration or children's art so unlike what I was used to. Most of all, I missed teaching the children the familiar carols, like "Away in a Manger" and "Little Donkey", and seeing their excited faces as they were ready to perform the nativity play for their parents when every child is a star.

It made the memories of my own children at that age even more precious and brought to mind the Christmas card that Matthew brought home when he was five of an angel with a black eye.

We'd sent Chris the airfare to visit at Christmas; otherwise he would have been all on his own. Jon was happily married living in Durham, Matt was living and teaching in Greece and Kate (the name Kathryn had adopted since leaving home) was living with her boyfriend. Kerry, especially, was looking forward to seeing Chris and having the wonderful opportunity of taking him to the art galleries in New York and Boston. At Logan Airport we scanned the crowds emerging from his flight and waited. They dwindled in number, then stopped altogether. But where was Chris? We stood anxious and helpless, wondering what to do if he'd missed the flight. After what seemed an eternity he appeared alone, looking very sheepish and obviously glad to see us still there.

'They took me in a room,' he garbled as I gave him a big hug. He'd been interrogated by immigration and had had to admit that he had no money and had no idea where we lived. Poor lad on his first flight and trip abroad what a greeting. If they'd have bothered to find us, we could have confirmed he was our son.

We had lots of invitations to friends' homes and Chris was impressed by their huge houses and their generosity. Bob, a retired chap married to Ann who was the school librarian, shared Kerry's interest in golf, art and fishing, so they invited us for Christmas Day. It was a cold buffet – rather low-key, but very nice. I'd been asked to take a homemade Christmas pudding and showed them our tradition of setting fire to the brandy. We didn't sit round a table and there were no crackers.

Boxing Day is unheard of, so the shops all re-open and people go back to work. When I went back to school on 2 January, it seemed I'd never left. It felt odd to me that no one child or adult mentioned Christmas. The children were happy to be in school again and I certainly had more confidence than when I'd begun the previous September. Brett, a little girl in my class who'd been particularly challenging the first term, said after a couple of days back in a familiar routine, "I like you Mrs Silk; you're the best teacher in the world, even though you do talk funny."

ICICLES AND ICE SKATING

After nearly four weeks, Chris went back to England laden. The good exchange rate meant that every pound in sterling was worth twice as much in dollars so we stocked him up with jeans and casual clothes, and he took bales of towels for Kate. He'd enjoyed visiting the art museum in Boston when the three of us had stayed at Sheila's for a few days. She was based there as one of the exchange teachers and we'd swapped houses so that she had more room for family to come and stay. We all liked Boston, probably because of its history and the English feel to it. Unlike New York and the modern cities in the west, the streets of Boston are not laid out on the grid system. The roads run in all directions and at funny angles revealing narrow cobbled alleys fronted by houses made of brick. The history of Boston dates back to the arrival of the Puritans from Europe. We walked the three-mile freedom trail which connects the city's most famous sites and learned about the organised resistance to the oppression from the British. It amused us when we later told our American friends about the visit, because they were amazed that we'd driven there in the first place and could actually find our way around.

They much prefer the familiar grid system where all roads are one-way and distances are measured in straight lines by blocks. We in turn were astonished when some friends admitted they'd never been to Boston, a distance of only 104 miles.

Bob also took Chris and Kerry to Yale University Museum of Modern Art where they saw an original Monet, and to a lesser-known place called Farmington. Hilltop at Farmington is not a typical example of a museum because its original purpose was a country house for a well-travelled rich American family of art lovers. It houses world-renowned masterpieces and rooms full of unexpected treasures. When we were invited for drinks and snacks during the holiday period, Kerry and Chris were never short of conversation openers. I noticed that they were always surrounded by a group of people eager to listen to an English voice.

It was so cold throughout January and February that school was cancelled on a couple of occasions due to black ice. Over 90 per cent of the children used the customary yellow school buses and the drivers would never take a chance in extreme weather conditions. They knew full well that should they be involved in an accident, litigation would follow. At one of our faculty meetings we'd had a lecture on how to avoid law suit costs and I learned that parents always win on procedural points, not on school philosophy.

On the way to watch ski jumping one Sunday with friends, we saw icicles like stalactites hanging from the banks by the roadside. They were big enough to impale a man. It was too cold to stand watching the jumping for long, so we adjourned to a diner where, surprise, surprise, pizza was ordered – which, when it arrived, was the length and breadth of the table.

When my class couldn't go out for recess because of the low temperatures, it was reflected in their bad behaviour. I'd started the term thinking I'd cracked this problem. Now we seemed to be back to square one. It made me cringe when the children were addressed in such a patronising manner by other members of staff who took them for Art and PE. Discipline always had to be positive, as in "I like your good manners, boys and girls" or "I need your listening ears". The offender's name was rarely used and I doubted whether this method would have worked in a school at home on a socially deprived council estate. Never before had I had behaviour problems that I couldn't deal with and I prided myself on the fact that I didn't need to raise my voice. Children loathe teachers who shout.

I had qualms when one weekend, Judy, the aide who worked in my room, invited Kerry and me to go ice skating on the lake that backed onto their garden. Neither of us had ever done it before and I had to admire Kerry for his guts. After my own feeble attempt, when I clung on to Judy and her ten-year-old daughter, not once daring to let go, I opted out to take some photos. Meanwhile Kerry, bless him, manfully had a go on his own and managed to stay upright until he turned and the force of the wind sent him flying across the ice, before he overbalanced and sat down with a bump. I filmed it all on video. The next day he was very stiff but still able to laugh about it and could exaggerate the retelling when we went to Kathy and Wayne's for dinner.

TEXAS, 14 FEBRUARY 1992

We left behind the snow and ice of New England and flew to Texas on Valentine's Day, arriving to a temperature of 70 degrees and daffodils in bloom. Our hosts were Mary, an American, and Robin, an Englishman, who lived midway between Fort Worth and Dallas. Robin was the cousin of Julie, a friend of mine in Cosby. We'd met on the occasion of Julie's wedding when as a favour to them their children had slept at our house for five nights. Mary, at the time, had repeatedly said, "If you folk ever come to the States make sure you visit and stay with us."

Neither of us anticipated that the opportunity would ever arise. Never say never really ought to be my motto. Mary was an expert at getting lost but through her we saw the most unlikely places. In a search to find a typical ranch, we ended up in a completely deserted yard. We walked around for a good twenty minutes without seeing a soul. Looking for help, we entered an office where on display sat expensive saddles and glistening bridles and spurs hung from the walls alongside cabinets holding solid-silver trophies. The name Tommy Mannion was engraved on a plaque by the door and we later found out that he bred and competed with world champion Quarter horses, the kind used by ranchers for the rounding up of cattle. Inside huge barns fitted out like no stables I'd ever seen, sleek horses chomped hay, only pausing to eye us curiously as we stood and admired their sheer physical beauty. As we drove away, I marvelled that no one had challenged our presence especially with all that priceless stuff on display. Or were we, in fact, being observed with someone on the standby with a gun? After all, this was America, where everyone has the right to bear arms.

We left the ranch and drove parallel to the Santa Fe railroad until we reached a small place called Ponder. Although there was only one street, it turned out to have associations with a pair of legendary bank robbers called Bonny and Clyde. The tiny store on the corner, which was formerly a bank, was, by repute, the first one that the pair had robbed. It now boasted a custom-made boot company, patronised by presidents and governors. We chatted to the proprietor who was busy hand-stitching a pair of boots. A selection of snakeskins in a variety of patterns and colours were hanging up or on display for customers to handle. After our query regarding food and drink, he directed us further down the empty street to where we found the aptly named Ranchman's Bar where we spent the next two hours.

The owner and his wife were fascinated by our British accents, such visitors were few, and we in turn were enthralled listening to his broad southern drawl. On the walls of the diner were newspaper cuttings with photographs of film stars and the crew who came to make the film of Bonny and Clyde in the 1960s.

On a visit to Dallas the next day, we saw the building from where the shot that killed President Kennedy was fired. We crossed the road along which the doomed motorcade had driven and walked to the Kennedy Memorial. This is an unprepossessing structure of four 30 to 40-foot high walls. They face inwards, each one made of nine individual smooth concrete columns that resemble planks of wood. What it was meant to signify was a mystery to us all. More impressive is the monumental sculpture called the Mustangs of Las Colinas, depicting nine life-sized mustangs galloping through water. From a distance the horses looked real, helped by the clever effect of the water spraying up around their feet. Robin took us to Fort Worth and explained the history. It was the last resting place for cowboys driving herds of Longhorn beef cattle heading north up the Chisholm Trail. Now the wooden penned stockyards stand empty and unused and down the street the boarded-up shops and old saloon bars are the only haunting reminder of days gone by. In sharp contrast we visited Billy Bob's, described as the world's biggest honky-tonk. Open seven days and nights a week, it has a seating capacity of 6,000, forty bars, restaurants and shops, and offers shooting games and snooker. You could even have a photo taken on a bucking stuffed steer. There's a Texas-sized dance floor, over which, centrally suspended, hangs a spotlighted silver saddle. At weekends there's competitive live bull riding and entertainment from well-known stars.

When I'd been writing Christmas cards in December, right out of the blue I remembered the address of a penfriend in Chicago. Her name was Judy Churchill and we'd written regularly from the age of ten till our mid-teens. I wrote it down before I forgot, 7739 Elm Grove Drive, Elmwood Pk 35, Chicago, Illinois. I posted a card; it was a long shot but worth a try. Amazingly her mum still lived there and she gave me Judy's phone number in San Antonio. We'd never heard of the place so looked on the map and found it way down south on the Mexican border. No way, we'd said. Imagine our surprise when Mary announced we were going to San Antonio for a couple of days. She worked part-time for American Airlines who also owned the Marriott hotels, so we all got free flights and reduced accommodation. San Antonio, with its chequered history under Spanish and Mexican rule, is delightful. We stayed opposite the River Walk, a place lined with open-air cafes and craft shops.

El Mercado, the restored Mexican market, was a sea of colour, smells and noise, full of knick-knacks, traditional ethnic pieces of jewellery and handmade toys and ornaments. That evening, we met Judy, her husband and her mum and ate in a Mexican restaurant famed for its authentic tortillas and fajitas. It was a thrill to meet after fifty years and find we still had a lot in common. We vowed to keep in touch. Next day we visited the Alamo, what's left of it. We watched a film first, which was a good job because I hadn't a clue what it was all about. I learned that there'd been a siege when the Texans wanted independence from Mexico. The Texans were seriously outnumbered and all were killed including

Davy Crockett. His name was only familiar because in 1955 there was a song promoting a Disney film called *King of the Wild Frontier*. I didn't see the film, but like everyone else my age, I knew all the lyrics.

PUBLIC SPEAKING
AND SPELLING

We arrived back in Connecticut to more snow and a temperature of minus 13. That evening, settled in front of a blazing fire in the grate, we devoured the pile of letters that had arrived in our absence. I loved reading the news from home. Jonathan had had a promotion at work and a significant pay rise and Chris was going to paint a mural on a wall in Lancaster. Ann wrote to tell us that Ben, our little Jack Russell, had put on weight, and enclosed a photo of him being shampooed in the kitchen sink. He didn't look impressed. Her passport had arrived and she was looking forward to coming over in April. David and Gill said they were bringing Tom, but Emma was revising for exams. They would be coming a week before the rest of the party. June would be arriving the day after Ann, without Peter who didn't want to come. She'd asked us whether it would be all right to bring her friend Doreen. We knew that she was nervous about travelling all that way on her own and were just glad that she'd have company. When I read that Christine at the farm had delivered unexpected twin lambs on Christmas Day I felt sad that this would be the first time for ages that I didn't take lambs to school at Easter. We couldn't wait to see family and friends. Although the American people we'd met were warm-hearted and generous, we discovered that they made glib promises. It was a case of out of sight, out of mind. It had surprised us when Mary admitted before we left Texas that invitations to visit, including ours, are given but folk are not serious and don't expect it to happen. Kerry was very disappointed when a couple we'd met at a party had promised to play golf and he waited in vain for a phone call. We missed friends arriving without warning saying "put the kettle on" as they walked in the door. In America, no one drops in to say hello without a prior invitation. We were experiencing a different culture with different values and learning to adapt. Another thing we noticed was the absence of children playing outside or with friends riding their bikes. Adults never just "go for a walk" or even take the dog out. Although dogs were sometimes tethered, most could roam freely in their own front yards. However, should they stray too close to the boundary, an invisible electric barrier was somehow activated by the dog's collar. I couldn't get used to using the term "yard" when referring to the large gardens. To me, the word brought up memories of Mammam's terraced house where all the properties were connected by back yards with washing lines and outdoor lavatories. Kerry commented on the absence of people his age in the shops and malls and I said jokingly that they'd all gone to Florida, were hibernating or were dead.

After an article and photo of us was printed in the *Hartford Chronicle* (Connecticut's oldest newspaper), a letter arrived for me from the Stafford Rotary Club. I was invited with my spouse to attend their International Night Dinner as one of the guest speakers. The club was beautifully set amidst lakes and trees, with a beach, swimming and fishing facilities. We arrived at 6.00 p.m. for cocktails, then Kerry and I were separated to sit at different tables each seating six men. There must have been at least sixty present, and apart from the waitresses, I was the only woman in the room. I was plied with questions throughout the meal and there was much laughter and far more noise it seemed from our table than those around us. Before I spoke, two lads, one from Holland and the other from Finland, talked about their life as students in the States. Whilst listening to the boys and indeed throughout the meal, my companions were constantly topping up my wine glass. Consequently, when I stood up and went to the front I felt quite squiffy. Without any notes I talked off the top of my head for nearly half an hour. It was a riot. When I finished, I was given a standing ovation; the applause was deafening. I caught Kerry's eye, he was grinning like a Cheshire cat and gave me the thumbs-up. I felt like a prime minister after his opening address at the spring conference. A couple of days later, a bouquet of flowers arrived with a note attached, saying, "Thanks from the boys at the table." I'd already been given a book about America, a pennant of the rotary club and an open invitation to visit again.

School ticked over with good days and bad, though my confidence in my own ability and my alternative methods of teaching was restored by the positive comments from parents, such as "Can you stay for second grade?" Or "Will you take Elsie to England with you?" These remarks far outweighed the disapproving looks I'd had from a certain member of staff.

Sometimes I wasn't surprised that the children were high when each week there seemed to be another excuse for a party. All the staff wearing green and a silly hat celebrated St Patrick's Day, and Kathy's class ate green scrambled egg and drank green pop. The following week should have been "Leap into spring day" when everyone went outside to fly paper planes. Unfortunately, it was cancelled because of torrential rain. On the horizon loomed a pizza party sponsored by Pizza Hut for the children who'd read the required number of books since November, then this would be followed by a visit from the Easter Bunny who doled out candy rabbits and marshmallow eggs.

As individuals I loved all my class especially when they made such innocent remarks. Recounting the events in a story, Ryan said something about the "happy guy". I was puzzled until I realised he meant the court jester. I was also told, "Too much cake lowers your IQ", and "the tooth fairy lives with God". My favourite, though, happened back in the first term when we were doing phonics. I'd asked for words beginning with v. Video, volleyball and violin were suggested before there was a pause. Then Andy, a shy, nervous little boy raised his hand.

'Voz,' he said and beamed.

'Good boy, a vase, vee ay ess ee.' I spelled it out as I wrote on the whiteboard.

'No-no-no,' he shook his head and waved a hand from side to side. 'Vee oh zee, voz,' he shouted. 'You know the wizard of Voz.'

It was a gem.

THE BRITS
HAVE LANDED

'I'll sue you,' Janice said to us as she wiped tears from her face. She'd just wet herself laughing at Derek who'd fallen off his chair because he'd been too free with the wine. He stumbled to his feet and grabbed hold of the back of the chair. 'S'jet lag,' he muttered.

'I need to go to bed.' It was probably a factor as they'd only arrived the night before and had been out and about with Kerry all day while I was at school. They were our first visitors, not counting Chris, and although they only stayed for eight days we crammed in a lot of trips. I'd learned from other staff members that we were actually allowed a set number of sick days per year. I knew that Sarah regularly took time off for going skiing so decided to skive that Monday in order to enjoy a long weekend in Vermont. I didn't even have to contact the school; just rang a supply agency that handled it.

Vermont is a pretty state with more hills and fewer trees than Massachusetts and Connecticut. White clapboard churches snuggle in the valleys and dairy farms hug the slopes. It's a state where until the mid-sixties there were more cows than people. Although the roads were clear, snow was piled at least ten feet high on the verges as we headed north to our destination. We were staying with Morna, the exchange teacher from Edinburgh. She'd specifically asked to be placed somewhere where she could ski and was in her element. We went to see her school, which was beautifully set. Most children arrived on skis, unlike our pampered lot, and they had the use of sledges at playtime. On the journey back we drove past acres and acres of red sugar maple trees. As the end of winter approaches and sap begins to rise, the trees are tapped for the sweet, sticky substance that is converted into maple syrup. The red buckets attached to the trees stood out in sharp contrast to the glistening white snow. We took Janice and Derek to New York, this time venturing to use a bus that went from Hartford into the city. It was a short walk from the bus station, but not one I'd do alone. It was a grotty side that we'd not seen on that first visit. There were tramps lying in doorways and a dubious-looking feller with a cigarette hanging from his lower lip who eyed us as we passed by. I squeezed Kerry's hand and quickened the pace. A scruffy man in a tatty raincoat was scrabbling in the bins and putting a variety of what looked like rubbish into a supermarket trolley. We headed for Central Park and watched the skaters, then took our visitors to all the places we'd enjoyed seeing at Christmas. It was a good practice run for going again when the family arrived in April. I was itching for the end of term, the cold weather seemed never-ending, and then I had a letter to say there was a debriefing that I was required to attend right at the end of term.

I shared a hotel room with Morna the following week in Boston where we met all the other exchange teachers based in New England. The meeting opened with introductions and a short talk, then there was a question and answer session. Everyone was clamouring to speak when teachers were given a chance to talk openly about the lack of discipline and respect. Over and over again the fact was stated that because all American children are expected to succeed they cannot handle failure. The teachers from France were the most vocal and it transpired that six had resigned and gone back home. My school didn't finish till the next day and Ann was due to arrive that evening. David and family had already been with us for a few days and it irked me that I was still working. Kerry picked me up that evening and after a meal together the five of us went to Logan Airport. It was great to see Ann and I was reluctant to be dropped off at the hotel for one more night. The next afternoon I flew back to Suffield in the smallest plane I've ever been in.

As it was only a forty-minute flight, there was just the pilot and nine passengers. I had to laugh when at the last minute a woman came tottering across the tarmac in high heels, a briefcase in one hand and clutching a hat in the other.

'Do you have a bathroom?' she shrieked.

'No,' said the pilot, 'but we'll wait for you, ma-am.'

Bradley, the local airport, was only ten minutes from our house. Kerry and I had got lost there one night when we'd been to Kathy's for a meal. We'd taken a wrong turning in the dark and gone round in circles for a good ten minutes, passing arrivals and departures several times looking for the exit. June and Doreen arrived the following day and although we'd never met Doreen, she bonded with Ann immediately as they were both smokers. Our party was complete.

Look out America, the Brits have landed.

LOON CABIN

June and Doreen barely had time to take a breath before we set off the next morning. We were going up country to Maine for four nights courtesy of a member of staff whose mother owned a holiday home. Maine is in the extreme north-east of New England with a spectacular coastline that stretches over two hundred miles. Stephen King, the novelist, was born there and as we drove along deserted highways that ran parallel to thick forests of dark, foreboding pine trees, it was obvious that he found his inspiration for horror stories right on his doorstep. Since there were eight of us, we'd hired a people carrier and travelled in tandem, the men in one vehicle and the women in the other. The main road had been cleared by snowploughs but we finally had to turn right onto a track leading between the trees. Although it was covered in snow, steep and slippery, I reached the top with no problem. However, the other car got stuck at the bottom, its wheels spinning unable to get a grip.

'Good job it's the men and not us,' said Ann. She and Doreen got out and lit a cigarette so I grabbed the camcorder. After much shoving and persuasion, Kerry managed to coax the car to the top while David and Tom walked behind to lighten the load. Set among the trees beside a frozen lake sat Loon Cabin. It was so named after a type of duck that arrives and stays every summer to breed and raise its young before it heads back to warmer climes. The separate garage was as large as an average bungalow at home and it amazed us that such a lavish property was only used for vacations. The smell of pinewood greeted us as we walked in and we stared, fascinated, at the carvings that decorated the staircase and a balcony overlooking the living room. There were loud exclamations of oohs and ahs followed by, 'Hey, come and look at this.'

'Wow, isn't it great?'

'Aren't we lucky, Maggie?'

'Bags I sleep here,' the latter from 11-year-old Tom who was sprawled on a bed. While the women found the duvet covers and sheets and set to making the beds, Kerry put the tins and cereals away, then Tom helped David to prepare a meal. Next morning I slipped outside with the camcorder while the others were getting breakfast, intending to film the view from the balcony without realising that Ann was already there swathed in a massive pink checked blanket. She was enjoying her first cigarette of the day, but with her dark hair and the way she sat hunched against the cold, she looked just like a Native American squaw.

I immediately started taking a picture, hardly able to keep the camera still for laughing. It was freezing and already the lens was beginning to mist up.

'Aw Maggie, you are awful. Isn't it beautiful?' She nodded towards the frozen lake as she tried to distract me. The others must have heard me laughing and only clad in their dressing gowns came out to enjoy the joke, but beat a hasty retreat as the cold air hit them. We went out each day exploring the area by car and spent the evenings in the warmth of the cabin playing Scrabble or cards. It was three days of non-stop noise and laughter.

Back in Suffield we did the familiar trip to New York with just a hiccup, when June refused to go in the lift up to the top of the Empire State Building.

'You've got a choice then,' said David bluntly. 'Come with me or stay here and get mugged.' As we bundled into the lift squashed together, he wrapped his arms around her and she hid her face in his thick fleecy jacket. In a matter of seconds, we were stepping out onto the 34th floor. We'd used the bus again from Hartford and before setting off to go back the driver gave his customary talk about no smoking anywhere on the vehicle. Halfway home, without any warning, he stopped in the middle of nowhere. It was pitch black and we all thought he'd hit something. However, with a face like thunder, he strode to the rear of the coach, burst into the restroom and emerged with a youth. Holding him by the scruff of his neck, he frogmarched him to the exit where he literally threw him off the bus and drove away, leaving him on the edge of the highway.

Ann was astonished and kept worrying about the poor lad, wondering how he would get home. His canvas bag was still on the seat.

ARRIVALS

Spring exploded in mid April. Daffodils burst into flower and the grass that had looked dead all winter seemed to turn green overnight. It was so unlike back home where the slow process of buds bursting into leaf and the anticipation of fresh green shoots emerging from the soil gave everyone such pleasure. The "snowbirds" (the folk who owned our house) came back from Florida and we had to move again. Luckily, we had a place lined up belonging to the grandparents of a little boy in my class. His granddad had been stationed in East Anglia during the war when he was only eighteen. I'd met the couple through Ryan at a school open day. They'd offered us the use of their home while they were away for two months camping in their RV (recreational vehicle).

The bungalow was spacious, surrounded by a large garden full of flowering shrubs and trees in blossom. By the middle of May it was hot and humid with the temperature in the high eighties. Kerry loved it and enjoyed cutting the grass, sitting half stripped on the motor mower, as he wove in and out of the trees and around the flower beds. It became impossible to sit outside in the evenings unless you were enclosed in a mosquito tent. We were told by a friend that the two cats she owned never went out from June to September. I was fascinated by the lightning bugs, tiny pinpricks flashing in the dark.

The end of term approached with the inevitable succession of party days and treats. A notice in the staffroom read "Sign up for breakfast at school", which would be strawberries and cream, Danish pastries, donuts, cream cheese and bagels. A potluck supper was served at Mel's home of pasta, sausages and burgers, and a farewell pizza party was to be laid on for me by the parents.

The day before I finally finished I had the afternoon off to go to Boston with Kerry to meet Jon and Katharine. However, the flight was cancelled and although we stood around for at least an hour with many other people waiting for an explanation, no reason was given and no information was forthcoming.

"Call tomorrow" was the only advice. I was gutted. As we walked into the kitchen and I went to make the ever cheering cup of tea, I noticed a folded piece of paper lying on the floor. I thought it was an old receipt and picked it up.

'Hey, look at this; where the heck has this come from? Did you drop it?' It was a Greek banknote. At that moment, Matt walked into the kitchen wrapped in a bath towel, his hair still wet from the shower. My disappointment over the cancelled flight was overcome by excitement at his unexpected arrival. He'd flown from Greece to Pittsburgh, then to New York, from where he got a ticket to Bradley. A taxi had dropped him off at the bungalow and a neighbour had let him in.

Jon and Katharine finally arrived the next day. Apparently, after leaving Gatwick, the pilot had turned back over Ireland due to technical reasons and everyone on the flight was taken to a hotel for the night. It was great to have half of our family together at the farewell party in the park. My class presented me with a huge balloon containing a pink sweatshirt and told me to sit on it to get at the contents. I must have gained nearly a stone in weight since I arrived in the States and could barely keep my balance for wobbling and laughing, cheered on by twenty-four children. The sweatshirt was decorated with handprints, one from each student in my class made with the help of parents. The following week two photos were published in the local paper, one of me with my class, the other with Kerry, the family and me.

'They must be short of news over here,' said Matt drily when he read it.

Expert tour guides by now, we took the kids to see New York and Boston, then because Jon and Katharine said they would love to see Niagara Falls we hired a bigger vehicle for the long drive. It was a 400-mile trip, but on arrival late in the evening we managed to find accommodation through an information bureau. For only forty dollars we shared a room in the Starfire Motel, that had two double beds and a third rather like a camp bed which they obligingly provided for Matthew. Having only seen black and white pictures in books, I'd imagined the falls to be pretty remote in the middle of nowhere, far away from civilisation. Therefore, next day, I was shocked to see how commercialised it really was. Like some tacky seaside resort back home, there were shops selling cheap-looking souvenirs and garish pennants and flags hanging outside, flapping in the breeze. Large people pushed their way through the large crowds clasping large ice creams or donuts and there was an overriding smell of fried onions. Despite my misgivings, the sheer volume of water going over the gorge was awesome and the noise it made cut out any background distraction from traffic or people. That evening, when the crowds had died down, we found the best view from the purpose-built tower. Laser lights lit up the falls and the forested area on the Canadian border, hiding the hype and razzle-dazzle immediately below us.

John and Katharine went back home after two weeks of intensive sightseeing, impressed by the added experience of meeting American families in their own homes and enjoying their generous hospitality.

Shortly after they left, we had to move once more when Ryan's grandparents returned. I thought of Mam and her address book with all its crossings out as she tried to keep abreast of where I was living. Had she been alive, she'd have loved to come and see us. We moved to Miriam and Dave's, my English friends who'd been very kind to me when I was homesick before Kerry arrived.

They were going to the UK for a month to see family and were pleased that we could house-sit. Chris came again when his term ended at university, then Kate with her current boyfriend and finally Emma, young Tom's sister. She'd been unable to come with the family at Easter because she'd been revising for exams. We did the same day trips to New York and Boston, but the kids were quite happy to explore the different shops in the local malls and to enjoy the hot weather. We had more invitations out from a younger group of parents who were keen to meet the teenagers. We usually sat outside where everyone was bitten by the infernal mosquitoes and the kids, in their element, tucked in to the enormous pizzas.

A bonus that we all enjoyed was the use of a swimming pool in a neighbour's backyard. The temperature was in the high 80s day after day, until one afternoon there was an almighty thunderstorm. I'd experienced thunder and lightning in Singapore but nothing like this. The wind got up and several inches of rain fell in an hour, flooding basements locally. We switched on the twenty-four-hour weather channel, which showed a tornado heading our way. We sat transfixed and scared, wondering what would happen.

EAST TO WEST-THE GRAND TOUR

Had the tornado not changed its course we might not have laughed and joked, as a week later we saw some of the damage and devastation it left behind. On 19 July when the rest of the family had departed, Kerry and I with Matt and Chris set off for our final adventure into the unknown. From Budget rent-a–car in Windsor Locks, we hired a large black Mercury with automatic drive and cruise control to make the long journey from east to west ending in San Francisco. A couple of tea chests had already been despatched to England, as all we needed for the trip was a minimum of lightweight clothing, cameras, binoculars, cash and credit cards and a series of road maps, which were free from the American AA. We had some addresses of possible stay-overs en route, but apart from that we had no plan of action. We'd decided that if we liked the look of the place we'd stop, otherwise we'd push on. From Connecticut we drove through Pennsylvania, Ohio and Indiana, getting into a pattern of stopping each day around four o'clock when the boys would go and check out possible accommodation. As they emerged from each motel that they inspected it was either a thumbs-up or a shaking of the head. The latter happened if the state of the room was not up to scratch or if what looked like undesirable characters were hanging around outside or in reception. Chicago, on the southern tip of Lake Michigan, was a pleasant surprise for us all. My image had been based upon a television series depicting a city of fast cars and wailing police sirens. However, its picturesque location along the lakeside immediately dispelled that illusion. It's a city of culture, with many fine buildings, housing art galleries and theatres. It's reputedly the cradle of jazz that dates back to the 1920s when there was a huge immigration of blacks from the south. We stayed two nights with my penfriend Judy's mum, who was thrilled to see us again. She told us that the name of the city was derived from a French rendering of the Native American word "*shikaakwa*". This translated as wild onion after it was noted in the 1600s that wild garlic grew abundantly in that area.

Kerry had once commented that the average Americans whom we'd met seemed disinterested in the history of their own country prior to the landing of the Pilgrim Fathers. There was almost a denial that the native population ever existed. On the other hand, we were fascinated with the names of places and rivers like Quinnetuk, Potomac, Milwaukee, which all had their roots in the old language of the tribes that inhabited that huge continent.

From Illinois, the interstate turned north to

Wisconsin and into La Crosse situated on the Minnesota side of the state boundary where we had another address to stay. That evening our hosts invited the boys to take charge of the barbecue, which like typical men was right up their street. We chatted and enjoyed a drink; it was a lovely end to the day after another long drive.

Next morning we had the sobering experience of seeing the devastation created by the tornado that had narrowly missed Connecticut the previous week. We were on the outskirts of Chandler looking for a farmhouse when we passed trees that had been stripped of leaves, branches and even bark. The remains stood like tall stickmen stuck in the ground, some with strips of paper caught round them flapping in the breeze. There was a high school with the roof blown completely away, the bricks tossed like matchboxes littering the surrounding countryside. A grain silo with its metal exterior twisted and buckled had also lost its domed roof. We got out of the car to take pictures. It was eerie and silent, no birdsong and no animals, the stillness only broken by the occasional sound of a piece of metal clanging on a broken iron gatepost. We spent that night on a working farm with relations of friends in England. Compared to the people I'd been with for a year, they were old-fashioned and still retained that simple charm and love of their own land, not of possessions from the modern materialistic world. They had a daughter who was born deaf, but instead of dwelling upon their misfortune they counted their blessings. Living in such an isolated community they were thrilled to have visitors and we had to turn down an invitation to stay longer.

Next day we headed into South Dakota on the I-90, which crossed over the Missouri River. Not knowing what to expect we followed signs into Badlands National Park. It was a bleak, inhospitable moonscape of ridges, gullies and weird shapes carved by the action of wind and rain over millions of years. We climbed up the slope to get an overall view, being careful to stay on the sandy path after reading a sign saying "Beware of rattlesnakes".

It was easy to see how it got its name and I didn't envy those early European explorers who must have dreaded getting lost, where, apart from the hidden danger of snakes, there would have been coyote and prairie dogs roaming at night.

THE BLACK HILLS
AND BEYOND

We continued our journey, briefly stopping by the roadside to take pictures of the four presidents, George Washington, Thomas Jefferson, Theodore Roosevelt and Abraham Lincoln, carved into the granite of Mount Rushmore. The driving was easy on the empty roads and soon in the distance we could see the legendary Black Hills, a group of low pine-covered mountains sacred to the Sioux. We followed the route driving through Deadwood, famous for its lawless reputation during the time of the gold rush in the 1800s. We learned that this whole area of the Black Hills was once territory of the Native American Indians who were given a treaty of ownership from the federal government. When the prospectors arrived looking for gold, they took over the land and there were bloody battles that left many dead on both sides, including over 300 women and children from the Indian tribes. The remaining original inhabitants were left homeless and defeated.

After one night in Spearfish, leaving North Dakota behind, we crossed the border into the state of Wyoming, where we stopped in Cody, reputedly the rodeo capital of the world. That evening we went to a show for my birthday treat. As I watched a mounted cowboy roping a calf whilst galloping and chasing it around the arena, I had to admire his horsemanship. He had the skill and ability to twist and turn on a sixpence, all the time whirling a lasso around his head ready for the chance to hurl it around the young beast's neck.

Yellowstone, established in 1872 as the world's first national park, was our next destination. Although we'd all heard of it through the famous cartoon character Yogi Bear, we really had no idea how big it was and what a memorable place it would prove to be. We'd hoped to lodge within the park but were greeted with no vacancies at all the motels, so had to exit into Idaho on the other side where we stopped at the nearest place called Mack's Inn. We stayed for two nights in a small but basic cabin that contained the essentials for cooking, sleeping and washing. The park extends over an area of nearly 3,500 miles, home to vast herds of bison as well as the numerous species of deer, including elk and moose, and wolves and grizzly bears. Visitors are warned not to feed animals from the car or even open the windows. Yellow posters depicting a charging bison warn people that to approach these massive humpbacked, hairy animals is extremely dangerous.

However, we watched in disbelief as folk with cameras in hand left their cars by the roadside and tramped over the grassy plain towards a herd that was grazing. Had they not read the signs stating that a bison could sprint at thirty mph and can weigh more than 2000 lbs, or were they just plain stupid?

We sat with hundreds of other visitors waiting to see the geyser Old Faithful, so named because of the frequency of its eruption every seventy-five minutes. It is capable of expelling up to eight and a half gallons of boiling water, sometimes as high as eighty feet. We could smell the sulphurous fumes emitting from the pools of bubbling mud long before we reached the boardwalks.

We left the park after two days, this time via the northern exit into Montana following the course of the Yellowstone River that flows through the scenic paradise valley. Cattle grazed in meadows of lush grass and their sheltered location stood out in sharp contrast to the harsh climatic nature of the place we'd just left. Wild flowers grew along the verges and at last we could turn off the air conditioning. It was bliss to open the window, letting the warm Chinook wind blow on my face and through my hair. Livingstone, our next overnight stop, was a hub of activity teeming with campers; some laden with bulging backpacks, in full camouflage gear with a hunters' rifle tucked under an arm, walking amongst fishermen carrying long rods, landing nets and buckets. It was the busiest place we'd been in since we left Chicago. Following the I-90 again we briefly crossed northern Idaho, spending one night in Spokane almost on the Washington state border. Our goal the next day was Seattle. In American history, it's a city that was settled comparatively late because of its remote location in the far west adjacent to the Pacific Ocean. Having just crossed the continent ourselves in the twentieth century with every modern convenience, we talked about the first pioneers who'd braved it unseen one hundred years previously. No maps, supplies limited to what they could carry on foot or horseback, no proper roads, and no idea that the terrain they were about to cross would be so full of hidden dangers. Seattle grew rapidly as the forested wilderness areas attracted lumberjacks, trappers and traders and the city prospered. We saw a clean, vibrant place buzzing with visitors, a fish market crammed with shoppers, busy restaurants famous for their seafood, and wide streets backed by modern high-rise buildings. In the evening we took a boat ride round the harbour, dining on board away from the hubbub of traffic. In the darkness, the city resembled a fairyland of twinkling lights under a black starlit sky. It was a magic end to the day.

VIEWS AND VOLCANOES

After leaving Seattle we headed south and that evening were once more installed in another cabin, this one more upmarket with magnificent views of Mount Rainier, a towering ice-clad volcano. Although it's currently dormant, it's not considered extinct and could one day blow its top. Our little blue-painted shack was the end one in a line of half a dozen, situated in a clearing of the forest. Each cabin was decorated with a hanging basket, a cascade of colour and smells, and a long trough crammed full of summer flowers. We explored the winding stony tracks that led into the forest, discovering clumps of pretty alpines alive with the buzzing insects and bees. As we sat outside enjoying the peace and quiet watching the sun go down, a hummingbird alighted on the basket fixed to our cabin. Not one of us had ever seen one and we sat transfixed not daring to breathe as it hovered, its long, thin beak seeking nectar in the flowers.

'Look at the contrast in size,' whispered Chris, referring to the tiny bird and pointing at distant Mount Rainier. 'This whole country is so full of superlatives. Biggest, highest, smallest, longest, widest; where does it end?'

We loved the location we were in, so decided to stay another night before going the short distance next day to see Mount St Helen. Another of Washington's snow-capped crown jewels until 1980 when puffs of steam appeared in March, signalling the end of the mountain's 120 years' sleep. The surrounding hills, formerly a beauty spot for nature lovers, hikers, campers and photographers, as well as loggers whose livelihoods depended on its trees, became a wasteland. An area of over 200 square miles was devastated two months after the initial puff of steam appeared. In May, a cataclysmic explosion took place following an earthquake. It created a mile-wide avalanche of molten lava, boiling water mud and rock. Although fifty-seven people perished, a photographer camping only eleven miles away survived. He was there to take pictures of the sunrise over the mountain and his series of photos taken at one-minute intervals, recorded before, after and during the whole event, provided the geologists and seismologists with vital firsthand information.

Twelve years later we were standing on the outermost fringe on dusty, stony ground, the nearest point permitted for visitors, looking over the dry, barren landscape beyond. Behind the few stick-like remains of trees immediately in front of us stretched mile after mile of empty hillside, broken only by small patches of green where the spring of new life was unfolding. No birds, no insects, no noise. Suddenly a tiny red chipmunk appeared close by, bringing hope that nature was beginning to fight back.

Next day we were in Seaside, Oregon, the largest and

oldest resort in the state and home to Marie's parents, a colleague of mine at school. We'd been travelling for more than a fortnight and when Kerry declared we were in need of R 'n R (rest and recuperation), we all agreed. Located right on the Pacific coast we spent three lazy days exploring and messing about on the fantastic beach, which stretched for miles in both directions. The weather was hot, not humid, tempered by a pleasant breeze from the water and unlike the east coast states there were no mosquitoes. Matt, who wore only his trunks and dark glasses with a makeshift head-covering making him look like Lawrence of Arabia, tanned quickly like my sister, and was soon a mahogany brown. On the other hand, Chris with his fair skin wore shorts but always kept on a thin T-shirt. It was a mystery to the whole family how Kerry with his red hair could expose his body to the sun without burning. He turned a golden tan with just a sprinkling of freckles.

Marie's parents were expecting us so we spent the final day with the whole family, eating, drinking and enjoying the typical American hospitality that we'd become used to.

We would have loved to stay longer in Oregon but had to push on as it was getting near to the time when we were due to drop off the car prior to flying home.

'Ca –li-fornia here we come, dah de dum de dum dum dum,' we sang, and then stopped abruptly because nobody could remember the words. We were on Route 101, the famous highway that runs all the way from the Canadian border to Mexico along the Pacific coast.

'Oh my, just look, you guys, at that ocean,' said Matt putting on an absurd American accent.

'It sure looks to be the biggest in the world,' added Chris. We all laughed. Everyone was in high spirits as this was the final leg of the journey. We'd been on the road for over three weeks, eating out every day for breakfast, lunch and dinner. We were looking forward to staying in a decent hotel for the last three nights, because apart from two homestays we'd slept in more than twenty different travel lodges. I started to record the end of our journey as Kerry drove slowly towards the Golden Gate, the bridge that spans the deep channel between San Francisco Bay and the Pacific Ocean. With my elbow resting on the window frame, I held the camera steady. Almost on cue, a great white cloud of mist enveloped us and we could see nothing.

'Damn, damn, damn. Never mind, eh? That's it boys, welcome to San Francisco.'

We booked into the Doubleday Hotel on Airport Boulevard, having dropped off the car. The bill for twenty-one days only came to $1,300, which when converted to sterling was about £720. It was the first time the two lads had ever stayed in a hotel and they revelled in the basic home comforts of a massive white bath towel and free shower gel. As Kerry and I relaxed on the supersized king bed, the boys lay sprawled each on their own double divan. Matt was scanning the hotel literature.

'What to do in the event of an earthquake,' he read aloud.

'Shut up, Jonah,' said Chris and chucked a pillow at him. He was reading the menu.

'Can we have a pizza brought to our room?' So we did.

Over the next couple of days we saw the sights, took a trolley car to Chinatown, ate large quantities of freshly caught seafood in an expensive restaurant on Fisherman's Wharf and enjoyed talking to complete strangers. Kerry and I were looking forward to going home but we were glad that the boys had been with us to share the amazing trip. Together we'd been through one of the most hostile environments on earth and witnessed first-hand the aftermath of a tornado and a volcanic eruption. We'd laughed a lot, eaten a lot, and learned a lot from the friendly folk we'd bumped into, who'd regaled us with true stories and legends not written down in any books.

POST AMERICA

Ben the little Jack Russell wasn't the only one to have put on weight. He'd been spoiled whilst living with Ann for the year but what was my excuse? Too many pizzas, too many glasses of wine with crisps and dips, and too much party food? When I saw myself for the first time on the films we'd recorded, I was horrified. At the party in the park I looked gross with a great moon face, flabby, plump upper arms and a big, fat derrière. My family and friends had been too polite to comment, but I resolved to get back to normal as soon as I could. Once in the old routine of school, dog walking, looking after two horses and riding (with the occasional burst of housework), I lost the excess pounds in two or three months. Kerry, who never ever put on weight and could eat what he liked, loved being home. He enjoyed the things he'd missed like sausages, black pudding, fresh bread and real English cheeses. Baking became a pleasure again, using a cooker I could rely on, so I made crab-apple jelly, jams, tarts and pies with hand-picked blackberries and apples. I took my class to visit the farm after harvest and they saw the grain piled high drying in the barn and the children picked up the corn seeds that littered the yard.

In the classroom next day I made bread with twenty-seven five-year-olds and one adult helper. It was a riot. They helped to weigh and mix the flour with yeast and warm water.

"Phoor, that smells like my dad's beer," someone said as they sat writing and drawing, waiting for the mixture to rise. Everyone was given a dollop to squeeze, stretch, knead and roll. The soft dough stuck to their little warm hands and fingers and sometimes lumps that were dropped on the floor were hastily retrieved by the adults and dusted down with flour; the end result being two trays of buns of different sizes and funny shapes, which when cooked smelled so delicious the children couldn't wait for them to cool.

Christmas time with concerts, carols and decorated rooms was sheer joy for me despite the increasing noise and excitement of things to come. I'd missed the anticipation and the build-up to concerts and parties that young children enjoy. With my class we actually sang 'The Twelve Days of Christmas' live on Radio Leicester, accompanied by me on guitar. I could only play three or four chords and those not always in the right order, but the children loved it and their singing drowned out my mistakes.

Although Kerry had managed to cope in temperatures way below freezing in New England, it was a dry cold compared to the damp English winters we get. After the first couple of years back home he again had flu and chest problems, and I was forever ringing the doctor who suggested that a spell in the sun might help. We tried it initially for a month when he went to Spain with Saga. He bloomed so it became an annual event extending to three months, usually from New Year until the end of March. I was happy in my job and without my wages we couldn't have afforded it. There was an added bonus of the school holidays when I was able to join him at half-term in February, which always coincided with his birthday.

I wrote to him weekly, filling the letters with news about the boys and Kate and the dogs. By then we'd acquired a Dalmatian called Toby, free to good home. The reason for that soon became clear. He'd come from a house with a toddler and was used to picking up food from the floor or the high chair, so the pattern was set. I grew wise to him stealing from counter tops, especially after he consumed a dozen Scotch eggs that had taken me a whole afternoon to make. The labour of love involved 1) hard-boiling the eggs and shelling them 2) rolling out the sticky sausage meat to wrap around each one, which despite all the flour in the world persists on clinging to your fingers 3) dipping them all in slimy yellow beaten egg yolk before rolling individually in a vivid orange breadcrumb coating and 4) finally deep-frying in the chip pan. They looked quite professional, so I'd left them to cool pushed well away in the corner of the worktop and gone to sit down with a hard-earned cup of tea. When I went back half an hour later to put them in the fridge, the plate was empty. I could have cried.

Our first grandson, Oliver, was born when Kate and I were in Greece visiting Matt. On my return, Kerry and I drove to Durham where Jon and Katharine were living.

It was hard to believe that Jon, that little lad who'd spent his first two years as a baby in Singapore, was now a proud dad and at last we'd become Grandma and Granddad.

Kerry went to Spain the following month and stayed until April. Earlier that year I'd begun a correspondence writing course and during the dark evenings alone I worked on the tasks that were sent. When it was time to have a go at producing something for a woman's magazine, I had an idea for a tongue-in-cheek account based on the five months' separation calling it *My Diary*.

MY DIARY

Drove Kerry to Birmingham Airport. He's off to southern Spain for the winter. Shall miss him but he benefits enormously from the dry climate.

22 November

Colleagues at work jealous of my newfound freedom. Although everyone like me is happily married, we often feel the need to have our own time and space. Much joking and laughing about my plans for the forthcoming three months. Toy boy mentioned. Ha, ha, not likely.

3 December

Great start. Had a marvellous weekend away with my friend June. All day shopping in York followed by a night in Harrogate. Spent Sunday at Knaresborough Edwardian Christmas Market. Tipped it down with rain and got soaked but we didn't care, too busy drinking hot toddy and eating mince pies.

Realised this evening I will have to wrap all the Christmas presents as well as write the cards. I hate wrapping, can't do it, keep losing scissors and Sellotape. Will tell Kerry I'm missing him.

Saw a rat in the stable while mucking out this morning. It's cold and dark down there at 6 a.m. Have to stick to routine of doing dogs and horses before I go to work. Toby the Dalmatian is still prone to chewing. I dread coming home after school to find another chewed chair leg or half the kitchen destroyed. He found the feather duster and all that remained was a single orange feather on a stick.

Flew to Spain to be with Kerry for Christmas and the New Year, had a lovely time.

Woke up to first snow of winter. Why does Britain grind to a halt? I was stuck in a traffic jam on the bypass for two hours. Tried vainly to tune into Radio Leicester. Pushed buttons and twiddled knobs for twenty minutes. Modern car radios are so complicated; bet Kerry could have done it in two minutes. Had a marvellous idea. Ring school on my new mobile phone, never used it before, found battery was flat. Decided enough was enough, so turned round at the next roundabout and went back home.

15 January

Third light bulb blew in as many days. Missing Kerry. Will write a long, chatty letter.

20 January

Heard noises in the roof last night. Too heavy for rats or mice. Think squirrels have moved in with the colder weather. Can't say I blame them.

26 January

Have had to change bedrooms. The racket in the roof is waking me up. Sounds like the squirrels are having a party or moving house. Early mornings and disturbed nights are taking their toll on me. I wonder if squirrels chew wires?

4 February

Phoned the environmental health department yesterday. A man came and looked in the roof; he showed me the squirrel droppings.

No evidence of rats up there, though I did see a HUGE one on the patio this week. He put a squirrel trap in the roof and some rat poison down in the garden where the dogs can't get at it. Am expecting two French teachers for a week and looking forward to some company. The winter evenings seem long and lonely. Wrote a chatty letter to Kerry full of horror stories about vermin.

10 February

Number plate fell off the car today, discovered it was just stuck on. Pathetic. At least I heard the clatter when it dropped.

20 February

Can't believe my bad luck. This morning when I opened the curtains on the landing, half the track fell on my head.

Shall have to tell the French ladies it's an English custom to have one curtain. My DIY skills are about as good as my present wrapping.

22 February

Cleaning house for visitors, guess what? The hoover was blocked; my good neighbour found it was full of hay.

7 March

Unusually foggy this week. Kate and I had a nasty scare in the field this morning. We thought we saw a figure standing motionless in the dark. Then Toby growled and his hackles went up. Too terrified to speak, Kate grabbed my hand and we ran. By the time we scrambled over the last stile we were laughing and wondered whether it really was someone.

8 March

Too scared to go same route this morning. Went in opposite direction towards farm. We took a big stick, a mallet and a can of hairspray just in case. Really missing Kerry.

20 March

Ben, our 13-year-old Jack Russell, is beginning to show his age. I think he is incontinent. Slipped on a pool of wee in the kitchen in my bare feet this morning, sat down really hard and hurt my wrist. Toby brought home a joint of cooked pork yesterday, daren't ask neighbours if they lost their Sunday dinner. Kate suggested giving him a Sainsbury's bag and asking him to fetch a chicken next time.

28 March

More snow and ice. Outside tap was frozen, had to lug buckets of water from the kitchen down to the horses. Surely spring and the light nights can't be far away.

3 April

Little Ben died on the early morning walk in the field. Kate was gutted and I was so upset I couldn't go in to school. We buried him later at the bottom of the garden. I decided that I'd had enough and would go to join Kerry as soon as we broke up from school.

I had no problem getting a flight and knew the kids would look after the dogs and horses for a week.

I never did send off my writing assignment and I gave up the correspondence course because of lack of time. Maybe when I retired things wouldn't be so hectic.

LESSONS IN LATVIA

For me it began with an advert in the church magazine. Volunteers wanted for a summer camp in Latvia to teach English to Christian students. I'd read it with interest and wondered whether Matt who was home for the summer would fancy the change. When I showed him the piece he gave it a cursory look, 'Hmm,' he said and went back to the book he was reading. However, the name Latvia held a peculiar fascination for me, probably because I'd never heard of the place and had no idea where it was. Out came the *Reader's Digest World Atlas* and I found Latvia's position on the Baltic Sea, between Estonia and Lithuania. The more I thought about it, the more I wanted to know. I began asking questions and found out it had only recently become independent, then a friend introduced me to someone who'd actually been. Although she'd enjoyed it, she made no secret of the drawbacks and the deprivation that existed in rural areas.

'Go for it,' said Kerry, 'you know you want to.' So I sent off an application. I heard two weeks later that my references had been taken up and expected an interview. However, when I had the letter with more details, complete with a list of volunteers, I was astonished to see my name already included. A couple of weeks later I drove up to Mexborough in Yorkshire to meet "the team". I wanted to know more about the facilities and the kind of accommodation we could expect. We were told that the camp was normally based in a school but that year it was probably in an art college in Bauska. Another place for me to look up in the atlas. There were half a dozen of us at the meeting and I thought I could relate to two of them, both men. There was something about the only female present that made me think twice and I wondered whether it was really wise to pay for my ticket there and then.

Back home that evening, I had misgivings. Deep down I was keen to go but I had reservations about the team and my own compatibility. The following day I rang the organiser and expressed my doubts. He seemed genuinely surprised and assured me that my teaching skills and experience and my apparent talent for spontaneous entertainment would be an asset. I had no doubts about the former but wondered what he meant by the latter. Would my wacky sense of humour and my idea of fun be acceptable to what had appeared to me was a group of serious-minded people?

I accepted the challenge and resigned myself to three weeks with no hot water for washing and no material comforts. Armed with a list of essentials I visited Boots the chemist, filled a basket and emptied my purse. There were tablets for water purification, antihistamine cream for bites, insect repellent, baby wipes, toilet paper, paracetamol, Savlon, plasters, Diocalm, but what else was on the list? Earplugs and candles? What did that mean? Were we going to be without electricity too, and what kind of noise necessitated the use of earplugs? Syringes were also recommended should we need to visit a doctor, so I managed to beg a few from a friend who was a district nurse. Along with T-shirts, shorts and trousers, I packed a travelling kettle and the continental adaptor. I hoped there would be somewhere to plug it in. Having been informed by someone that the food to expect would be cabbage cooked in twenty different ways, I also took numerous packs of biscuits along with tea bags, instant milk, coffee and boxes of cuppa soups. My suitcase was heavy and my hand luggage cumbersome, filled with books, pencils, paper, rubbers, felt pens and little gifts for students.

Gatwick was bustling with long queues of people jostling each other, babies crying and small children running around unsupervised. I suspected they were all bound for the sunshine, two weeks' all-inclusive in Lanzarote, Spain or Florida. There were nine of us in our group and I felt rather smug as we walked straight up to the empty desk of Baltic International. *This'll be no holiday,* I thought; *it's an adventure*. Anyway, what's three weeks in a lifetime? I was soon to find out.

ROOM 407

The art college in Bauska turned out to be a former agricultural college in Mezotne, a remote village of half a dozen houses and a few surrounding small farms. From the airport at Riga, we boarded a local bus and were driven through lush green countryside along an almost deserted main road. When we turned onto a minor road, we soon noticed a difference. We became enveloped in a cloud of dust that obscured anyone or anything passing by. Then the bus began to weave about from side to side and we thought the driver was losing control until we realised he was avoiding the huge potholes. It didn't really matter which side he was on because there was no other traffic. The small wooden homesteads we passed looked old and in serious need of repair. Broken panes of glass were clearly visible and, through wide open doors, the interiors looked dark and dingy. After losing our way we finally turned onto an even narrower dirt track before the bus stopped in front of a massive concrete block of flats. My heart sank. It looked grey, cold and foreboding even in the afternoon sun. It reminded me of pictures I'd seen in post-war films of Russian or German headquarters where people were sent to be interrogated.

Dragging our cases over the stony track, we followed our host up three steps into the building. We entered into a gloomy-looking entrance hall where in a corner was placed a beautiful vase of flowers. A lady directed us to the end of a long corridor where we stood while she unlocked room 407. Five of us who were to share this room filed in until the ones at the front stopped short, causing us behind to bump into each other. We edged forward to see what was wrong. At first no one spoke, until a voice piped up, 'At least we're not sleeping on the floor like last time.' The speaker had obviously been before. I looked in dismay at the low, iron-sprung beds and the dirty, stained mattresses. On each one, there was a coloured blanket and a filthy-looking pillow. Meanwhile, Dorothy had opened the door of the "en suite".

'You ain't seen nothing yet,' she joked, pointing to a handbasin resting at an angle. It was supposed to be attached to the wall but there was only one hinge. The result of this was that water tended to run left and collect, leaving a dark stain where it refused to drain. The toilet looked even worse. There was no seat and no top on the low-level cistern where a ballcock floated in the rusty water. The lavatory pan was likewise stained brown and a foul smell like fields after muck spreading filled the cramped space. Dorothy, bless her, a former nurse and ever practical, rummaged through her belongings to find j-cloths and a bottle of Savlon.

She made a plastic apron from a supermarket bag and, wearing rubber gloves, set to work. The rest of us looked around the bedroom with a growing sense of dread. Beside each bed was a small locker decorated with stickers of pop stars. Against one wall was a built-in cupboard with no door handles. The walls were papered in a faded, dull brown and green leaf pattern and from the ceiling hung a dirty glass chandelier. A small metal-legged table stood under the big sash window that was bedecked by tatty yellow curtains and a piece of dirty grey net. We covered the available surface with water bottles, purifying tablets, water filter, coffee, tea and mugs. By then Dorothy had finished her chores and though the toilet facilities still looked and smelt uninviting, we knew that in the circumstances they were clean and hopefully germ-free. We'd been told to take soft toilet tissue and one wise person had even taken nappy bags knowing that in rural Latvia the sewage system cannot cope with paper. Our temporary dining room that day was an empty bedroom down the corridor. No inhabitants, but full of furniture and paraphernalia crammed into cardboard boxes. We all squeezed into chairs and, sandwiched between the table and beds, looked forward to our first meal since leaving England. It consisted of tinned sardines and sprats, fresh tomatoes, pickled gherkins, coleslaw from a jar, cold carrots and peas straight from another jar, and thick slices of rich brown rye bread spread liberally with peanut butter. We were all so hungry we tucked in.

Whilst waiting for the students to arrive that afternoon, we decided to explore the area. There were no proper roads in the immediate vicinity, only dirt tracks, and when a vehicle did pass we almost choked on the cloud of dust that was thrown up. Tethered cows and storks grazed side by side in the lush grassy pastures that were unfenced and without hedges. An elderly-looking lady appeared wearing a headscarf and wellingtons. In one hand she carried an old-fashioned tin bucket and in the other a small stool. When she sat down beside one of the cows and began to milk it, I would have loved to have taken a photo. Instead we waved and smiled as she turned her head to look at us.

She shouted something back in Latvian but whether it was a greeting or not we had no idea.

That evening we met our students for the first time when we ate together. They were aged between eleven and twenty-three, boys and girls from all over the country. They'd arrived by bus and car and we later discovered that two girls had even completed their journey by combine harvester. They viewed us with curiosity as they drifted in to the school canteen to sit down at long wooden tables. I enjoyed the pork fritter with potatoes and coleslaw and really liked the warm pink fruit drink with its thick chunks of apple and plum in the bottom of the glass. As each little group finished eating, they stood up and chorused, "*Pal Dias*" before they left.

Back in our room, not wanting to be eaten alive by mosquitoes, we closed the window before switching on the light. The tatty curtains didn't quite meet in the middle so we used a bath towel to cover the gap. We drew lots to see who would wash first and while the lucky person went off to dabble in the cold water we tried to arrange our beds. The mattresses were dirty, old and lumpy, sagging in the middle but at least we all had our own clean sleeping bag. Nobody wanted to use the pillows and we made do by folding clothes and wrapping a bath towel round them. That night we discovered that we all snored, although some of us hotly denied it. The next morning Paul, who was sharing the adjoining room with Brian, came into us scratching his arms like mad and complaining. He showed us angry red marks all over his body. On examination by our team of experts we decided they were probably flea bites. Unfortunately flea powder hadn't been on the list of essentials but we reckoned that the insect repellent might be as effective, so we all sprayed our mattresses and removed the sleeping bags and other stuff to store in a suitcase during the day.

We met the students in the education block at ten o'clock and they took a short question and answer type test in order for us to group them according to their ability in English. I was to take the beginners, the biggest group, fifteen in all, while the other three groups varied between four and seven students. Because of the significant difference in numbers, I was assigned two helpers; Dorothy and Brian, who had had no teaching experience but were more than happy to help in a practical way. Most of the work I did was role play and conversation and instead of sitting formally at desks, we always sat in a circle. There was fun and laughter from our classroom, which apparently could be heard by the other classes along the corridor. Often we were questioned about what was going on and I guessed that a few girls and boys were somewhat envious by the free and easy approach to learning. One student actually asked to be moved down a class to join us.

I'm never at my best first thing in the morning until I've had a cup of tea and been left to come round. However, on that first day of school, we were rudely awakened at 6.30 a.m. by the sound of a tuba playing at full blast. The noise came from two loudspeakers on our corridor and because there were students on the second and third floors, it had to be loud to be effective. By the end of the first week we managed to wake before the reveille and even had a cup of tea in bed. The first person to get up filled the kettle with purified water and with great care plugged it in. The two-pin socket in the wall, like the handbasin, was very loose and the slightest wiggle once you'd plugged in the kettle created an alarming blue flash. It was a bit like the instructions on a firework, light the blue touchpaper and stand well back.

My relationship with Dorothy blossomed that week, although she'd been the reason initially why I'd nearly backed out of the trip. She had a soft Irish accent and a lovely sense of humour. One evening the two of us went out with Paul to a small bar he'd found close by. There were probably nine or ten unshaven old blokes in the tiny room, obviously regulars, who turned, grunted at us and carried on with their game of dominoes. However, a good-looking, single, younger chap with the bluest eyes I've ever seen on a man smiled and asked to join us to practise his English. Dorothy was smitten and turned on the Irish charm. We didn't leave until 11 p.m. by which time Paul had had a bit too much to drink or maybe it was the unaccustomed mixture he'd knocked back. We held him, one each side, and steered him back to our room trying in vain not to laugh or make a noise that would wake the others.

One evening, we decided to ask for permission to take our two classes into town as a change from the classroom. At first there was opposition, but we made a point of all the advantages the students would gain from the exercise and our request was granted.

DAY TRIP TO BAUSKA

The students stood chatting in groups as we waited at seven in the morning for the first bus of the day. Because we were staying in such a remote area there were only three buses anyway, the early one, the next at midday and the last at six in the evening. Fortunately we were at the terminus, perhaps not so lucky for people who would get on later en route. Four adults with me, Dorothy, Paul and Brian, plus twenty-one youngsters, laughing and joking, climbed aboard. Initially we were all seated, but as the bus stopped frequently along the dusty road to pick up more passengers it was noticeable that our youngest members gave up their seats. It was a bit of old-fashioned courtesy that seemed to be absent back home. The folk who got on looked surprised to see it so packed but they smiled and nodded at us. They were mostly older ladies, each wearing a headscarf and clutching a wicker shopping basket. Their drab clothes contrasted sharply with the bright T-shirts, pretty blouses, shorts or miniskirts that our students were wearing. A small bunch of flowers placed in a jam jar was somehow balanced on the shelf by the driver, a lovely touch in the old bus. The wooden slatted seats were hard and unforgiving as the tyres bumped and jumped on the unmade roads. We'd set off so early many students had missed breakfast, so when we arrived in Bauska we found somewhere for them to sit and they tucked into rye bread sandwiches of cheese or peanut butter. Before we went off to find the ruins of a castle we'd heard about, we needed to find a bank to change some traveller's cheques. It was hard to believe that although we'd been in Latvia for five days, we'd still managed on less than eight pounds per person. Travellers were only allowed to take a small amount of local currency into the country.

The bank in Bauska was a clean, modern building so in we trooped taking a student with us who spoke enough English to translate our needs. I noticed that the girls working on computers nearby each had a small vase of flowers on the desk and for a short while amid the modern technology of telephones and fax machines I felt we were back in England. Suddenly, Dorothy said, 'I bet they have decent toilets in here, I'm going to ask the manager.' Without hesitation, she walked through the open door straight into his office.

'Do you speak English?' she asked, switching on her usual Irish charm.

'Yes, a little,' he beamed at her and I squirmed. Was he expecting a rich investor about to deposit a few thousand lats? I could hardly believe her nerve.

'May we use the toilets, please?' Looking a little taken aback he rose and took a key out of his pocket, beckoned and we followed. The toilets were clean and smelled fresh despite the ever present rusty water.

After several students had also availed themselves of the facilities, we were about to leave when someone noticed that Brian was missing. We looked around, then heard a faint tapping coming from the toilets.

'Oh blimey, he's shut in,' Paul said. The door must have automatically locked when the last person came out. We couldn't help laughing despite the fact that people were staring at us and shaking their heads.

'Climb through the window!' Paul shouted. Meanwhile, our interpreter girl had summed up the situation and gone to find help. A smart, young office worker appeared waving a key. She unlocked the door and stepped inside. It was empty. An open window swayed in the wind. We made our apologies and still laughing beat a hasty retreat. It set the mood for the day as we headed for the castle. From the noticeboard outside the entrance we could see scaffolding and men at work. It was plain that restorations were in hand and that we were the only visitors. We explored the ruins, climbing up and down endless stone steps and peering through windows and holes. From the very top, where a red and white Latvian flag fluttered in the summer breeze, we could see over the surrounding countryside. There was just a bridge going over the river where a couple of youths were having fun splashing and shouting upstream, a few small buildings, then miles and miles of lush green vegetation and woods as far as the eye could see.

The sun was hot and by the time we'd been there half an hour we were all ready for a drink and a sit down. We found a cafe called Kafenica Lana just up the road, so we all brushed through the bead curtain from the sunlight into the relative coolness of a tiny room. The young girl behind the counter gaped at the sudden invasion as we crowded round and ordered four cups of coffee. She was only able to provide two initially because of the lack of boiling water so the men waited while the heater was refilled.

Most of the students were happy with a can of fizzy drink. They also bought small bags of sweets and soft bars of confectionery that looked like nougat with free stickers of pop stars enclosed in the wrapper. As there were only three tables and customers were arriving for a snack lunch of savoury pancakes, we told our crowd to wait outside.

As the primary object of the day was to practise English, we looked for some shops where we could ask the students questions in a real-life situation as opposed to role play. We found a small department store but as soon as I walked in I felt as though I was stepping back in time. Right back to when I was ten and was in the shoe department of Grimsby Co-op with Mam looking for new sandals at Easter. There were only two floors. On the ground floor, long shelves stretched the whole length of the room. At right angles to these stood several glass-topped cabinets in which goods were displayed – to look at but not handle. There were no boxes of soft toys, no rows of pens, pencils or crayons to choose from. Four or five assistants were standing behind the counters, where we could see further items on display. It was quite disconcerting to have to ask and point each time I wanted to look at something and I felt guilty when

I handed it back and shook my head. We take browsing and handling for granted and it's half the pleasure of shopping when you're able to change your mind. A little boy in a check shirt and wearing red shorts was standing gazing at a big plastic tipper truck next to a sign saying "*Preces Bernie*" which meant "children's things". We all moved to the far end where ladies' and children's dresses, skirts and jumpers hung together in no apparent order. The upper floor, reached by a flight of concrete stairs, seemed to be half empty. There were fewer displays and only a couple of assistants. There seemed to be only general haberdashery including buttons, cotton, needles and wool. I felt uneasy as I stood and fingered some key rings desperately searching for something to buy as a souvenir. I was aware that I was being watched and wanted to get out. The students were pacing the aisles already looking bored, so we made our exit.

Once outside when I explained what we were looking for, two of our lads showed us the way to a small museum. From outside it looked like a deserted warehouse with huge wooden doors below a crumbling façade. However, a sign written in both languages said, "Exhibition of Folk Applied Art" and the door was ajar. We climbed the stairs that led into a long, low-ceilinged room where swathes of cotton and woollen cloth in beautiful colours and patterns were tastefully displayed. Two artisans in working smocks stepped forward with a smile.

'Welcome, please feel free to touch the things and ask questions.' There was a table full of handmade clay mugs and ornaments with ethnic designs that reminded me of the Native American art I'd seen with Kerry. I chose a very fine-glazed mug and a little cone made to resemble a bell. A piece of plaited string was threaded through the top, holding a tiny, tiny ball of clay that served as the clapper. It made the sweetest, soft tinkle. We each bought something and a lady wrapped them carefully in newspaper. They would be a lovely memory of an unusual working holiday.

By then it was mid afternoon and after trailing around in the heat, the four adults were beginning to wilt. We found a park where we could sit in the shade with most of the girls, while the lads kicked a ball around. Some local children, boys about nine or ten years old, joined in with the big lads and our boys made sure that the younger ones got a fair share of the ball. As we got ready to go to the bus stop, just a five-minute walk, I noticed that the little lads were looking at our carrier bags that still held a few sandwiches.

'Would you like them?' I asked, gesturing and pointing. They looked puzzled. One of our girls laughed, then asked them in Latvian. Their response was immediate and they pounced on them like hungry little wolf cubs. We gave them what drink was left and the thing that pleased me most was when our boys gave them the football. We left them waving to us, their mouths stuffed with bread and with very happy faces.

THE WIZARD OF OZ

There were eight of us sitting in room 407 on beds, chairs and the floor.

Everyone was racking their brains. We'd been asked to give an evening of entertainment but the request had not been well received and not one idea had yet been forthcoming.

'How about the *Wizard of Oz*,' I suggested. I was answered by blank looks.

'Listen; there are just enough of us to take part with me as narrator; if I write it, will you all be in it?'

There was a silence before Dorothy broke it with, 'Can I be Dorothy then?'

'I'll be the Scarecrow,' added Trish, quick as a flash.

'All right, I'll be the Tin Man,' said Paul.

Allison agreed to be the fairy, Vic the Lion, Brian the Wizard and Heather, Toto the dog.

'I can make plaits out of black dustbin liners,' Dorothy said, 'and big pink bows with j-cloths.'

'I'll use those net curtains for the fairy', said Allison, 'and start collecting silver paper from the kids' sweets for a wand. You can borrow my straw hat, Trish, for the Scarecrow.'

'Thanks,' she said. 'I won't need to dress up, just collect a load of straw to shove down my clothes the next time we go out.' Everyone laughed; I could tell they were warming to the idea.

'But how the heck will I dress the Tin Man?' Paul asked.

'Hah, no problem, have you ever been in the kitchen?' I said. 'There are pans with lids in various sizes ranging from hat size to dustbin size. Even if you can somehow strap just a couple of lids to your arms or legs it will create the illusion.'

For the next two days, I spent every spare moment working on the script. The vocabulary had to be basic enough for the students to listen to with an easy storyline that they would understand.

We went through the finished piece together and made a list of unfamiliar vocabulary. During the next lesson we spent time explaining the meanings of some words, including scarecrow, tornado and precious, brave, rusty and straw. With Brian and Dorothy helping me out, we kept our class in fits of laughter as we tried to demonstrate some of them through actions or role play.

On the evening of the performance, the cast waited anxiously. I knew they were terrified of forgetting the words and tried to reassure them, saying that it didn't matter, I'd have the script and give them the cue. Even if they ad-libbed, no one would know. To everyone's credit it was a success and after hysterical laughter from the audience every time the tin man moved, the cast began to enjoy it, too. Words were hesitant, some totally forgotten, but the rendering of the songs "Somewhere Over the Rainbow" and "We're Off to See the Wizard" was a choral symphony. Dorothy looked a picture with her black plaits and pink bows sticking out at right angles under her straw hat. Toto's floppy sock ears and plaited string tail dangled on the floor and the fairy looked magnificent in her see-through off-white gown that trailed behind her like a wedding dress. The lion was coy and acted his part well. Someone had found a big yellow shawl with tassels perfect for a mane and Vic had attached two ears of painted cardboard and drawn whiskers on his face with a black pen. After the tin man was given his heart by the wizard, Paul did a jig, making the pan lids held on by string clatter as they swung to and fro. The audience loved it and there were howls of laughter. We took a final bow to loud applause and sang an encore. I don't think anyone ever did notice that the rainbow painted on the backdrop of the scenery was upside down, starting with violet at the top and finishing with red. Whoops!

OFSTED VISIT, 1995

Each time I visited Kerry in Spain, I was impressed with the amount of Spanish that he'd learned. He'd been going to Spanish lessons in the hotel and though it was basic he could manage to order from a menu and even ask for directions when we got lost in the car. He always said that he'd been no good at languages when he was at school and was quite happy for me to use what French or German I knew when we went to Europe on coach trips. The only time he couldn't cope was when we were pulled over by the police on a quiet road. They looked closely all over the hire car, spoke to each other, wrote something down, then in sign language conveyed to us that they needed to see our passports. We handed them over and, after studying them for a good three or four minutes, gave them back and waved us on. We didn't have a clue what it was all about.

I'd been glad of Chris's company in the evenings while Kerry was away because he was able to help me with the computer. I'd bought it to use for my writing course but because I'd never even had basic typing skills, there was so much to learn. Although we'd had a computer in the classroom for some years, I usually left it to the children to help each other. Lots of them by then had a computer in their own home and were growing up with it. It was far harder for teachers of my generation to pick up. I was happy being ahead of my friends as the owner of a mobile phone, albeit the size of a spectacle case and difficult to keep safely tucked in a pocket.

In March that year Chris went to look at a house in Littlethorpe with a view to renting. He said that at his age, twenty-five, it was time to go it alone if he could afford it. I would miss him but knew he was right. After all, Jon had never come back after finishing at Durham, and Matthew had been teaching in Greece since he left university.

The pressure at school started to build when we got the date for our first Ofsted inspection. The new system had only been introduced in 1992 and instead of a single inspector on one day of the year, a whole team of four or five would come in for a week. We'd all heard horror stories from friends who'd gone through the ordeal. We started to have staff meetings every lunchtime and learned that we'd have to produce lesson plans for six weeks in advance of the date. I thought it was potty because, quite frankly, with young children there are often hiccups to any lesson. One of the worst things to happen to me was when a child was violently sick all over his own workbook plus the book of the poor little lad sitting beside him. They'd both burst into tears while the whole of the class, looking on in horror, said, "UGH!"

Although I worked to a weekly plan it was quite likely

to go off at a tangent, usually as a result of a question or remark from a child. A lot of my work was spontaneous but I always got good results. I decided that I was too near to the age of retirement to bother about worrying. Then another bombshell hit us when we were told that we were overstaffed and two teachers would have to leave at the end of the term. Everyone was really fed up, knowing that after working so hard for the inspection two of us would get the push.

To my surprise on the last afternoon before the Ofsted team departed I was called into the head teacher's office to be congratulated by them. They'd been impressed with the overall look of the room, with my methods and by the way my class listened and responded. We'd been doing a topic on large vehicles like buses, lorries, vans and trucks. I'd taken my class to visit the farm where they'd actually touched and talked about the tractors and I'd put photos on the wall showing the comparative size of each child standing in front of a massive back wheel of a tractor.

I couldn't wait to get home and tell Kerry what they'd said. I was bursting with pride.

"I knew you'd be OK," he said. He was always telling me that I should stop doing schoolwork in the evenings. Even so, I could tell by his face that he was as thrilled as I was.

The following evening all the staff went to the pub to celebrate the end of the inspection. I thought there'd be a mention of my achievement and at least a round of applause but not a word was said. I plucked up the courage a week later to ask the head why I hadn't been acknowledged publicly. She replied that she didn't want to upset the rest of the staff. We all had to reapply for our jobs but after one person handed her notice in because of an impending house move, only one teacher was dismissed with redundancy pay. I wish I'd jumped in first, with an offer to resign with a pay-off, because by then I'd made up my mind to only do one more year.

UNITED NATIONS, 1997

While Kerry was in Majorca for three months during the winter, in January that year June offered to go with me to Heathrow to meet a girl from Japan who'd be living with us until the summer. I'd read a leaflet left on the staffroom table that was asking for host homes. The girls involved in the scheme were not students but were all in work and had leave of absence for a lengthy period. They were funding themselves and wanted to experience life with an ordinary English family. They were expected to fit in with the daily routine. Snow was forecast on the evening that we planned to leave so we left Cosby not long after midnight in case there was a hold-up. However, traffic was light and when we arrived about half past three, all the roads into the airport were deserted. After driving through the main tunnel three times, desperately looking for the exit to the long-term car park, I had to flash down a man who was driving a Heathrow car.

'Follow me,' he said and took us for the fourth time back through the tunnel to our destination.

The plane landed on time around 6 a.m. and as the Japanese passengers came trundling through with their baggage, June and I gawped. We were looking for a girl in her twenties with black hair, wheeling a red suitcase. Every fourth or fifth passenger could have been her, because we had no idea that all the Japanese girls have long, straight black hair and that red seemed to be the popular choice in luggage that year. After June, in her enthusiasm, had approached at least three girls who'd looked at her blankly shaking their head, it was Yukari who spotted us. We don't seem to realise in the UK just how much our hair is a part of our identity. It can be short or long, straight, wavy or curly, blonde, ginger or black and varying shades of brown and grey.

Yukari was charming, her English was good and she told us in the car that she'd been saving for a long time to fund her trip. As she was gazing out of the window from the back seat of the car, she was admiring the abundance of trees and the large open spaces. Suddenly, she exclaimed, 'Oh! What is that?' I glanced over to a field on my right.

'They're sheep,' said June. 'Don't you have sheep in Japan?'

'Only in zoos.' We couldn't help laughing.

We got on very well and she enjoyed going to school with me every day. She sat with a small group and told them about Japan and showed them the art of origami. She made them all little birds, which they coloured and took home and a few even tried to make their own.

The children liked her and her English improved as she started to use phrases and colloquialisms, which are not normally learned in a foreign language lesson.

In February I got bronchitis and was away from school for over three weeks. I felt lousy and spent most of the time lying on the settee reading and dozing. Kate and June were very good and looked after Yukari. June took her on a couple of coach trips, one to York, the other to Bath, and when Kate or Chris walked the dogs she loved going with them. She was most surprised that we were allowed to go across fields or even walk round the edges. I explained that those paths had been in use for so many years as a means of getting from one village to another, that they had become part of our national heritage.

I had letters, drawings and cards from all the children in my class saying how much they missed me, and the staff sent a lovely bunch of flowers. It was unusual for me to be away for more than a day. When Ann came down from Ormskirk to stay for a few days it cheered me up and we played Scrabble and talked about John, who was then terminally ill with cancer.

On Saturday, June took Ann and Yukari to the sweater shop factory sale in Leicester and they all came back laden with bargains. I had to laugh at Ann as she opened her bag and tipped the contents out onto the floor. She held up a knitted garment and waved it at me.

'Look at these waistcoats, Maggie, how much do you reckon I paid?'

'I've got no idea, not much knowing you.'

'50p! I'm going to take them to Scrabble club and sell them for £1.50.' She was so like Dad; he'd always been a bit of a dealer that no one seemed to question when he came home with "something a customer had given him in return for a favour".

I had plenty to talk about in my letters to Kerry and he wrote regularly, though reading between the lines I think he was looking forward to coming home at Easter. We'd have lots to talk about, as I'd soon be handing in my notice at the start of the summer term.

He was so thrilled that I was packing it in because it meant I'd be free to go with him at any time of the year. John died during the spring and although it was expected, it was still a shock for me to lose a sibling. All the family went to Marshchapel in Lincolnshire for the funeral.

Chris moved out after Kerry came home and although Yukari was with us, we had two spare bedrooms again. It was a real United Nations when another French lady came for five days in May, followed by more folk from America in June and July. My exchange partner Louise from Connecticut, with her new husband Jason, came for a few days on their honeymoon, so I organised an English afternoon tea. June and Yukari helped to make the sandwiches and I made dozens of small fancy cakes. No pizzas and no donuts. Unbeknown to Louise, I invited as many children and parents as I could from the class that she'd taught. Five years on, they were all twelve or thirteen. They were as thrilled to see her as she was surprised to see them. We were lucky with the weather that afternoon and spent the whole time in the garden. Although in teaching it's hard not to favour certain children, I knew that that particular year group, the same one I'd taught on my return, was one of the best. They were motivated, bright and considerate, with a lovely sense of humour. No wonder Louise had wanted to stay on for a second year. Compared to all the problems I'd had to deal with, her experience had been a walk in the park.

Yukari had a Japanese friend called Kiyoe who'd come with her on the same flight, but who was staying on the other side of Leicester. We'd met her on several occasions and they'd both been out with Kate and Chris in the evenings.

Kiyoe wanted to stay for a further six months in order to enrol into an English language class and to experience a typical Christmas in our country. However, it wasn't convenient for her host family so I said she could come to us.

When the time came for Yukari to leave, she was in tears. She'd enjoyed herself so much especially the food and the English pubs. She'd put on over 5kgs. When I asked her what her favourite meal had been she said, 'Frog in the pond and apple crumble.'

'What did you say?' Kate asked. I couldn't help laughing.

'She means toad-in-the-hole.'

NO MORE SCHOOL

I did retire one year early the following summer, having checked with the authorities that it wouldn't affect my final teacher's pension. I'd intended to work till I was sixty but after the fiasco of the post Ofsted inspection I'd had enough. I was pleased with myself that I'd clocked up over thirty years working full-time, only taking a break of eight years when the children were small. A lot of my friends who'd started when I did had retired much earlier or gone on to part-time. Kerry showed his delight by booking a holiday to South Africa for three weeks. It felt strange to me to be going away in September, almost like I was playing truant, and it came as a big shock when we encountered a totally different culture to what we'd expected.

We were situated in a small resort on the coast not far from Durban and on the first morning after breakfast, everyone gathered for a briefing. We were told that although there were sharks in the vicinity the area was netted so it was safe to swim in the Indian Ocean but only between the set barriers, a distance of about two or three hundred metres.

'Fat chance of you or me going in,' I whispered to Kerry.

Then we were informed that there were no local taxis and it wasn't wise to use public transport whether by train or bus.

'On no account walk along the road out of the nearest village; it's unsafe,' continued the holiday rep.

By then all of us were shuffling in our seats, folk were muttering and probably like us were wondering just what we could do. There were inclusive tours that we did enjoy. We managed to see zebra, impala, a gnu and crocodiles in a wildlife reserve, but best of all was the massive rhino. He crossed over from left to right within two metres of our stationary jeep and even though a ranger was sitting beside us with a rifle I held my breath when the great beast stopped. We'd been told earlier that if one ran at a vehicle it could overturn it in seconds. He turned to look at us before plodding off into the undergrowth and even when he'd disappeared I could still feel my heart thumping. No one had dared move to take a picture.

Officially apartheid, the system of racial segregation, had ended in 1994, but as we travelled by coach through both town and rural areas it was obvious that there was still ill feeling between rich whites and poor blacks. We passed large properties belonging to white landowners. Twelve-foot-high walls topped with razor wire and a sign on the electric gates that read twenty-four hour armed response surrounded them all.

Kerry had spoken to a shopkeeper in the village who told him that he never went anywhere in the car without a mobile phone and a gun.

Six of us from the hotel paid for a private tour to

Durban where we were made to stay together at all times. Nevertheless, we were so impressed with the engaging manner and local knowledge of the young South African couple in charge that we booked another trip.

A few days later, we travelled from Durban with more tourists in a couple of 4 x 4s up the Sani Pass, the only vehicular route over the Drakensberg Mountains into Lesotho. The spectacular single-track stony road twisted and snaked up and up; it seemed to the top of the world. It was a hair-raising experience as I sat next to the driver on the side where the edge of the road dropped abruptly hundreds and hundreds of feet down to the boulders and rocks below. Every time the driver pointed out something of interest, he took one hand off the steering wheel. We could tell by his face that he was doing it deliberately to scare us as he grinned and pretended to swerve. I was never so pleased to get out of any vehicle when we finally reached the top and stumbled into the Sani Mountain Lodge for a reviving drink. Lesotho is a landlocked kingdom made up of highlands. Like Tibet, the Basotho have a unique mountain culture herding goats and sheep. Smoke spiralled into the air from the chimneys of round mud huts nearby. We were privileged to go into one of the dwellings where the woman who was expecting us was preparing a local dish. We sat on multicoloured blankets on the floor while our guide talked and translated questions that were asked. It was difficult to judge the age of the woman as the effects of poverty, combined with the harsh climate, hot by day and frost at night, had taken their toll. Several small children were sitting outside, each wrapped in their own blanket and all wearing brightly coloured wellington boots. We'd taken sweets and biscuits for them and knew that included in the price of our tour was a sum of money intended for the family.

When we got home we both agreed it was an experience rather than a holiday, but overall Kerry had enjoyed the warm climate and taken some wonderful photos of people, places and wildlife.

ACCOMODATION
NOT PROVIDED

There was no lock on the bedroom door, so I pushed my suitcase and a small bedside cabinet against it. All ninety rooms were unoccupied except for mine on the first floor and a flat on the sixth that was home to a young caretaker and his wife.

What was I doing staying in a former convent that was completely isolated in the mountains of Switzerland? You might ask.

"You're mad," they said.

All my friends had warned me but I suspected they were secretly wishing they dared do the same. At the age of sixty I was off again to live and work right by Lake Geneva for a year. Unfortunately, accommodation was not provided. It was only eight years after I'd come back from America. The first year after I retired I'd enjoyed the freedom and the fact that we could go away at short notice but I was soon bored. I knew that I still had some useful working years ahead so had applied for voluntary service overseas. I was interviewed at Eltham Palace and was accepted, but there was a delay in finding me a suitable placement. I'd said I didn't want to go to Africa because I knew from in-depth research and questions that primary education over there wasn't given a top priority. Schools were often poor, lacking in basic equipment and mainly situated in remote village areas. People I spoke to at a workshop, who'd had firsthand experience, told me that electricity could be off for hours, water might need to be drawn from a well and toilets were basic and sometimes shared. Housing at its best would only be one room, for eating, living and sleeping in. On the other hand all secondary schools were generally in towns and had things we take for granted like running water and flush toilets.

Then I was offered a post in Tuvalu, an atoll island miles from anywhere in the South Pacific. My first reaction was excitement at this exotic location and the more I found out, the more it appealed to me. Then my hopes were dashed when I discovered the job would entail visiting the neighbouring small Gilbert and Ellis islands. Transport would be by motorboat, which in rough weather might not be able to get close enough to the shore in which case I'd have to jump into a waiting rowing boat. I knew my limitations so looked for something a bit more suitable and by sheer good luck found one. I was going to work in a bilingual kindergarten and primary school in Switzerland. I sincerely hoped my school French that had long been dormant could be rekindled.

With my balcony door wide open until dusk, the only sounds were cowbells. I could see them in the distance grazing in the lush meadows. They looked like toy farm animals, their size dwarfed by the size of the surrounding snow-capped mountains. I stood and gazed in awe at the natural beauty.

Later that evening, with the doors closed and shutters pulled down, the only noise I could hear was the blood pounding in my head. The sound of complete silence has to be experienced before it can really be understood. I drifted off to sleep thinking about some of my favourite stories that I'd read when I was ten or eleven like, *The Chalet School Girls* and *Heidi*.

Next morning, in order to catch a train, I had to get up so early that it was still dark. I managed to feel my way along the wide, empty corridors, fumbling for the unfamiliar light switches, down to the kitchen on the ground floor. It was eerie; the only noise was coming from my slippers shuffling on the stone floor. No wonder Maria left the convent so soon in the film *The sound of Music*.

Three days later, I did find somewhere to live much nearer to work; it was advertised in the local supermarket. I called it my Swiss Wendy house. But had I gone from the sublime to the ridiculous? It was actually a cattle shed that had been converted for a holiday letting. There was one tiny room on the ground floor and an equally small one above reached by a vertical wooden ladder. The only safe way to descend was backwards. I soon learned to be extremely careful, especially after downing two glasses of wine. The loo and shower room were outside next to an enormous terraced area. That was complete with a rocking chair, a table with candelabra and bedecked with fairy lights. Every evening I sat outside with my French bread and a glass of red wine, admiring the changing autumn colours on the trees that covered the slopes of the opposite mountainside. Eventually, when it got dark, the mosquitoes drove me in and I reluctantly retreated to the small table inside. I wrote lengthy, wildly exaggerated letters to Kerry, friends and family.

The elderly Swiss couple who owned the place lived in a house close by. They spoke no English but sometimes when I got home from school, there was a present; a bar of chocolate balanced on the door handle or some fruit on the step. One Saturday morning, there was even an international *Guardian* and some warm croissants. I thought I'd really landed on my feet until in November I woke to cold, damp bedroom walls. The holiday season was well and truly over.

Goodbye Wendy house, time to move again. I didn't want to leave my little cattle shed, not least because I'd miss the treats like nutty bread and custard pastries left by the landlady.

I flew home to England at half-term in order to drive back in the car with Kerry. As usual he would be going to Spain for his winter sojourn and it meant I could get about a lot easier, not relying on a lift or a bus. We stayed initially in the cattle shed and he was charmed by the set-up, especially the view from the balcony. Then one day while I was at work, he found another flat. It was advertised on a board in a supermarket. We went to look and decided it was ideally situated, not far from school and within walking distance of a bakery for my daily bread. Every morning I met the same folk walking home carrying two or three baguettes wrapped in paper, who always greeted me with a cheery "*bonjour*". I had a lovely neighbour on the same floor called Pia. She was Swiss/German and spoke three languages. She seemed thrilled to have an English-speaking person moving in next door and showed me where everything was. The washing machine and drying racks were in the basement and she explained how everyone in the flats had an allocated day and time to use it.

The school, a private one, catered for children of all nationalities, but because we happened to be in the part of Switzerland that was French-speaking most of the children spoke the language. However, there were also a number of students from England whose parents worked at the Nestlé headquarters in Vevey. Every morning the children had classes in their mother tongue but in the afternoon they swapped to English or French for two hours. As I was working in the nursery with an English girl and a French girl, we had to use a language that the little ones were familiar with. I became a surrogate grandma to a little German boy because I was the only one who could talk to him. His parents were grateful that I helped him to settle in so quickly. There was also a five-year-old Chinese girl who clung desperately to her grandmother every morning. Neither of them understood any English. I cuddled her for five minutes until she stopped crying and by the end of the week, she just sat and sucked her thumb. Then she noticed the piano. She pointed to it and looked at me. Using hand gestures, I asked her if she wanted to play. She nodded, smiled for the first time, then taking my hand led me across the room. I lifted her onto the stool fully expecting her to hit the keys at random, typical of any small child. I was astonished when she began to play from memory a familiar piece of classical music. She was in her element as her little fingers flew over the keys. Parents just arriving, teachers setting out picture books and children already playing with toys stopped what they were doing and watched in amazement. As Melody, we later discovered her English name, finished the piece she turned to me for approval and spontaneously everyone began to clap. Happy at last, we let her carry on until she'd had enough.

For me, and probably the children, the afternoons were more of a challenge. Although I only had nine in my group, their ages ranged from four to eleven and they spoke little or no English. We were supposed to teach in English the whole time but it would have been useless because they couldn't understand even basic commands.

I did what I'd done in Latvia; singing, games and role play. Some of the time they sat and coloured prepared worksheets, naming animals, parts of the body and colours. It worked well and I began to realise it was a two-way process because I was learning everyday phrases and words that children use.

I started having French conversation lessons with Monique, a friend of Pia's. She wanted to improve her English, so again it worked both ways. She cut items from the newspapers for me to read, then asked me questions; it was good fun. She was a bit older than me and could remember fleeing France during the war with her parents and little brother when she was only five years old. They left Dunkirk and walked cross-country through German occupied territory sleeping in barns. They managed to reach Switzerland without once being stopped where they joined relations. They never returned to live in France.

Kate came to stay for a week and loved it. I took her to the places I was familiar with, including a journey up a single-track railway to the top of a mountain where snow was already lying. One of the young French teachers who lived in a village some distance from Vevey invited us to a St Nicholas party. It was snowing in Vevey when we left that evening but we had a lift from another colleague. The snow got heavier as we went up and when we arrived, there were already about thirty people there – friends and neighbours. The room was in semi-darkness the only light coming from candles set in tangerines on every flat surface available. There was a sweet smell of spices. We all sat around a table laden with different kinds of bread, a huge variety of French cheeses, nuts and a fruitcake. We were served with hot mulled wine and drank cinnamon tea that was delicious. We finished the evening by singing carols. It was a lovely start to the festive season.

I'd planned to fly directly from Switzerland to Spain for the Christmas holidays, but the price was prohibitive and it worked out cheaper for me to go home and fly from East Midlands. We had a good Christmas dinner in the hotel and the old ladies sitting with us who knew Kerry were singing his praises. They said what a lovely man he was and had heard lots of stories about me. I was quite embarrassed about that, but so proud of him.

On New Year's Eve, there was a dance in the hotel and we joined in with the celebrations. I made the silly mistake of leaving my handbag under the table when we all got up to sing "Auld Lang Syne". When I went back to sit down, it was gone. Complete with money and passport. The next day, New Year's Day, we went to the little one-manned police station in Mijas to report the theft. The man on duty, although he spoke no English, understood. He sat before an old typewriter and with two fingers laboriously wrote an incident report. He gave us a copy and said it would be necessary to go to the British Embassy, which wouldn't be open on a public holiday. The following day, we got a bus to Malaga.

The embassy was packed. We were appalled at the strong language and derogatory comments coming from certain people sitting waiting or pacing around the small room. I was almost ashamed to be English. I was relieved that we had the relevant documents from the police and that Kerry could confirm his identity. We didn't have to wait for long and the official whom we saw seemed pleased to speak to someone who was in genuine need. He issued me with a temporary passport just to get me back to the UK. In fact, it was a piece of paper stamped with the British Embassy logo and a signature.

'Now don't go losing that, Mrs Silk,' he said as he handed it to me, but there was a twinkle in his eye and we knew he was just joking.

I arrived home with only a few days before I was due back in Switzerland. Instead of getting a new passport through the normal channels, possibly taking six weeks or longer, I needed to get one immediately. This would involve going to the nearest office in Peterborough, where in extenuating circumstances it could be issued the same day. June agreed to go with me on the train. We always enjoyed a day out together, guaranteed to be a laugh or a disaster.

It was easy to find the office which was already packed with about a dozen people sitting waiting. There were four officials on duty at the post office-like counter, so we hoped it wouldn't take long as we wanted to look round the town and have a meal. As we sat at the front, it was impossible not to overhear the conversation between the clerk and the man directly in front of us.

'Well, where did you lose it?' asked the woman.

'In the car park.'

'Which car park?'

'The car park at Sainsbury's.'

'Where was your passport?'

'In my back pocket.'

'Do you always take your passport to the supermarket?'

The man had a foreign accent and the woman continued to grill him. Even to us, he didn't seem quite genuine. She was getting more and more annoyed.

'I hope we don't get her,' whispered June. We did.

I approached her with a smile but it wasn't returned. I explained the situation.

'Have you brought an eligible person to confirm your identity?'

This meant someone with a profession who'd known me for at least ten years.

'Yes, my friend and neighbour Mrs Rooke.'

'What is your profession?' she asked June.

'I was a school secretary for fifteen years and before that worked for the civil service all my life.'

'H'mph,' snorted the woman. 'It doesn't really meet the criteria but in this case will have to do.' She turned back to me.

'Have you got your flight details?'

'No, when I rang for information it was an automated system and the robot didn't tell me that.' I was getting really fed up with her rudeness.

'I can't issue a new passport without confirmation of your flight. You'll have to ring and ask them to fax it here.'

'Where's a phone?' asked June.

'The payphone's over there, here's the number for EasyJet.' She dismissed us with a wave of the hand.

'Next please.'

'Cor, what a bitch, we drew the short straw there,' I whispered out of the corner of my mouth.

EasyJet was brilliant. A man answered immediately and, after asking my name and the date of travel said, 'Don't worry, Mrs Silk, here it is. I'm faxing it straightaway.' It was such a relief.

We'd been told to go back in a couple of hours to pick up the new passport, so went off to get a welcome cup of coffee. After that we went to look round Peterborough Cathedral. I'd no idea that the tomb of Katharine of Aragon, Henry VIII's first wife, was there. I didn't enjoy history at school and relied on a good memory to recall facts for exams, with no real understanding of events. I realised much later that this was due to poor teaching. Unlike schoolchildren today, we had no television or theatre to bring history alive, and were not encouraged in the classroom to challenge or question a point of view.

When we went to pick up the new passport I said thank you, resisting the temptation to add, "Have a nice day," to the same sour-faced woman who again dealt with us.

I returned to Switzerland, looking forward to the snow and the possibility of learning to ski again. I'd only done it once in my life back in Germany in the sixties, and still had the American certificate to say I'd participated.

However, after a few weeks back in the kindergarten, I had tonsillitis for the second time in three months. Whether it was due to stress at work, my age, or I was just run down, I didn't know. I saw a doctor who gave me medication and also said that my blood pressure was too high. That confirmed it. I rang Kate.

'I think I'm packing it in; the early mornings are getting to me. I have to leave the flat and be down in Vevey by half past seven every day in order to park the car. Sometimes it can take me fifteen minutes to even find a space, then it's quite a long way from school and another ten-minute walk.'

'Ok, come home, what's the problem?'

'Well, what will people say?'

'It doesn't matter what they think: you've been, you've tried it and it's not for you. Where's the shame in that?'

I took her advice and rang the manager at home and asked if I could go round and have a chat. I felt guilty leaving mid-term but hadn't signed a contract, just verbally agreed to do one year. I explained the situation and was pleasantly surprised at her reaction. She reassured me by saying that I'd made a positive contribution to the staff, introduced some fresh ideas and was popular with both the parents and the children, who'd be sorry to see me go.

My friend Sue in Cosby, who'd kept an eye on our house and entertained my American exchange partner Louise, agreed to fly over and accompany me on the long drive home. I'd dangled the carrot of a free week's holiday, excursions included, and she jumped at the offer. She was in her element when I took her to Montreux, just up the road a few miles, where we saw a huge statue of a man playing a guitar.

'Wow, it's Freddie Mercury,' she said; she was overawed.

'Who's he? I've never heard of him.'

'You must have done; he was the lead singer in Queen.'

We found out that he'd bought a house and a recording studio with a view of the lake, so Sue wanted to have a look round to see if we could find it. We never did.

The drive back to England with an overnight stop in France took a couple of days and was 777 miles from Vevey to Cosby.

Within a couple of weeks, I was back in the familiar routine doing supply work for two local schools. I had plenty to tell Kerry in my letters, who was still in Mijas until the end of March. I wrote and told him that I felt proud of Kate, who appeared to have matured and become quite forceful and articulate.

She was fed up at work and had threatened to leave her job if they didn't sort out one of the chaps with an attitude. However, I told Kerry, things seemed to have simmered down lately so she was hanging on. I guess they thought too highly of her to let her go lightly.

I had a long letter from Yukari and read it aloud to Kate and Chris.

'How is your farther in raw? My sister has a new baby she is glowing very fast and has eight mouths.'

'Blimey,' said Chris, 'she must be radioactive.'

VISIT TO JAPAN, MILLENIUM YEAR

In August 1999, I came across the following article in the church magazine.

> *Why not join Bishop Tim and a group from the Leicester Diocese visiting Japan in the spring of 2000. Leicester's contact with the diocese of Yokohama goes back to 1885 and has included several visits in both directions. Accommodation during the trip will be in hotels and in the homes of our Japanese hosts giving the opportunity for members of the party to gain an insight into the pattern of life in a Japanese household. There will be between ten and twenty people comprising clergy and laity. If you are interested in going make an application by the end of August.*

Having only recently hosted Yukari and Kiyoe for eighteen months, I'd learned a lot about Japanese culture. The thought of an opportunity to stay in homes and experience life at firsthand would be a chance of a lifetime. I sent off for further information, read it and applied. A reply received told me that due to an overwhelming response, there would be interviews in October. Although there'd be a party of twenty, eleven were already taken by clergy from the Leicester diocese. This meant the competition to go was for only nine places. I didn't think I had much chance. At the interview I sat facing seven people sitting in a semicircle, two wearing clerical white collars.

When I was asked the question, "Have you travelled abroad before?'" I was embarrassed to list the places where I'd lived and worked and felt as though I was showing off. At the end of the meeting they told me I would hear whether I was successful early the following week. The day of the interview was Tuesday. By Friday, a letter arrived saying I'd been accepted.

In March 2000 we flew with Japanese Airlines on a jumbo jet, twelve hours non-stop to Tokyo. It was a thrilling start to the fortnight when I got up in the early hours to have a walk and stretch my legs. As I crept to the back of the plane, everyone else, eyes covered, appeared to be sound asleep. I looked out of the window to brilliant daylight and miles and miles of shiny blue ice reflected by the cloudless sky. *Wow, I thought, were we really over Siberia?* The minute I sat down, a very pretty Japanese stewardess approached and asked me whether I'd like a drink. I was grateful because I rarely sleep on a long flight.

Diocesan representatives who were fluent English speakers met us at the airport. From there, we travelled by coach to Yokohama where we checked into a hotel. Exhausted, I slept well that night.

The next morning we visited the beautiful Commonwealth War Cemetery. It was a thought-provoking and emotional start to the week. The separate sections have been designed as part of an informal landscape garden, each area distinguished by plants and trees imported from the homeland of those that lie in them. Silver birch, oak, elm and mountain ash are among the trees introduced into the United Kingdom section. English cottage garden flowers, namely hollyhocks, daisies, lily of the valley, pansies and dahlias, flourish alongside flowering shrubs. Tasmanian snow gums and eucalyptus trees are a feature of the Australian section and maples and sycamore represent Canada.

From there we travelled to a museum, where we were shown various artefacts dating back to the period when Christianity was banned. For 300 years Christians worshipped secretly but thousands were discovered and martyred by the Shogun government. A bigger tourist attraction, both figuratively and literally, is the famous Kamakura Daibutsu or Great Buddha. The huge bronze statue was originally inside a temple that was swept away by a tidal wave leaving the Buddha unharmed. Again, after an earthquake in 1923, the base was destroyed but not the body. Since then repairs have been made, making it possible for the main part to move freely and prevent damage in the event of a further natural disaster.

From the window of the coach, I was surprised to see an abundance of electric cables, wires and pylons everywhere. The towns and cities seemed overshadowed by the ugly mass. I was puzzled until I realised the reason.

In the event of an earthquake, a regular occurrence, power would be the first essential to be needed and restored. Practicality and access therefore was far more important than appearance.

As we all had two different experiences of homestay, our insight into Japanese culture was as wide and varied as that of family life in the UK. In my own case, the first couple with whom I stayed were relaxed and friendly and in many respects quite westernised. Michiko spoke English exceptionally well, whereas Katsuhiko her husband spoke very little.

They had a small miniature Dobermann called Steve who didn't like strangers and had even bitten Katsuhiko, who showed me the scars.

On the second day when he was at work and I sat alone in the living room, the dog was in the kitchen where Michiko was preparing a meal. I saw the door slowly open and the little dog walked in. I froze.

He looked at me.

'Hello Steve,' I said, waiting for the worst to happen. He jumped straight up onto my lap. Two minutes later, when Michiko came into the room, I was still sitting there stroking him. She gaped.

'He's never done that with anyone,' she said.

'I expect he can smell mine.' I laughed but was so relieved that he'd taken to me. That evening it was suggested that we cycle to church the following morning. However, when we woke up it was raining hard, so we went to Chiba on the train. As we walked to the station lots of people cycled past us, each one clasping an umbrella thrust forward against the downpour. I was glad they hadn't expected me to do the same. The church service was mostly in Japanese but, along with five more folk from our group and a parallel translation, we tried to follow in a fashion, usually reaching amen before everyone else. At the end, the whole congregation, about twenty-five, came together in the schoolroom. After a meal we introduced ourselves, telling the gathering a little about our own parish. Gallons of green tea were dispensed and we were given postcards, gifts and souvenirs.

The next day, knowing my background in education, Katsuhiko had arranged a visit for me to a local primary school. A taxi driver duly arrived to pick me up. He looked more like a personal chauffeur in his black uniform, peaked cap and spotless white gloves. He touched the tip of his hat, led me to the already open door, smiled and with a hand gesture asked me to be seated. I felt like Japanese royalty. I was warmly welcomed by the headmaster and again invited to share a cup of green tea before we toured the classrooms. The youngest children were curious to hear English being spoken and one or two brave souls said hello or good morning. This set the rest of the class giggling. I had to laugh because that's exactly what all children do in similar circumstances.

In the afternoon Michiko took me to Chiba, a modern, clean city where in the department store I was horrified to see how expensive everything was. I only bought five postcards and they came to £4.00. For the first time in my life, I went on a monorail. Having seen it beforehand suspended from an overhead track, I wasn't that keen and needed a bit of persuading. We took the train again to Tokyo to meet the rest of the group at the end of my stay. I felt as though I was leaving an old friend, not someone I'd only met three days previously. We vowed to keep in touch.

The next night, we all stayed in a convent. We each had our own bedroom; very basic, with just a bed, a side table and a chair. The toilet facilities, which were shared, were right at the end of the corridor.

On the table was a torch, an addition I'd also noticed in the hotels. *That's useful,* I thought, *I could use it in the night to go to the bathroom.*

Then the real reason for it occurred to me. It would be essential in the event of an earthquake if all the lights went out. When four of us went to wash before dinner, we used the toilets for the first time.

'Hey Maggie,' shouted Davina from the next cubicle, 'what are these three buttons for?' I hadn't noticed them placed on the right-hand side of the seat.

'Press it and see,' I said.

'I daren't, you do it.' I liked Davina. She was the youngest in our group, only twenty-one, but despite the difference in our age she seemed to have tagged on to me. Sometimes I'd gone with her to find a McDonald's so she could fill up on burger and chips, as she wasn't adapting very well to the local food. I laughed.

'OK, here goes.' I pressed the top button and a jet of

warm water shot up. 'Ooh, that's nice, I wonder what this one's for?' I pressed the middle one and a blast of warm air was directed to the same area. There were screams of laughter as they all tried it; this was a story to be retold and embellished when we got home.

My homestay the second week couldn't have been more different. Luckily I was not on my own but shared the experience with a lovely lady called Ena. Our hostess had been a Christian for most of her life but seemed to be overshadowed by and much in awe of her husband. He was a strict Buddhist, an extremely clever man who'd been in the medical world and highly respected in his particular field. With hindsight, I think alarm bells should have sounded when his welcome letter arrived. He was a specialist in hypertension and endocrinology and in London in 1964 he gave a talk entitled "Mathematical models of Steroid Hormone Metabolism". He listed the songs that he was able to play on his violin while his wife sang the words. They included "Annie Laurie", "Bluebells of Scotland", "Comin' Thro' the Rye" and "The Last Rose of Summer"; all Old English or Scottish folk songs that no one born after 1960 would have heard of. I got the impression that since he'd retired he rather resented the absence of the esteem and acclaim he'd received in the academic world. He showed Ena and me to our bedrooms on the top floor, telling us on the way that he allowed his wife to be a Christian. We daren't look at each other. Our separate rooms were big and empty apart from the futon in the middle of the floor sitting on a tatami mat. He'd provided us each with a pair of slippers for indoors, having left our outdoor shoes in the porch.

'However,' he said, 'it is strictly forbidden that you go to the bathroom in the same slippers. Please use the ones provided for that purpose.' I didn't tell him about the times when I forgot at night. After going to the loo I'd be in the bedroom halfway across to the futon when I realised I was wearing the wrong slippers. Wood and paper screens closed onto a balcony that overlooked the front garden and street. Again, in no uncertain terms, we were told never to touch them because they cost a lot of money. No expense was spared during our three days with him. We were taken to a tea ceremony where Ena and I were expected to kneel on the floor for half an hour. The ceremony is steeped in tradition and involves slurping green tea from a dish after turning it so many times clockwise then anticlockwise. We didn't have a clue what was going on and finding it difficult to kneel for so long, we gradually slumped to sit sideways. The highlight was a visit to the Noh Theatre. It's a formalised and unrealistic type of drama, a favourite with the former rulers of Japan commonly called Shoguns. Half an hour would have been long enough but we actually sat for a solid four hours.

In order to stay awake, I began to write a few notes on the back of my programme:

JAPANESE KABUKI

Some thoughts written down during the performance of a play that is going on and on.

I am so bored I cannot understand a thing. All the howling (there are no words) sounds like my Dalmatian when the phone rings. There is a man on the stage, dressed as a woman in a pretty Japanese dress; he is wearing a white face mask. At least a dozen people around me are asleep, including my host, his niece and Ena. She is the other lady in our group of twenty who are visiting Japan. The theatre is only half full and most people seem to have come in for a siesta. On the stage they are chanting and pulling faces as though they have stomach ache. One man's costume is so long the legs are dangling on the floor at the back. I am waiting for him to trip up. A Japanese flute occasionally screeches an accompaniment, while two men kneeling on the left are hitting a hand-held drum. After each strike they pause a few seconds and then howl before hitting it again. The man dressed as a woman is now holding a fan. Each step he takes is in slow motion, when one foot is barely placed in front of the other.

Another half an hour has gone by. Ena will be sorry when she wakes up and realises she has missed it all. I must stay awake; it would look bad if we both dozed off as I'm sure the tickets were expensive. Now the man sounds like a cow separated from her calf after giving birth. More chanting; will it never end? Another man is strutting about like a turkey cock looking for a fight. He occasionally stamps his foot and sings in a high-pitched voice, but it's all being done in slow motion.

Four men on the right are kneeling. Now and then they bend forwards, wave their arms in the air and almost prostrate themselves as though greeting the Pope. This is accompanied by a blood-curdling howl.

I think it's going to end; they are leaving the stage. Please God. Forty minutes later, I am struggling to stay awake. The old man *with a fan is walking with his legs so close together, he looks as though he is dying to go to the toilet. Up and down, back and forth, I'm sure if I could see his buttocks they would be tightly squeezed together. He has such a worried frown on his face and only once dares to stamp his foot. The four choir men kneeling behind him are singing in Japanese. It probably translates as something like, "hang in there mate, it's not long until this performance is over."*

Ena, on waking up says, 'There's not a lot you can do with a fan.'

By the end of our visit to Japan, we'd all been lucky to partake in and sample so many different aspects and traditions of local culture. We'd travelled on the bullet train, had afternoon tea and scones in the British Embassy with the high commissioner and been wined and dined by total strangers who'd taken us into their hearts.

On the very last day, my two Japanese girls Yukari and Kiyoe made the long journey halfway across the country to spend the day with me. I found it hard to believe that I was seeing them again, this time on their own home ground. It was something I'd never even contemplated in Cosby when we'd said a final goodbye only two or three years previously. We never stopped talking and they wanted to know first about the family and second about the things and places we'd seen in Japan. They were astounded when I gave a very graphic picture of the tea ceremony and the Noh Theatre. I showed them a photo of the second home where I'd stayed with Ena.

'H'oh,' gasped Yukari. I loved listening to her accent and broken English. 'He very rich man. I never go to theatre or tea ceremony.' Neither had Kiyoe or anyone they knew. We had such a lot to catch up on and the day went too quickly. They both said they would see me in England next time. A promise they kept.

I was missing Kerry and was well ready to go home. I couldn't wait to tell him all the funny things we'd done and seen.

Ann died in October that year after fighting breast cancer. She'd been so cheerful and brave the last time I saw her in hospital in Liverpool.

'Wheel me outside, Maggie, so I can have a cigarette. It won't make any difference now,' she'd said.

After my own experience only ten years previously, I was gutted, assuming that she would come through it as I had. It made me realise how lucky I was.

A YEAR OF EVENTS, 2001

Kate was dismayed.

'You can't sell this place, it's our family home.'

Kerry and I had made the decision to move house because we were asset rich and penny poor. It was true that all the good times, and a few bad, had been at Elmtree Road but the family itself had all moved away. Jon, Chris and Kate each had their own house, while Matt, now home from Greece and working, was negotiating a mortgage. We'd paid for the boys to go to Loughborough Grammar School, a decision we never regretted despite the fact that the fees took all of my salary for over ten years. Kerry had retired after his first heart attack during Chris's final year there. Then when the boys all went on to university, because our income had dropped to half, they all got a state grant. We'd never had savings for a rainy day because normally there was no money left at the end of the month.

Elmtree was a big house and the heating bills were enormous so we figured we could save money by buying a smaller, modern property. We must have looked at over a dozen before we found the perfect one. It was built by a man to his own specification and was only eight years old. Because we'd had visitors staying from the United States and France the previous year it was still practical to have four bedrooms and two bathrooms. However, the footprint of the house was much smaller and everything in it was fresh and right up to date. Elmtree Road was only on the market for two days.

Kerry went to Denia in Spain in early January for three weeks, so the house move was arranged for the time he was away. Although he never complained I could see that he tired easily and spent more time reading and doing crosswords. He'd even stopped going to the golf club on a Tuesday evening to play cards. I spent the days on my own filling boxes and trying to offload memorabilia. Easier said than done. There were piles of schoolbooks belonging to the boys and Kate as they'd progressed from the infants right until they left at eighteen. School reports, which I couldn't resist reading, and a variety of handmade Xmas, birthday and Mother's Day cards. They all ended up with the stuff I was keeping, along with the mounds of photographs of the children growing up.

On moving day, the kids were brilliant. June came to help and worked with Kate getting the kitchen organised and making endless cups of tea for the removal lads and us. She and Peter had moved to Oadby the previous year, only six or seven miles away, but a bit too far to pop in every day. I was already missing her. Matt and Chris came straight after work to shift the heavy furniture into place and finally about 9 p.m. we sat round the table with a Chinese takeaway and a bottle of champagne.

By the time Kerry came home everything was more or less in order, so he was able to enjoy getting to know the house before he went away again, this time to Majorca for just three weeks. Unbeknown to him, I'd arranged to go and stay for the week of his birthday on 15 February. I was well ready for a break myself what with moving, walking the two boxer dogs, doing days of supply teaching and fitting in a couple of boys at home for lessons. I arrived at his hotel in the early afternoon having left home just after 5 a.m. to get my flight from East Midlands. Kerry's face was a picture when he opened the bedroom door. He was overwhelmed and flung his arms around me. He didn't look at all well and finally admitted he needed to see the hotel doctor. Early next morning and within hours of seeing the doctor, he'd been admitted to hospital in Palma to have tests.

I was worried sick. I hardly slept that night and straight after a hasty breakfast was in a taxi on my way to the hospital. He'd been moved to ICU (intensive care unit) where visiting was only half an hour. He was all wired up being monitored, but was responding to treatment and already looked a better colour. He told me that an ECG had detected an irregular heartbeat and further blood tests and an X-ray had revealed a kidney problem. It seemed to me that I'd barely sat down and taken it all in before I was ushered out again by a nurse, who said that if I returned at 7 p.m. that evening I could talk to a doctor. It wasn't worth doing the two-hour journey back to the hotel so I trailed aimlessly round Palma. I walked through the grotty back streets but everywhere was closed because it was Sunday. I managed to find an English cafe right down near the harbour and sat for ages with a drink and something to eat. I felt desperately lonely and needed someone to talk to. *Snap out of it,* I told myself, *at least you were here, people in the hotel are concerned and the weather's good.* The doctor I saw later couldn't say a lot but was fairly reassuring. I took a taxi back because it was quicker and arrived in the hotel just in time to catch a late evening meal. This was the pattern for the next eight days, Kerry finally coming out of intensive care after six but having to stay in till the insurance people could book a suitable flight. Every evening Kate phoned, which lifted my spirits. She said that half the village knew Dad was poorly and people were constantly ringing or stopping to ask her how he was.

I also had a designated insurance man called Mike, who phoned regularly and said not to worry about anything as it would all come together as soon as they were informed by the hospital that Kerry was fit to fly home. I was impressed by their service and personal care of customers. The birthday week that I'd booked had already run into ten days. Finally, two days later, we were both on a flight home to Manchester. Kerry was taken to the airport by taxi where I was already waiting, having arrived on the hotel shuttle bus. We had priority boarding and he was transported onto the plane in a wheelchair where we sat together right at the front. At Manchester Airport we were met by Medic–transport and enjoyed a ride back to Cosby in a very comfortable Mercedes. Kate was there to meet us. She'd been so worried and had been on the point of flying over to join me had her dad stayed in any longer. I was physically and emotionally drained and had the best night's sleep for almost three weeks, only woken by Kerry, bless him, bringing me a cup of tea.

That year would prove to bring another personal crisis for the family, a national disaster for the British countryside and the farmers and an international incident that shook the world.

Ten days after Kerry came home from Spain feeling better than he'd felt for years, I noticed a rapid deterioration. I asked the surgery to arrange an immediate consultation with a specialist, as there was obviously something very wrong. We were given an appointment for the very next day. I told the doctor and nurse that it had taken them ten days in Palma to balance his tablets and that he'd come home on top of the world. I also added that what upset me the most was the fact that no one had even looked at, or attempted to translate his notes that the hospital had wisely given to us. Kerry went through all the same tests again and this time we were hit by a bombshell. A different consultant, who didn't mince his words, said the news wasn't good. His heart was enlarged, meaning it was weak and damaged and there was little they could do without significant risk.

He was brusque; his forthright manner upset me. Then he said he could barely understand how Kerry had managed to go for twelve years without medication since his first heart attack in 1989. It had been severe and he'd nearly died then. He advised us to move into a bungalow and together enjoy what time there was left. I was stunned and left the hospital in tears. I couldn't take it in. That evening Chris arrived with a bottle of red wine then Matt came, closely followed by Kate. We sat around the kitchen table.

'We're not moving. We'll have a stairlift installed,' I said.

'Dad just loves it here,' said Kate. 'Neither of you would survive another move. You've only been here five minutes.'

Chris suggested getting a mobility scooter.

'He'd love that, he could still go and fetch his paper and even get to the golf club if he wanted to see his mates.'

Their positive attitude was rubbing off on me and I knew that together we'd all try to carry on as normal. When Kerry eventually came home he was on several different medications, but was looking infinitely better. He was bright and cheerful, again determined to put on a brave face.

Meanwhile, around the country, farmers were facing the biggest outbreak of foot and mouth disease since 1967. Despite restricting the movement of cattle, it continued to spread. It created a crisis in the British countryside and all public footpaths, farm parks and zoos were closed. Over ten million sheep and cattle were destroyed and the final cost and loss of revenue to farmers and the tourist industry amounted to over £4 billion.

Oliver, having turned five and home for the school holidays, came to stay for a week at Easter. June and I took him on the train to Leicester where we headed for the New Walk Museum. There was a dinosaur exhibition and like all five-year-olds he'd been doing them at school. He could recognise some and was able to pronounce their names. At one point when June and I chatting had wandered into the next room, we heard a little voice calling excitedly, 'Auntie June, Auntie June, come and look at this dung beetle.' It was a gem.

One afternoon, Matt and I took him and the two boxers to Burbage Woods. After a lovely walk, we headed for the little cafe and sat outside in the sun. There was water provided for the dogs and having seen to them first we secured them by tying the leads to the leg of the wooden bench. As we sat in the warm sun, I could faintly hear in the distance the noise of an approaching train.

'Look, look, Oliver, there's a train coming.' The line from Birmingham to Leicester was directly behind us up on the embankment. He couldn't wait to get back to the house to tell Kerry.

'Granddad, Granddad, we saw a virgin in Burbage Woods.' It was such an innocent remark but so funny that I wrote to the letter page in the local evening paper and it was published.

The summer that year was a good one weather-wise and in July seven of us went away for a week in Dorset.

At the time of booking the holiday, we had no idea that Kerry wouldn't be fit to go.

However, he admitted that he couldn't face the long journey and was content to stay at home to enjoy the new house and garden. I felt happy knowing that there were enough friends and neighbours keeping an eye on him.

The new vicar Philip had also got into the habit of popping in at least once a week. He'd only been in the village since January, having changed his role from being a chaplain in the Leicester hospitals to looking after the two churches of Cosby and Whetstone. He'd even come to see Kerry during the first few days we were back after the emergency in Majorca. He was a wonderful support and Kerry liked him. I desperately needed a break to unwind and the boys and Kate were more than ready for a holiday.

The caravan site was a good one, with plenty of space between the two vans and enough room for sitting outside. It had its own children's playground, a swimming pool and a games room for the big lads. Kate, her friend and her little lad Ollie's age had one caravan and Matt, Chris, Oliver and me shared the other.

The first day started off hot so we headed for the beach, where we hired a windbreak and an umbrella for shade. Ollie's hair was a paler shade of Kerry's, a light auburn, but his skin was fair and I knew we'd have to lather the suncream on and make sure he always wore a sun hat to protect the back of his neck. The boys, big and small, paddled in the water, then built a massive sandcastle together topping it with turrets and flags. I sat in a deckchair laughing as I watched the two little ones trying to bury Matt's feet and legs. He let them get so far before he deliberately wiggled a foot or toe and with shouts of frustration they started again. The girls had packed a pile of sandwiches, some fruit and bottles of water, so we stayed until mid afternoon. From the beach at Charmouth we could see Golden Cap, the highest point on the south coast of Britain, and decided it would be worth going up next day to see the view. That evening the boys went to the supermarket for stuff to cook on the barbecue, so Kate and I took the two little lads in the pool.

Later we sat outside enjoying the warm end to the day, eating hot dogs with onions, beefburgers, and a big mixed salad prepared by Matt. He was particularly good at cooking having learned a lot in Greece and was never afraid to experiment. When June and I went over to stay with him, we'd gone to the market where all the locals shopped. We were amazed at the variety of vegetables, different sorts of lettuce and different sized tomatoes. They were piled up on plastic sheets and the Greek women bought them by the kilo, not in the pre-packed bags that we were so used to.

We did climb up Golden Cap the next day; it was well marked by a grassy track but was quite a challenge. Chris kept the little boys amused by kidding them that trolls lived in the rabbit holes.

'Listen,' he whispered, beckoning to them before he got down on his knees. 'Can you hear them?' They squatted beside him, each putting a hand to an ear exactly like him.

'Yes, I can hear something,' they said together.

'Shhh, they'll go away if you make a noise.'

I filmed it all on camcorder so that Kerry, John and Katharine would be able to see it later.

On 11 September, events took place that shook the world when two hijacked planes crashed into the Twin Towers of the New York Trade Center. We watched in horror at the live images on television as the second plane hit and, shortly after, the two buildings slowly began to collapse. Not much later, it was announced that a third hijacked plane had crashed into the Pentagon, then a fourth in Pittsburgh. As the news unfolded, it became even more shocking. The harrowing footage on television resembled an American disaster movie. Throughout it all, it was heart-warming to hear and read about the extraordinary bravery of human beings who risked their lives to help the injured and comfort the dying. Over the ensuing weeks the sheer number of people killed, maimed or still missing became clear. So many countries were affected that the whole world realised this was the beginning of an entirely different kind of war.

ANIMALS
AND CHILDREN

Somebody once said, quote: Never work with animals or children.

I tend to disagree because, for most of my life, those times for me have been the happiest and often the funniest. Work, home and leisure revolved round both.

I was doing a day's supply in the local primary school. It was with a class of five-year-olds who were only in their first term. At that age animals and pets are a popular topic, so we were making a graph of children's pets. The class was responsive and the children wriggled and squirmed on their chairs, waving a hand in the air in order to attract my attention. We began the bar chart with the usual tally of cats, dogs, rabbits and budgies. Then, one little girl said she had a parrot.

'Wow, that's different,' I said, turning to start a new column on the whiteboard.

'What colour is it?' asked a couple of children together.

She paused, 'Err... red 'n yeller 'n blue and black, I think.'

I had to hide a smile before saying, 'Where does it live; in a cage?'

'No, no, no.' She was sure about that. 'It lives on the curtain rail.'

I was really taken aback. 'Ah, so where do you feed it?' I was busy imagining this parrot flying freely around the room, dropping feathers and excrement on the furniture and any folk present.

'It has a saucer on the rat's cage,' she said as if this was the most natural thing on earth.

On priceless occasions like that, all teachers of young children wish they had a moment to write down the hilarious and sometimes bizarre things that children say. There just isn't time and the lesson has to go on.

In a different school with a slightly older class, we were talking about the Royal family and in particular the Queen. After discussing her crown and asking when she would wear it, the children's answers varied from when she had important visitors to when she went to the bank, or when she was reading in bed. However, the funniest replies to where do you think she eats her meals were, in a Royal pub or in a posh restaurant.

Supply teaching and looking after the puppies, two young boxers that we'd recently acquired, kept my mind focused in the months that followed when I finally lost Kerry. He died in the hospice in May 2003. I thought I was prepared after coping with his ill health for so many years. But nothing prepares you. The realisation that you will never ever see your loved one again takes a long, long time to accept. Life seemed empty with no purpose and, as with the arrival of our first baby, I had to learn to cope, but this time on my own. The children were a great support, coming round after work or ringing regularly but they all had their own lives and I tried hard to hide my feelings when I was having a bad day. I joined a class and started learning Spanish, immediately enjoying it and having something new to look forward to each week. I accepted all the supply teaching that was offered and was on call in three different village schools. I carried on doing lessons at home and somehow muddled through the first year. In the second year, I decided that I was ready to have a holiday on my own. It would be strange, so I deliberately chose a singles' walking week. We were based on a little-known Greek island called Evia. It was a huge success because I was with a group of people who all shared the same interest. That week gave me the courage to book a dream holiday that Kerry and I had planned to do one day: A trip to Canada with a cruise to Alaska. After a long flight to Calgary and a couple of nights spent in Banff for sightseeing, our party of forty-nine people boarded a coach for the long journey to Vancouver. I was the odd one out sitting alone in the front seat. The coach driver was an expert on birds and could spot a bald-headed eagle from such a distance that he was able to tell us exactly where to look as we got closer. He told us some interesting facts about the building of The Canadian Pacific Railway that sometimes ran parallel to the road we were on. I suddenly felt lonely and very jealous of the couples nearby laughing and talking. *I* should have been sharing this with Kerry. By the time we stopped en route for a coffee break, I'd made up my mind that on arrival in Vancouver I was going to fly home whatever the cost.

Back on the coach, the first to be seated, I watched people chatting and taking photos of the view. As they climbed in and returned to their seats, most of them acknowledged me with a smile. Then, one lady stopped.

'Would you like me to sit with you?' she said.

I couldn't believe it.

'I'd love it but what about your husband?'

She laughed, 'He won't care; I'll just go and tell him.'

That act of kindness meant so much and needless to say I decided to carry on with the holiday. I got to know the couple very well and usually joined them for a drink in the evening when we'd talk about the trips we'd been on. They came from Bristol. Her name was Mo and his was Bernie, though I called him Captain Birdseye after he said he was an ex-sailor. I kept him amused and exasperated by referring to the front and the back of the ship and using the expression upstairs and downstairs. I could remember the names when he told me but not necessarily apply it to the right place.

Shore excursions were chosen and paid for in advance and I joined a small group of ten or eleven to visit a wild animal sanctuary. We were met off the ship and taken in a motorboat for a short ride to an island. The man who owned and worked the site could only be described as an eccentric, but he was dedicated to his job. He housed and nurtured abandoned or injured wild animals including wolves, pine martens and elk. He had a snowy owl and a raven that his son had taught to do tricks. We stroked a young silver fox and he showed us a wolf cub that he was raising to walk on a lead. There were half a dozen more wolves in a high-fenced compound that eyed us as they paced restlessly around their enclosure. They'd all been rescued but once treated and handled by man it was impracticable for them to be released back into the wild where they would probably have been killed by their own kind. Standing in front of us he looked like a character from a film or a storybook, with his green dungarees, peaked cap and quirky smile.

'Would you guys like to make the wolves howl?' he said, then without waiting for an answer continued. 'Throw your heads back like this, pucker your lips and howl as loud as you can.' We looked at each other and grinned, then everyone feeling rather daft did what he said. The joint effort of the noise we made resembled a howl and the effect on the wolves was instant. They stopped pacing, threw back their heads and howled in response. The noise they made was blood-curdling and stomach-churning. It was such a menacing sound that we stood in silence before anyone spoke.

'Boy, that was eerie,' said a man in our group.

'Scary,' said a little girl and we all nodded.

The three elk we saw at close quarters looked very similar to reindeer. They were also in a pen but close enough to be touched.

'Would any of you guys like to feed them?' he asked,

picking up a handful of hay. As no one in the group volunteered, I said I'd like to. I could tell by his face that he was surprised as I hand fed them and gave them a pat.

'You are one brave lady,' he said. Everyone laughed and some took a photo. It was no different from feeding horses which I'd been doing all my life; nevertheless, I took his praise as a compliment. Something to tell the kids.

PHOTOS
AND MEMORIES

I've been sitting at the kitchen table dealing photos as in a card game for four players. I want to make an album each for the children. I thought it would be easy after I'd located the photos shoved into empty bottom drawers and plastic ice cream containers stacked on top of a wardrobe. However, it's been difficult to know where to start. I've already chucked away all the ones of only scenery, ships and sunsets. I don't know where they were taken. Kerry was the serious photographer and used to take all the photos on holidays with the children. Before cameras became digitalised and more sophisticated, thus much easier to use, he'd fiddle for ages with the settings making sure that the subject was correctly focused and all that palaver. The kids used to tease him saying, "Come on Dad, if you don't hurry up the ship will have sailed over the horizon or that stunning mountain will have gone to look for Muhammad."

They all had a wicked sense of humour. He took it in good fun and seldom got rattled. However, in later years on holiday without the family, I tried to persuade him to place me in the corner of a picture, at least just to give me a reminder of where we were.

I'm not getting very far because I keep stopping and trying to remember which holiday we were on. I'm talking to myself as usual, something I've done a lot since I've been on my own.

'I'm sure that's Scotland; no, it can't be, we had a white estate car when we had that boxer. I know that's Cornwall because I remember we took Kate's friend, Emma, and it rained. Look at them grinning in their shorts and yellow anoraks. Where the heck was that castle? I bet it's in Wales, just look at Chris's skinny legs; he must have been twelve or thirteen.' I remember all the lads in their teens were skinny and ate like horses. Sometimes, after finishing a big Sunday dinner of roast beef with Yorkshire pudding and vegetables, followed by apple pie or crumble someone would say jokingly, "What we having for tea, Mam?"

This job is taking longer than I thought. I put the kettle on for a cuppa.

I open the next blue and white pack, thinking it would have been easier if I'd written the date and event on the outside. Hindsight is a wonderful thing but heigh ho off to work I go, just like the dwarfs in *Snow White*.

Now, whose wedding was that? Family, obviously, because the boys are wearing suits. They hated dressing up; a bit like me. I'm much more comfortable in my dog walking gear and a pair of wellies. Matt's scowling; I'll have to email him that one. Kate doesn't look too thrilled either; she only looks to be about nine. I know what she'll say when I show it to her. Chuck it away Mum, though I'll bet she remembers who was getting married. I put the two pictures to one side.

Aw… Look at their first school photos. Weren't they sweet? Why did they have to grow up? Well, if they hadn't I wouldn't have the grandchildren, would I? I'm blessed now with two boys and a girl. Oliver is taller than Jon, his dad; Kieran, Kate and Scott's little lad, was born in 2005. He's a joy but, just like his mother used to be, is a stick of dynamite ready to explode at any time the fuse is lit. I love him to bits but am equally exasperated on occasions. Like the rest of the family, he's inherited a sharp sense of humour. Kate admits she can see herself in him.

Matt's little girl, Penny, born in 2011, is half Chinese. He brought her to England for the first time when she was three and a half and she charmed everyone. Despite Cantonese being her first language, she adapted so quickly. She's bubbly and bright but I just wish that they lived nearer, at least in Europe. I've been to China five times but have to admit that long-haul travel is losing its charm.

Chris is very like his dad, in that he's artistic and into photography. He lives with his two dogs, goes shooting and has a big social circle within the village. Chris says he's willing to babysit Kieran now that he knows he won't break if he drops him. Kieran worships both him and Matt.

I still haven't finished the photos but I've made a good start. Four big piles carefully secured with an elastic band are ready to go into four separate albums.

Perhaps I'll write down my ambitions made at ten years old and stick a copy in the back of each book.

1.　　　*To become a teacher – tick*
2.　　　*To travel all over the world – tick*
3.　　　*To marry a man in uniform – tick*
4.　　　*To have four children – tick*

I have very few regrets, the biggest being that Kerry didn't live long enough to enjoy Kieran and Penny or to see Oliver grow up into a fine young man. I wish I'd asked Mam more questions about her background and bless her for keeping all my letters from Singapore. Despite our differences as children, I miss Ann, who died in her early sixties. I think, in a weird way although she constantly bullied me and called me names, she helped to make me what I am. Strong enough to stand up and face my fears.

Lindsey County Council Education Committee

Bursar Primary (Junior) School.

.... July 1947 .... *Examination.*   Class   VA

Dear Sir (Madam),

    I beg to forward Margaret Goodbutts .... Report in the Midsummer Examination, and ask your interest in the same.

Yours faithfully,

E. P. Peak

Head Teacher.

ATTENDANCES: Possible No. ....   Actual No. ....

Subject	Marks Possible	Marks Gained	Remarks
Reading	100	95	Very good.
Composition	100	94	Very good indeed.
English	50	48	Excellent
Arithmetic Mental	100	50	Poor result; can do better.
History Mechanical	100	89	Good
Geography Problems	100	80	Good.
Needlework Comprehension	50	42	Good.
Total	600	498	

Number in Class 45   44 Examined   Position in Class 9

General Remarks: If Margaret had been more careful in mental work, she would have had an even better position. All her other work is of a very good standard and she should do well.

Class Teacher. E. Barrett.

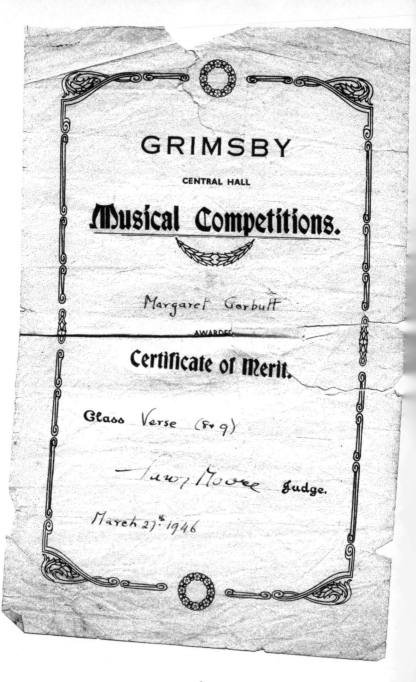

GRIMSBY

CENTRAL HALL

𝕸usical Competitions.

Margaret Garbutt

AWARDED

Certificate of Merit.

Class *Verse (8 & 9)*

Nancy Moore Judge.

March 27ᵗʰ 1946

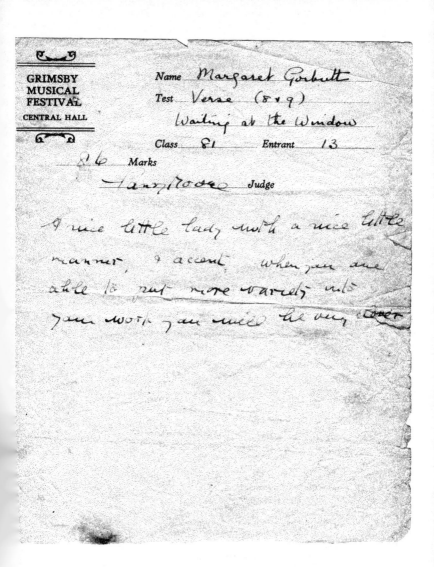

GRIMSBY MUSICAL FESTIVAL
CENTRAL HALL

Name *Margaret Corbett*
Test *Verse (8 x 9)*
Waiting at the Window
Class *81*   Entrant *13*
86 Marks
Harry Rooke Judge

A nice little lady with a nice little manner, & accent. When you are able to put more variety into your work, you will be very clever.

"A nice little lady with a nice little manner & accent,
when you are able to put more variety into your work,
you will be very clever."

Diocese of Leicester Japan Link Group Visit to Japan
9-23 March 2000
Leader – The Right Reverend Tim Stevens, Bishop of Leicester

DRAFT ITINERARY

Thursday 9th

pm	Travel to Heathrow Airport by coach from Leicester
17:00 pm	Check in
19:00 pm	Depart for Japan – Japan Airlines JAL402 (Terminal 3)

Friday 10th

15:45 pm	Arrive at Narita (Tokyo) International Airport, met by the Bishop of Yokohama Travel to Yokohama by coach Check in at Yokohama International (Kokusai) Hotel ; 2-16 Minami-saiwai, Nishi-ku, Yokohama 220-0005

Saturday 11th

am	Sightseeing in Yokohama Diocese – including Oiso Christian Museum, Kamakura Daibutsu (Buddha) by coach, accompanied by the Bishop of Yokohama
5 pm	Evensong at St Andrew's Cathedral Church, Yokohama
5:30 pm	Welcome Reception & Supper at St Andrew's Hall, hosted by Bishop of Yokohama Travel with host families to their homes in Yokohama Diocese. Overnight stay

Sunday 12th

Go to church with the host families and stay overnight

Monday 13th

Spend the day with the host families and stay overnight

Tuesday 14th

am	Travel with host families to Tokyo Station by train
11:00 am	Meet up with the Leicester Group. Sightseeing in Tokyo by coach Stay overnight at Nazare Convent in Tokyo ; 4-22-30 Mure, Mitaka-shi, Tokyo Tel : 0081- 422- 48- 4560 ; Fax : 0081- 422- 48- 4601

Wednesday 15th

10 am	Visit St Paul's Boys (Anglican) School in Tokyo, met by the Headmaster and Mr Imai, Master of Music and Revd Akiba, Chaplain
10:30-11:20	Bishop Tim to address 250 pupils at assembly
11:20-12:30	Tour of school
13:00	Lunch at school by the invitation of the Headmaster
pm	Brief visit to St Paul's University Theological Dept (where majority of Japanese prie are trained), met by Revd Nishihara, Lecturer and Theological Adviser of Provincial Office) Free or Sightseeing?
6:30 pm	Attend a Special Service jointly presented with Japan Anglican Provincial Office (NSKK) *Celebration of the New Millennium and Prayer of Reconciliation* at St Andr Cathedral Church, Tokyo *Bishop Tim preaching, St Paul's Boys Choir singing Stay overnight at Nazare Convent in Tokyo

411